Armed Group Structure and Violence in Civil Wars

This book examines whether differences in the organizational structure of armed groups shape patterns of human rights violations in civil wars.

Since the end of World War II, civil wars have been characterized by extremely high numbers of civilian casualties. However, the exact extent of civilian suffering varies across time, conflict, and geographic region. Recently, a new strand of research has emerged, primarily focused on studying the dynamics underlying the variation in civilian abuse by examining the characteristics of the armed groups and how these characteristics influence the armed groups' behavior towards the civilian population.

With reference to principal–agent theory, and data on the organizational structure of more than 70 armed groups, and information gathered from personal interviews with combatants, the author's analysis functions both on the level of the armed group and the individual combatant.

Offering a unique insight into how factors such as recruitment methods, hierarchy, and organizational commitment may affect the likelihood of civilian abuse by combatants, this book will be of much interest to students of political violence, civil wars, war and conflict studies, security studies, and IR in general.

Roos Haer is a Senior Research Fellow at Konstanz University, Germany, and has a PhD in International Relations.

Routledge Studies on Civil War and Intrastate Conflict
Series editors:
Edward Newman
School of Politics and International Studies, University of Leeds
and
Patrick Regan
Kroc Institute for International Peace Studies, University of Notre Dame.

This series publishes theoretically rigorous and empirically original scholarship on all aspects of armed intrastate conflict, including its causes, nature, impacts, patterns of violence, and resolution. It welcomes work on specific armed conflicts and the micro-dynamics of violence, on broad patterns and cross-national analyses of civil wars, and on historical perspectives as well as contemporary challenges. It also seeks to explore the policy implications of conflict analysis, especially as it relates to international security, intervention and peacebuilding.

Understanding Civil Wars
Continuity and change in intrastate conflict
Edward Newman

Territorial Separatism in Global Politics
Causes, outcomes and resolution
Edited by Damien Kingsbury and Costas Laoutides

Armed Group Structure and Violence in Civil Wars
The organizational dynamics of civilian killing
Roos Haer

Armed Group Structure and Violence in Civil Wars

The organizational dynamics of civilian killing

Roos Haer

Routledge
Taylor & Francis Group

LONDON AND NEW YORK

First published 2015
by Routledge
2 Park Square, Milton Park, Abingdon, Oxon OX14 4RN

and by Routledge
711 Third Avenue, New York, NY 10017

Routledge is an imprint of the Taylor & Francis Group, an informa business

British Library Cataloguing in Publication Data
A catalogue record for this book is available from the British Library

Library of Congress Cataloging in Publication Data
A catalog record for this book has been requested

ISBN: 978-1-138-82936-7 (hbk)
ISBN: 978-1-315-73714-0 (ebk)

Typeset in Times New Roman
by Wearset Ltd, Boldon, Tyne and Wear

To my family who hardly ever asked why this is still going on but never gave up believing it will be done.

To all the Congolese who allowed me to take their thoughts, their experiences, their suffering and sorrow, their knowledge and hopes with me.

To all my friends who brought life and fun to me.

To those staying with me in difficult times.

And those who kept me happy.

Contents

Figures

Tables

Abbreviations

AAH	Asa'ib Ahl al-Haq
ACCU	Autodefensas Campesinas de Córdoba y Urabá
ACLED	Armed Conflict Location Event Dataset
ADF	Alliance of Democratic Force
ADP	Alliance Démocratique des Peuples
AFDL	Alliance des Forces Démocratiques pour la Libération du Congo-Zaïre
AFL	Armed Forces of Liberia
AMB	al-Aqsa Martyrs' Brigades
ANC	African National Congress
APLA	Azanian People's Liberation Army
AQIM	Al-Qaeda in the Islamic Maghreb
ASG	Abu Sayyaf Group
ATTF	All Tripura Tiger Force
AUC	Autodefensas Unidas de Colombia
AWB	Afrikaner Weerstandsbeweging
BBC	British Broadcasting Corporation
BIAF	Bangasamoro Islamic Armed Forces
BLA	Baluchistan Liberation Army
BLTF	Bodo Liberation Tiger Force
BOP	Bayesian Ordered Probit
BVES	Bureau Volontariat pour les services de l'Enfance et de la Sante
CAPA	Centre d'Apprentissage Professionnel et Artisanal
CNDD	Conseil National Pour la Défense de la Démocratie
CNDP	Congrès National pour la Défense du Peuple
CNRD	Council of Resistance for Democracy
CPI-M	Communist Party of India-Maoist
CPN-M	Communist Party of Nepal-Maoist
CPP	Communist Party of the Philippines
DDR	Disarmament, Demobilization, and Reintegration
DHD	Dima Halam Daoga
DHD-BW	Dima Halam Daog-Black Widow faction
DRC	Democratic Republic of the Congo

ELN	Ejército de Liberación Nacional
EPLA	Eritrean People's Liberation Army
EPLF	Eritrean People's Liberation Front
ETA	Euskadi Ta Askatasun
EU	European Union
FAPC	Forces Armées du Peuple Congolais
FARC	Fuerzas Armadas Revolucionarias de Colombia
FARDC	Forces Armées de la République Démocratique du Congo
FARF	Forces Armees pour la Republique Federale
FDD	Forces pour la Défense de la Démocratie
FDLR	Forces Démocratiques de Libération du Rwanda
FIAA	Front Islamique Arabe de l'Azawad
FLN	Front de Libération Nationale
FMLN	Frente Farabundo Martí para la Liberación Nacional
FNI	Front des Nationalistes et Intégrationnistes
FNL	Forces Nationales de Libération
FPR	Front Patriotique Rwandais
FRPI	Forces de Résistance Patriotique d'Ituri
FSLN	Frente Sandinista de Liberación Nacional
GAM	Gerakan Aceh Merdeka
GIA	Groupe Islamique Armé
GICM	Groupe Islamique Combattant Marocain
HAMAS	Harakat al-Muqāwamah al-'Islāmiyyah
HAND	Human Rights and Advocacy Network for Democracy
HPC	Hmar People's Convention
HRM	Human Resource Management
IFP	Inkatha Freedom Party
IGO	Intergovernmental organization
INLA	Irish National Liberation Army
INPFL	Independent National Patriotic Front of Liberia
IPEC	International Programme on the Elimination of Child Labour
IRA	Irish Republican Army
IRC	International Rescue Committee
ISI	Islamic State of Iraq
JEM	Justice and Equality Movement
JI	Jemaah Islamyia
JSS	Jana Samhati Samiti
JVP	Janathā Vimukthi Peramuṇa
KNU	Karen National Union
KR	Khmer Rouge
KRA	Kuki Revolutionary Army
LAV	Laissez l'Afrique Vivre
LeJ	Lashkar-e-Jhangvi
LPC	Liberia Peace Council
LRA	Lord's Resistance Army

LTTE	Liberation Tigers of Tamil Eelam
LURD	Liberians United for Reconciliation and Democracy
MAGRIVI	Mutuelle des Agriculteurs du Virunga
MCC	Maoist Communist Centre
MCMC	Markov Chain Monte Carlo
MFDC	Mouvement des Forces Démocratiques de Casamance
MFDC-FN	Mouvement des Forces Démocratiques de Casamance-Front Nord
MILF	Moro Islamic Liberation Front
MK	Umkhonto we Sizwe
MNJ	Movement for Justice in Niger
MODEL	Movement for Democracy in Liberia
MONUC	Mission de l'Organisation des Nations Unies en République Démocratique du Congo
MPCI	Mouvement Patriotique de Côte d'Ivoire
MPGK	Mouvement Patriotique Ganda Koy
MPIGO	Mouvement Populaire Ivoirien du Grand Ouest
MS-13	Mara Salvatrucha
NALU	National Army of the Liberation of Uganda
NDFB	National Democratic Front of Bodoland
NDFB-RD	National Democratic Front of Bodoland-Ranjan Daimary faction
NGO	Non-Governmental Organization
NLFT	National Liberation Front of Tripur
NPA	New People's Army
NPFL	National Patriotic Front of Liberia
NRA	National Resistance Army
NRM	National Resistance Movement
NSA	Non-State Actor
NSCN	National Socialist Council of Nagaland
NSCN-IM	National Socialist Council of Nagaland-Isaac-Muivah faction
OCQ	Organizational Commitment Questionnaire
ONLF	Ogaden National Liberation Front
OPC	Oodua Peoples Congress
OSAM	Organizational Structure of Armed Movements
PAC	Pan Africanist Congress
PAIGC	Partido Africano da Independência de Guiné e Cabo Verde
PARECO	Patriotes Resistants Congolais
PFLP	Popular Front of the Liberation of Palestine
PIJ	Palestinian Islamic Jihad
PIRA	Provisional Irish Republican Army
PITF	Political Instability Task Force
PKK	Partiya Karkerên Kurdistan
PLA	People's Liberation Army
PRIO	Peace Research Institute Oslo
PULO	Patani United Liberation Organization

PWG	People's War Group
RCD	Rassemblement Congolais pour la Démocratie
RCD-CP	Rassemblement Congolais pour la Démocratie-Christian Pay faction
RCD-K	Rassemblement Congolais pour la Démocratie-Kisangani
RCD-K-ML	Rassemblement Congolais pour la Démocratie-Kisangani-Mouvement de Libération
RCD-LN	Rassemblement Congolais pour la Démocratie-Laurent Nkunda faction
RCD-ML	Rassemblement Congolais pour la Démocratie-Mouvement de Libération
RCD-N	Rassemblement Congolais pour la Démocratie-National
RENAMO	Resistência Nacional Moçambicana
RRA	Rahanweyn Resistance Army
RTC	Résistance Tchadienne Clandestine
RUF	Revolutionary United Front
SATP	South Asia Terrorism Portal
SB	Shanti Bahini
SIMI	Students Islamic Movement of India
SL	Sendero Luminoso
SLA	Sudan Liberation Army
SLA-MM	Sudan Liberation Army-Minni Minawi faction
SLDF	Sabaot Land Defence Force
SLM	Sudan Liberation Movement
SNA	Somali National Alliance
SPLA	Sudan People's Liberation Army
SPLM	Sudan People's Liberation Movement
SPM	Somali Patriotic Movement
SSDF	South Sudan Defence Force
START	Study of Terrorism and Responses to Terrorism
SWAPO	South-West African People's Organization
TTP	Tehrik-i-Taliban Pakistan
UCDP	Uppsala Conflict Data Program
UIFSA	United Islamic Front for the Salvation of Afghanistan
ULFA	United Liberation Front of Asom
ULIMO	United Liberation Movement of Liberia for Democracy
ULIMO-J	United Liberation Movement of Liberia for Democracy-Johnson faction
ULIMO-K	United Liberation Movement of Liberia for Democracy-Kromah faction
UN	United Nations
UNITA	União Nacional para a Independência Total de Angola
UNRF II	Uganda National Rescue Front II
UPA	Uganda People's Army
UPC	Union des Patriotes Congolais

UPC	Union des Patriotes Congolais
UPDS	United People's Democratic Solidarity
USC	United Somali Congress
VHP	Viśva Hindu Pariṣad
vivo	Victim's Voice
ZANU	Zimbabwe African National Union
ZAPU	Zimbabwe African People's Union
ZIPRA	Zimbabwe People's Revolutionary Army

Acknowledgments

Writing is never a solitary effort, and there are many people that I have to thank for having the energy and the ability to complete this work together with me. I offer my sincerest gratitude to Katharina Holzinger, Susumu Shikano, Thomas Elbert, Lilli Banholzer, Marius Bayer, Inna Becher, Johannes Dingler, Thomas Duttle, Bettina Duval, Sophie Esselink, Valentin Gold, Stephan Grohs, Sebastian Haunss, Silke Hell, Michael Hermann, Harald Hinkel, Joop van Holsteyn, Aline Iragi, Johanna Jobst, Antje Kirchner, Daniela Kromrey, Anna Maedl, Mass Walimaba Katangira, Nadine Meidert, Anja Osei, Huib Pellikaan, Annett Pfeiffer, Yvette Peters, Heike Riedke, Karin Schemmann-Schoernack, Gerald Schneider, Michael Schumacher, Sjard Seibert, Frederik Trettin, Anna van der Wandt, Martin Welz, Kathryn Uhrig, Eva Maria Vögtle, Roland Weierstall, Nina Winkler, Marion Woelki, and for all those friends and colleagues that I forgot to mention but were crucial during the writing process of this book. Finally, I thank my family for supporting me throughout the process. More than anything, they kept me focused on all the things in life that are really important.

Introduction

Although the idea of a conventional regimented war, as codified by Clausewitz (1989 [1832]), is still widely present in most people's minds, it is largely misleading nowadays. Collective violence no longer primarily concerns two state armies facing each other in a well-defined area and shooting at each other (Azam 2006: 53). Instead, internal conflict involving many state and non-state actors has been the dominant form of conflict throughout most of the post-World War II period (Gleditsch *et al.* 2002). These conflicts have affected close to one quarter of all countries in the world and are characterized by extremely high numbers of civilian casualties (Zahar 2001: 43). Civilians are then also no longer isolated from the events on the battlefield. Rather, the most dramatic and prevalent threat to noncombatants nowadays arises in internal armed conflicts (Balcells 2010: 295–296; Bruderlein 2001: 22).[1]

Fearon and Laitin (2003) for example, have estimated that these conflicts have caused the death of more than 16.2 million people. Harff (2003) even assessed that as many as 22 million civilians have died since the end of World War II, more than all battle-related deaths of all internal and international wars together since 1945. However, the exact extent of civilian suffering varies across time, conflict, geographic region, and more important for this study, it varies across armed groups. Some insurgent groups, such as the Ugandan National Resistance Army (NRA), exhibit restraints in their relationship with noncombatants, while other armed groups, such as the Rwandan Interahamwe, have intentionally target civilians on a very large scale (Humphreys and Weinstein 2006: 429).

In exploring this variation in civilian abuse, the starting point of this study is the idea that targeting civilians is potential costly for armed groups. It violates the principal of noncombatants immunity and discrimination as enshrined in the Geneva Convention IV relative to the Protection of Civilian Persons in Time of War (1949), which require that belligerents must distinguish between combatants and noncombatants, and orders to refrain from targeting the latter (Downes 2006: 156). Targeting civilians and violating the Geneva Convention might then also upset international actors, which can lead to their involvement in the war. They can, for example, freeze economic assets or send military troops. Additionally, coercive tactics undermine the civilian base of support for warring parties

(Valentino *et al.* 2004). Mao already bequeathed that those who take up arms against authority must have the explicit support (or at least the tacit complicity) of the population among whom they live, if they are to swim among the masses like fish in the water (quoted in Mkwandaire 2002: 181). In other words, insurgent groups depend on civilian populations for resources necessary to sustain their war, and they risk this support when they utilize violence (Humphreys and Weinstein 2006: 429; Wood 2009: 1). As a member of the Irish Republican Army (IRA) explains:

> Without the community we were irrelevant. We carried the guns and planted the bombs, but the community fed us, hid us, opened their homes to us, turned a blind eye to our operations.... Part of me wanted the community to day: We need you, as you need us.
>
> (Collins 1997: 225; Bloom and Horgan 2008)

The costly nature of this violence raises an important question: what motivates armed groups to target civilians when doing so appears to be a suboptimal strategy and morally wrong? Why do armed movements appear as anything but fish in the water? To put it differently, why do some warring factions abuse noncombatants whereas others do not?

Those studies that have approached the topic of violence against civilians, also called one-sided violence, have focused on two strands of explanatory factors.[2] The first batch of studies has identified regime type as the key predictor (Downes 2006: 153). However, scholars who evoke democracy as an explanation disagree over the effect that it has, and this dispute reflects the norms versus institutions division in the broader democratic peace literature (Downes 2006: 159). According to some scholars, democracies are less likely to target civilians primarily because they adhere to liberal norms that proscribe killing innocent people. Valentino *et al.* (2004: 382) for example, argue: "If democratic values promote tolerance, nonviolence, and respect for legal constraints, then democracies should wage theory wars more humanly than other forms of government." Studies of democratic institutions, however, imply just the opposite: democracies are more likely to target noncombatants because the vulnerability of their leaders to public opinion makes them wary of incurring heavy costs in the battlefield for fear of losing home support. This fear could compel democratic elites to target noncombatants to avoid costs or to win the war quickly (e.g., Reiter and Stam 2002; Downes 2006: 153–154).

A second strand of studies suggests that the decision to resort to violence is made with an expectation that it improves the strategic position of the actor who employs it. According to these theories, violence against civilians is not arbitrary, but rather represents a frightening rationale due to changes in the overall strategic environment (e.g., Kalyvas 2006; Wood 2009: 3). This idea tends to get missed in traditional human rights literature, but is increasingly taken up by scholars in the field of international relations (Keen 2000: 25–26). Most notably, Kalyvas (2006) argues that changes in territorial control and informational asymmetries drive the decision to use violence. Other scholars have similarly argued that insurgents (or states) may use terrorist tactics during periods of setback or when they otherwise find their environment working against them, using violence as a means to induce communal loyalty (Byman 1998), enhance their bargaining position (Lake 2002), or induce humanitarian resources for predation (Hoffman 2004). Hultman (2007) for example, argues that civilian killing is a strategy often employed by rebels whose power is declining relative to the government. By targeting civilians, these actors can impose extra costs on the government since the latter is ultimately responsible for the protection of the civilian population. This argument can also be found in the work of Downes (2006: 170). He argues that civilian victimization is driven by its perceived necessity: leaders of armed groups may see themselves as having little choice but to target noncombatants. They believe that targeting the noncombatant population allows them to continue fighting, reduce casualties, and possibly win the war by coercing the adversary to quit.

Both explanatory strands of literature tend to focus on the context of violence and have largely ignored the actor's choice and responsibility (Mitchell 2004: 15). Do not misunderstand: in order to explain the variation of civilian abuse across armed groups, it is useful to know whether these environmental settings, such as the level of democracy, come with civilian abuse. However, the intentional killing of civilians is a policy – not the inhuman outcome of impersonal, slow-shifting economic, political, historical, or international substructure (Mitchell 2004: 17–18). In other words, if we want to uncover the much-needed dynamics underlying the variation in civilian abuse, it is necessary to devote attention to the characteristics of the armed groups, actors (state or non-state) that use armed force to accomplish a various spectrum of goals (Eck and Hultman 2007; Gill 2012).

Only few academic studies have given attention to the characteristics of these kinds of violent groups and how these characteristics influence their behavior towards the civilian population. This lack of attention stems from the fact that the field has been dominated by studies focused on approaches of realism and liberalism, which mainly focus on the nation-state, or on the relations between nation-states in the international system (Carey and Poe 2004: 4–5). Those studies that moved beyond this theoretical orientation have primarily argued in line with the so-called new war perspective. According to this perspective, one of the central characteristics of these new wars is the blending of the criminal and the political, and all the competing armed groups are expression of this unique process (Kaldor 1999). This idea leads often to the adoption of the isomorphism hypothesis as a central common-sense assumption; armed groups are treated as a constant factor and differences between them are glossed over (Gutiérrez Sanín 2007: 2). Consequently, practitioners and scholars alike lose a significant part in their interest in armed groups. This is surprising, particularly if the international community wishes to influence the behavior of these groups in order to protect civilians. If we aspire to generate a more pragmatic approach to dealing with these groups, the first step is to move beyond this isomorphism hypothesis and examine the difference between armed groups and how these difference influence their (violent) behavior. Only then might the policy community be able to develop effective warning systems or more capable policies for resolving existing conflicts (Jones and Carter 2001: 238–240). To account for this lack of attention, this study focuses on the following research question: do differences in the organizational structure of armed groups shape broad patterns of human rights violations against the civilian population, and if so how?

Structure is conceived here as a broader construct describing processes governing internal operation as well as the similarity and insularity of the members (Pynchon and Borum 1999: 347). These processes determine how preferences are aggregated, how choices unfold over time, and how armed groups set expectations about future interactions (Whitford 2002: 168). The effect of the armed group's organizational structure on their behavior towards the civilian population is examined by drawing on the principal–agent theory, in which I contend, in line with the strategic explanation of civilian abuse (see above), that civilian victimization is the result of a strategic and rational decision of the leader (Valentino 2004). I argue in Chapter 1 of this study, that the faithful execution of this order is conditioned, like in any other delegation relationship, by the amount of influence or control that the leader can pose over her troops. Her level of control depends on whether she can overcome two problems inherent to any delegation relationship: the problem of adverse selection (i.e., she does not know whether she hires the right people) and of moral hazard (i.e., she cannot tell for sure that her orders are executed).

In Chapter 2 and 3 of this study, I argue that the leader can overcome these two problems by employing four strategies that transform the organizational structure of her armed group in a way that it increases her level of control over her troops. Two of these strategies are focused on overcoming the problem of adverse selection by improving the recruitment and selection capabilities of the leader. This she can do by offering particular kinds of incentives to attract a certain type of combatant and by recruiting new members from one and the same social network. The problem of moral hazard can, on the other hand, be overcome with strategies that are focused on improving the monitoring and sanctioning capabilities of the leader: she could structure the armed group more hierarchical and try to create organizational commitment among her troops.

For each of these four strategies, two hypotheses are derived: one for testing the relationship on the level of the armed groups (i.e., the meso-level) and one for testing the effect of these strategies on the level of the individual combatant (i.e., the micro-level). Unfortunately, for both levels comparative information is missing; there is no dataset available that records comparative information of many armed groups across the world. Additionally, there is no publicly available information available on the strategies of the individual combatants. Consequently, in this book two new datasets are constructed.

To examine the effect of these four strategies on the violent behavior of armed groups, I have created the first dataset on the basis of a self-developed Web survey among 400 armed group experts. This dataset records information on the internal structures of around 70 armed groups across the world. In Chapter 4, I discuss the developed research design, the operationalization of the key dependent and independent variables, the selection of the armed groups, and the construction and implementation of the Web survey. In Chapter 5, I analyze the resulting armed group dataset with a Bayesian approach and test the four hypotheses.

To investigate the effect of these four strategies on the level of the combatant, I have created a second dataset on the basis of 95 quantitative interviews held with (former) combatants in the Democratic Republic of the Congo (DRC). The research design and the variables underlying the interviews are discussed in Chapter 6. In this chapter, I also focus on the challenges that scholars might encounter when doing research in these conflict-affected areas. In Chapter 7, I empirically analyze with Bayesian methods the 95 interviews and present the results. In the final chapter, the conclusion, I summarize the theoretical approach and the empirical findings and discuss the broader research implications of this study.

By examining these four strategies on the level of the armed groups and of the individual combatant, I presume that armed groups are not unitary actors. Rather, I consider them as collective organizations composed of individual combatants. If we want to verify that the identified causal mechanisms linking the organizational structure to civilian abuse are robust, without running into the problem of ecological fallacy, we would have to make sure that these mechanisms are also present at lower levels of analyses, i.e., on the level of the combatants. Likewise, it is incorrect to explain the violent behavior of combatants by not referring to the armed groups in which they are embedded. Taking this into account, I extend the micro-level part of this study by focusing on an additional research question: how are individuals molded into committed combatants by armed groups? In other words, which strategies can these groups employ to create committed fighters? In answering this question, I examine whether armed groups employ the same kinds of economic management strategies as legal public and private firms do to create committed employees.

Only when these two levels of analyses are combined, is the international community able to develop preventive programs or more effective Disarmament, Demobilization, and Reintegration (DDR) programs. Bøås and Hatløy (2008: 34) for example, state that attempts at reintegration of combatants must be made with an understanding of the civil war, not just at a state level but, perhaps especially, at a micro-level. A greater understanding of what makes them more likely to target civilians will enable the development of more effective and sustainable processes and policies to bring them fully back out.

Notes

1 Civilians are often not defined in the literature. See Walzer (1977) for a useful discussion. For the purpose of this study, I use the terms "civilians" and "noncombatants" interchangeably and define it in line with the Geneva Convention IV (1949); a civilian or noncombatant is any individual who does not take an active military role in the conflict.

2 Throughout this study the concepts of "one-sided violence" and "civilian abuse" are used interchangeably. One-sided violence is defined as the direct and intentional use of armed force by government of a state or by a formally organized group against civilians (Eck and Hultman 2007).

References

Azam, Jean-Paul. 2006. "On thugs and heroes: Why warlords victimize their own civilians." *Economics of Governance* 7(1): 53–73.

Balcells, Laia. 2010. "Rivalry and Revenge. Violence against Civilians in Conventional Civil Wars." *International Studies Quarterly* 54(2): 291–313.

Bøås, Morton and Anne Hatløy. 2008. " 'Getting in, getting out': militia membership and prospects for re-integration in post-war Liberia." *Journal of Modern African Studies* 46(1): 33–55.

Bloom, Mia and John Horgan. 2008. "Missing Their Mark: The IRAs Proxy Bomb Campaign." *Social Research* 75(2): 579–614.

Bruderlein, Claude. 2001. "The End of Innocence: Humanitarian Protection in the Twenty-First Century." In *Civilians in War*, ed. Simon Chesterman. London: Lynne Rienner Publishers, 221–235.

Byman, Daniel. 1998. "The Logic of Ethnic Terrorism." *Studies in Conflict Terrorism* 21(2): 149–169.

Carey, Sabine C. and Steven C. Poe. 2004. "Human Rights Research and the Quest for Human Dignity." In *Understanding Human Rights Violations. New Systematic Studies*, eds. Sabine C. Carey and Steven C. Poe. Aldershot: Ashgate, 3–15.

Clausewitz, Carl von. 1989[1832]. *On War*. Princeton: Princeton University Press.

Collins, Eamon. 1997. *Killing Rage*. London: Granta.

Downes, Alexander B. 2006. "Desperate Times, Desperate Measures. The Causes of Civilian Victimization in War." *International Security* 30(4): 152–195.

Eck, Kristine, and Lisa Hultman. 2007. "One-Sided Violence Against Civilians in War: Insights from New Fatality Data." *Journal of Peace Research* 44(2): 233–246.

Fearon, James D. and David D. Laitin. 2003 "Ethnicity, Insurgency, and Civil War." *American Political Science Review* 97(1): 75–90.

Geneva Conventions. 1949. "The Geneva Conventions of 1949 and their Additional Protocols." www.icrc.org/eng/war-and-law/treaties-customary-law/geneva-conventions/ (August 8, 2014).

Gill, Paul. 2012. "Terrorist Violence and the Contextual, Facilitative and Causal Qualities of Group-based Behaviors." *Aggression and Violent Behavior* 17(6): 565–574.

Gleditsch, Nils Petter, Peter Wallensteen, Mikael Eriksson, Margareta Sollenberg, and Hårvard Strand. 2002. "Armed Conflict 1946–2001: A New Dataset." *Journal of Peace Research* 39(5): 615–637.

Gutiérrez Sanín, Francisco. 2007. *Organizing Minors: The Case of Colombia*. Working paper, Ford Institute for Human Security.

Harff, Barbara. 2003. "No Lessons Learned from the Holocaust? Assessing Risks of Genocide and Political Mass Murder since 1955." *American Political Science Review* 97(1): 57–73.

Hoffman, Danny. 2004. "The Civilian Target in Sierra Leone and Liberia: Political Power, Military Strategy, and Humanitarian Intervention." *African Affairs* 103: 211–226.

Hultman, Lisa. 2007. "Battle Losses and Rebel Violence: Raising the Costs for Fighting." *Terrorism and Political Violence* 19(2): 205–222.

Humphreys, Macartan and Jeremy M. Weinstein. 2006. "Handling and Manhandling Civilian in Civil War." *American Political Science Review* 100(3): 429–447.

Jones, Bruce D. and Charles K. Carter. 2001. "From Chaos to Coherence? Toward a Regime for Protecting Civilians in War?" In *Civilians in War*, ed. Simon Chesterman. London: Lynne Rienner Publishers, 237–262.

Kaldor, Mary. 1999. *New and Old Wars: Organized Violence in a Global Era*. Cambridge: Polity Press.

Kalyvas, Stathis N. 2006. *The Logic of Violence in Civil Wars*. Cambridge: Cambridge University Press.

Keen, David. 2000. "Incentives and Disincentives for Violence." In *Greed and Grievance: Economic Agendas in Civil Wars*, eds. Mats Berdal and David M. Malone. Boulder, CO: Lynne Rienner Publishers, 19–41.

Lake, David A. 2002. "Rational Extremism: Understanding Terrorism in the Twenty-First Century." *Dialog IO* 1(1): 15–29.

Mitchell, Neil J. 2004. *Agents of Atrocity. Leaders, Followers, and the Violation of Human Rights in Civil War*. New York: Palgrave Macmillan.

Mkwandaire, Thandika. 2002. "The terrible toll of post-colonial 'rebel movements' in Africa: towards an explanation of the violence against the peasantry." *The Journal of Modern African Studies* 40(2): 181–215.

Pynchon, Marisa Reddy and Randy Borum. 1999. "Assessing Threats of Targeted Group Violence: Contributions from Social Psychology." *Behavioral Sciences and the Law* 17(3): 339–355.

Reiter, Dan and Allan C. Stam 2002. *Democracies at War*. Princeton: Princeton University Press.

Valentino, Benjamin, Paul Huth, and Dylan Balch-Lindsay. 2004. "'Draining the Sea': Mass Killing and Guerrilla Warfare." *International Organization* 58(1): 375–407.

Walzer, Michael. 1977. *Just and Unjust Wars: A Moral Argument with Historical Illustrations*. New York: Basic.

Whitford, Andrew B. 2002. "Decentralization and Political Control of the Bureaucracy." *Journal of Theoretical Politics* 14(2): 167–193.

Wood, Reed M. 2009. "Draining Their Sea?: Rebel Capability and Violence toward Civilians in Civil Conflict." Presented at the Annual Meeting of the International Studies Association, New York.

Zahar, Marie-Joëlle. 2001. "Protégés, Clients, Cannon Fodder: Civil-Militia Relations in Internal Conflicts." In *Civilians in War*, ed. Simon Chesterman. London: Lynne Rienner Publishers, 43–65.

Part I
Theory

The internal organization of armed groups

1 Principal–agent theory and armed groups

Recent years have been characterized by a heightened academic interest in organizations. It is in the context of organizations that collective action is most effectively coordinated, that prisoner's dilemmas are most readily overcome, and that stable social decisions are most likely made (Kiewiet and McCubbins 1991). The organizational bases of collective action are many – firms, bureaucracies, associations, committees, leagues, representative assemblies, but also armed groups. What the most prominent forms of organizations have in common, however, is the delegation of authority to take action from the individual or individuals to whom it originally endowed (Kiewiet and McCubbins 1991: 23). When talking about organizations and delegation, one quickly arrives at the agency theory that explains various aspects of delegation. In the following chapter, I explain the basic concepts of the principal–agent theory and how this is related to armed groups.

Development

Agency theory was first formulated in the field of economics. In 1971, Spence and Zeckhauser (1971) published an article in which the framework was presented that clarified the dilemmas of dealing with incomplete information in insurance industry contracts. By the 1980s, economists working on insurance models had defined the issues, concerns, and canonical result of the principal–agent theory (Holmström 1979; Shavell 1979; Miller 2005). From its roots in economics, agency theory has developed along two lines: positivist (empirical) and principal–agent (theoretical) (Jensen 1983). The two streams share a common unit of analysis: the contract between an actor that delegates and one that receives the extra responsibility. Both research strands also share common assumptions about people, organizations, and information. However, they differ in their mathematical rigor, dependent variable, and style. Positivist researchers have primarily focused on identifying situations in which the actors involved in the delegation are likely to have conflicting goals and they then describe the mechanisms that limit the actions of the actors that receive the extra responsibility (Eisenhardt 1989). Principal–agent theory researchers, on the other hand, are concerned with a general theory of the principal–agent relationship, a theory that can be applied to employer–employee, lawyer–client, buyer–supplier, and other agency relationships. This paradigm involves often careful specification of assumptions which are followed by logical deduction, and mathematical proof (Eisenhardt 1989).

Terry Moe (1984) made the translation of the agency theory to political science, where it has become very influential. However, within political science the differentiation between the two streams is less emphasized and one generally speaks about principal–agent theory without acknowledging the two strands. Most political scientists are, however, primarily concerned with the positivist stream of the agency theory. They apply the theory and describe the mechanisms that solve the problem of agency loss. Only few political scientists have been concerned with the theoretical principal–agent stream, i.e., which delegation contract is the most efficient under varying levels of outcome uncertainty, risk aversion, information, and other variables (Eisenhardt 1989). However, when political scientists first applied the principal–agent theory, not only were the two strands largely disregarded but also further differences emerged from the original economic formulation (Waterman and Meier 1998). In its new formulation, it was postulated that the principal and agents in political settings share the same characteristics as they would do in economic settings.

The first applications of this theory in political science was in the field of American and comparative politics, in which the theory has become the basis for an extensive set of studies relating to the delegation to bureaucracy and legislative committees (see e.g., Banks and Weingast 1992; Mitnick 1973; 1975; 1980; Moe 1982; 1984; 1985; Kiewiet and McCubbins 1991; McCubbins and Schwartz 1984; Wood and Waterman 1991; 1993; 1994; Scholz and Wei 1986). The most important finding from these applications is that the previously widespread view among scholars – that all-powerful bureaucrats often run amok in the policy process – is dramatically overstated, if not false (Nielson and Tierny 2003). The agency theory has also been taken up by international relations scholars. They have applied it to the study of international organizations, noting several similarities between domestic bureaucracies and multilateral bodies (e.g., Brown 2010; Pollack 1997; Nielson and Tierney 2003). Especially in the field of European Union (EU) studies, principal–agent models and the theory of delegation have been increasingly applied (Kassim and Menon 2003). This is in large part due to the fact that the theory is explicitly concerned with complex inter-institutional interactions, which is an inherit aspect of the EU (Kassim and Menon 2003). As a result, the principal–agent model offers a way of grasping the institutional complexity of the EU without relying too much on the intergovernmentalist versus neofunctionalist debate that historically dominated the field (Pollack 1997; Kassim and Menon 2003).

Principal–agent theory has achieved widespread recognition in political science and research has proliferated (see Miller 2005 for a good overview of the application of the principal–agent theory in political science). However, within security and conflict studies, principal–agent theory has seen relatively little use (Rauchhaus 2009: 873). Some scholars have, however, applied the theory to the study of civil–military relations. Deborah Avant (1993; 1994) was one of the first that borrowed insights from the principal–agent theory to explain different propensities for innovation across British and American military organizations. Risa Brooks (2000) also uses the theory to compare how different patterns of civil-military relations produce different grand military strategies. Amy Zegart (1999) uses it to explore the design of national security agencies at the start of the Cold War.

However, applications of the principal–agent theory to the study of armed groups and their behavior towards the civilian population almost do not exist (Johnson 2008). An important exception forms the study conducted by Gates (2002). Although only limitedly focused on the internal dynamics of armed forces, Gates (2002) developed a model to demonstrate that geography, ethnicity, and ideology play an important role in determining military success, deterring defection within the rebel group, and shaping recruitment. Also Hovil and Werker (2005) use the principal–agent theory as a basis in their study to anti-civilian violence in Western Uganda. They found out that a high level of violence towards the Ugandan civilian population was the result of a divergence of interests, unequal access of information, and contracting limitations between the financier and the insurgents. To put it more precisely, civilians were victimized by the Allied Democratic Forces (ADF), so that they could keep their outside funding. Also the study conducted by Butler *et al.* (2007) forms an exception and use the principal–agent theory to investigate sexual violence committed by government security forces. The authors start their theory with the assumption that when combatants are given a high degree of slack, they are more likely to perpetrate incidences of sexual violence. After controlling for factors likely to increase the incidence of sexual violence, such as military size and ethnic fractionalization, they found that, where agents are more accountable and subject to tighter control, sexual violence is less likely perpetrated. Note, however, that their dependent variable is the number of incidences of sexual violence, not the number of sexually violated victims.

Assumptions

The principal–agent model is an analytical expression of the agency relationship, in which one party considers to enter into a contractual agreement with another in the expectation that the latter will subsequently choose an action that produces outcomes desired by the former (Moe 1984). In other words, principal–agent scholars assume that social life is a series of contracts, in which the "contracts" are between (two or more) parties (Perrow 1986: 224). One, designated as the agent, acts for, on behalf of, or as representative for the other, designated the principal, in a particular domain of decision problems.[1] Examples of agency relationships are legion. For instance, in the doctor–patient relationship, the doctor is the agent hired by the patient, the principal. But the cooperative executive of a company and her subordinates as agents is also a good example. Note that the cooperative executive is in turn an agent for the shareholders (Pratt and

Zeckhauser 1985: 2). In sum, essentially all contractual arrangements can be approached with this particular theory (Ross 1973).

As these examples tend to suggest, a principal may delegate to an agent for various reasons. Delegation is then also the basis of the principal–agent theory and several factors motivate a principal to give up some authority over outcomes by delegating it to an agent. One of the most important functions of delegation is to save costs. Delegation allows principals to internalize costs associated with arm's length transactions as well as to realize efficiency gains associated with specialization. Principals may lack time and task-specific expertise to carry out all required operations and will consequently contract an agent to perform a specified job or jobs (Byman and Kreps 2010; Egan 1998; Salehyan 2010). They might also delegate to increase the credibility of their commitments or to displace responsibility for unpopular decisions (Fiorina 1977; Epstein and O'Halloran 1999). For example, delegations to enforcing agents with high discretion such as an independent central bank signals commitment, since granting enforcement authority to this agent makes it less possible for the principal to back out of its pledge (Byman and Kreps 2010). Also delegating warfare to private security companies is a good example of displacing responsibility for unpopular decisions, such as the use of violence against the civilian population. The principal might also seek to delegate to agents in order to ensure that the principal's preferences are acted upon well beyond the duration of the principal's tenure (Byman and Kreps 2010). Delegation resolves then also the problem of policy-making instability since delegation to an agent that shares and implements policies is one way to enact change over the longer term when the principal's power may wane or when other principals may assume greater power (Byman and Kreps 2010; Pollack 1997; McKelvey 1976; Riker 1980).

Given some motivation for relying on an agent, the principal offers the agent a contract. The principal has the first mover's advantage, which resembles the Stackelberg game in which the leader and the followers move sequentially (Von Stackelberg 1934). Consequently, the principal is endowed with all of the bargaining power and can make a "take-it-or-leave-it" offer to the agent (Sappington 1991: 47). However, the offered contract must satisfy the so-called participation constraint of the agent, i.e., the agent's compensation must be at least as great as his opportunity costs. If this condition is not met, the agent will not be made better off by entering into the relationship and will decline to sign the contract. Assuming that the participation constraint is satisfied, the principal's goal is to delegate tasks and responsibilities and to specify a corresponding schedule of compensation in such a way that the agent is motivated to best serve the principal's interests rather than shirking or sabotaging (Kiewiet and McCubbins 1991: 27–28).

If information flowed costless and perfectly, principals would know what their agents knew and what they were doing. They could be confident that agents were operating as if they were principals themselves (Pratt and Zeckhauser 1985). But in real life, complete and full information is rarely freely available to all parties. Agents' possess more information about their tasks than their principals do, though principals may know more about what they want accomplished (Pratt and Zeckhauser 1985: 3). It is the very nature of delegation that results in this information asymmetry. However, note that the exact nature of this information is unclear in most circumstances (Mitnick 1986). In the more mathematical applications of the principal–agent model, this is a lesser problem since ambiguities in these studies can relatively easy be removed. However, most principal–agent studies lack a clear definition or idea on what this information connotes (Waterman and Meier 1998).

In the study of armed groups and their behavior, much information is common to both the agent and the principal. For instance, both know the nature and the general identity of their enemies and they often share a common history and political memory. However, each actor has also private information that is discerned only dimly by the other. The agent's status as an expert on the management of violence confers significant informational advantages over the principal in areas like tactics and logistics (Feaver 2005). Of course, the extent to which the military agent's expertise exceeds that of the principal, even in the arcane of operational art, varies with the backgrounds and biographies of the agents involved (Feaver 2005). Likewise, some information is private to the principal. For instance, only the principal knows exactly how to judge various risks and how these judgments translate into preferences and outcomes (Feaver 2005: 69).

In addition to an asymmetry of information, the relationship between the agent and principal is complicated by the fact that there exists also an asymmetry of preferences between the two players. This asymmetry in preferences is most notable when speaking about effort. Effort is a disutility to the agent, however, it has a value to the principal in the sense that it increases the likelihood of a favorable outcome (technically, the distribution of the outcome to a higher effort stochastically dominates that of a lower effort; that is, the probability of achieving an outcome that exceeds any given level is higher with higher effort) (Arrow 1985: 38). The result of this setting is that a natural conflict of interest occurs; the cost for one is the revenue for the other: the wage paid is revenue for the agent and a cost for the principal, while the effort and action of the agent favors the principal is costly for the agent (Macho-Stadler and Pérez-Castrillo 1997: 5).

In economic settings, such as in the marketplace, these conflicts are often over the amount of effort expended by the agent. He wants to make as much money as possible while the principal wants to pay as little as possible for services (Waterman and Meier 1998: 185). In these kinds of settings it is then also not implausible to imagine that an agent would produce no work if he gets away with it. In political settings, such as the bureaucracy, with a focus on policy instead of profit, goal conflict may not always be so clearly apparent. In these settings, conflict is more likely to be over the course of action the agent has to pursue (Kiewiet and McCubbins 1991: 24). However, assessing the course of action, i.e., how efficient an agent has fulfilled his job, is tremendously difficult. Brehm and Gates (1994: 192) for instance, argue that even if the subordinate's production were fully visible with zero monitoring costs, production is itself ambiguous. A good example is the civil-military setting. It is reasonable to posit that both civilian principals and the military agents want the same thing: security for the state. However, they might disagree on how to provide that security, in general and especially in particular settings (Feaver 2005: 59).

Even more controversy surrounds the topic of goal variance in armed movements and how this relates to human rights abuses. In some studies, scholars have simplified the analysis by assuming that "the act of repression has no utility" (Gartner and Regan 1996). In other words, the principal does not receive any benefits in victimizing the civilian population. Butler *et al.* (2007) for example, assume that governments (i.e., the principal) lose control over their security forces and that this loss of control increases the number of incidences of sexual violence perpetrated by out-of-control agents. In other words, they assume that principals do not have the intention to victimize civilians and that their agents go on a rampage as soon as they realize that they are not controlled. However, recent literature on genocide and mass killing offers a compelling alternative view. Valentino (2004) for instance, argues that mass killing is an intentional tactic employed by political and military leaders in pursuit of their strategic objectives. Or as he has formulated (2004: 2):

> Previous theoretical studies of genocide have tended to diminish the role of leadership on the grounds that the interests and ideas of a few elites cannot account for the participation of the rest of society in the violence. My research, however, suggests that society at large plays a smaller role in mass killing than is commonly assumed. On the contrary, the impetus for mass killing usually originates from a relatively small group of powerful political and military leaders.

This strategic understanding of human right abuses neither implies that commanders always evaluate objectively the problems they face nor that they accurately assess the ability of civilian victimization to resolve these problems. Nevertheless, principals might consider civilian killings as an instrumental policy – a brutal strategy designed to accomplish leaders' objectives and counter what they see as their most dangerous threat. Note that this brutal strategy is often a policy of last resort. Principals commonly experiment with other, less violent, or even conciliatory means in the attempt to achieve their objective. However, when these means fail or are deemed too costly or demanding, leaders are forced to choose between compromising their most important goals and interests or resorting to more violent methods to achieve them (Valentino 2004: 67). For example, Daly (2002) note when talking about the military strategy of the Ḥarakat al-Muqāwamah al-ʾIslāmiyyah (HAMAS), that although some of their attacks are successful against military strategies, most are carried out against civilians. As the HAMAS training manual notes: "it is foolish to hun the tiger when there are plenty of sheep around."

If we approach civilian killings from this strategic perspective, benefits of civilian abuse accrue to the group rather than to the individual member and the cost of committing the abuse is applied to the individual rather than the group (Humphreys and Weinstein 2006: 433). As a result, the logic of this proposed argument is a reversed version of that of Butler *et al.* (2007): the principal endorses, rather than restrains, the abuse of the noncombatant population. From this illicit principal–agent perspective, an organization that functions effectively in pursuit of its overall objectives can thus serve to increase abusiveness if its leaders are motivated by a desire to kill or destroy civilians (Humphreys and Weinstein 2006: 433). Following this reasoning, it is assumed that if a principal controls her agents, they are more likely to commit human rights abuses against the civilian population and if these abuses occur that the principal has ordered it. At the same time, it is assumed that agents prefer not to victimize civilians at all.

This sketched relationship between the principal and her agents and the two inherent problems (information asymmetry and preference asymmetry) might have severe consequence for the civilian population. In the next two chapters, these two problems are explained in more detail. More importantly, potential strategies are discussed that help the principal to overcome these two problems and increase her control over her troops. In turn, I argue in the upcoming chapters that this increase of control has severe consequences for the civilian population in conflict-ridden countries.

Note

1 In order to make things clear throughout the different chapters, I decided to define principals as female and agents as males.

References

Arrow, Kenneth J. 1985. "The Economics of Agency." In *Principals and Agents: The Structure of Business*, eds. John W. Pratt and Richard J. Zeckhauser. Boston: Harvard Business School Press, 1–37.

Avant, Deborah D. 1993. "The institutional Sources of Military Doctrine: Hegemons in Peripheral Wars." *International Studies Quarterly* 37(4): 409–430.

Avant, Deborah D. 1994. *Political Institutions and Military Change: Lessons from Peripheral Wars*. Ithaca: Cornell University Press.

Banks, Jeffrey S. and Barry R. Weingast. 1992. "The Political Control of Bureaucracies under Asymmetric Information." *American Journal of Political Science* 36(2): 509–524.

Brehm, John and Scott Gates. 1994. *Working, Shirking, and Sabotage. Bureaucratic Response to a Democratic Public*. Ann Arbor: The University of Michigan Press.

Brooks, Risa. 2000. *Institutions at the Domestic and International Nexus: The Political-Military origins of Strategic Integration, Military Effectiveness and War*. PhD diss., University of California, San Diego.

Brown, Robert L. 2010. "Measuring Delegation." *The Review of International Organizations* 5(2): 141–175.

Butler, Christopher K., Tali Gluch, and Neil J. Mitchell. 2007. "Security Forces and Sexual Violence: A Cross-National Analysis of a Principal–Agent Argument." *Journal of Peace Research* 44(6): 669–687.

Byman, Daniel and Sarah E. Kreps. 2010. "Agents of Destruction? Applying Principal–Agent Analysis to State-Sponsored Terrorism." *International Studies Perspectives* 11(1): 1–18.

Daly, John. 2002. "Suicide Bombing: No Warnings and No Total Solutions." *Jane's Defence Weekly*, 17 September 2001.

Egan, Michelle. 1998. "Regulatory strategies, delegation and European market integration." *Journal of European Public Policy* 5(3): 485–506.

Eisenhardt, Kathleen M. 1989. "Agency Theory: An Assessment and Review." *The Academy of Management Review* 14(1): 57–74.

Epstein, David and Sharyn O'Halloran 1999. *Delegating powers: A Transaction Cost Politics Approach to Policy Making under Separate Powers*. Cambridge: Cambridge University Press.

Feaver, Peter D. 2005. *Armed Servants. Agency, Oversight, and Civil-Military Relations*. Harvard: Harvard University Press.

Fiorina, Morris P. 1977. "The Case of the Vanishing Marginals: The Bureaucracy Did It." *American Political Science Review* 71(1): 177–181.

Gartner, Scott S. and Patrick M. Regan. 1996. "Threat and Repression: The Non-Linear Relationship between Government and Opposition Violence." *Journal of Peace Research* 33(3): 273–288.

Gates, Scott. 2002. "Recruitment and Allegiance: The Microfoundations of Rebellion." *Journal of Conflict Resolution* 46(1): 111–130.

Holmström, Bengt. 1979. "Moral hazard and Observability." *The Bell Journal of Economics* 10(1): 74–91.

Hovil, Lucy and Eric Werker. 2005. "Portrait of a Failed Rebellion. An Account of Rational, Sub-Optimal Violence in Western Uganda." *Rationality and Society* 17(1): 5–34.

Humphreys, Macartan and Jeremy M. Weinstein. 2006. "Handling and Manhandling Civilian in Civil War." *American Political Science Review* 100(3): 429–447.

Jensen, Michael C. 1983. "Organization theory and methodology." *Accounting Review* 56(2): 319–338.

Johnson, Patrick. 2008. "The Geography of Insurgent Organization and its Consequences for Civil Wars: Evidence from Liberia and Sierra Leone." *Security Studies* 17(1): 107–137.

Kassim, Hussein and Anand Menon. 2003. "The principal–agent approach and the study of the European Union: promise unfulfilled?" *Journal of European Public Policy* 10(1): 121–139.

Kiewiet, D. Roderick and Mathew D. McCubbins. 1991. *The Logic of Delegation. Congressional Parties and the Appropriations Process*. Chicago: The University of Chicago Press.

Macho-Stadler, Inés and J. David Pérez-Castrillo. 1997. *An Introduction to the Economics of Information: Incentives and Contracts*. Oxford: Oxford University Press.

McCubbins, Mathew D. and Thomas Schwartz. 1984. "Congressional oversight overlooked: Police patrols versus fire alarms." *American Journal of Political Science* 28(1): 165–179.

McKelvey, Richard D. 1976. "Intransitivities in multidimensional voting: models and some implications for agenda control." *Journal of Economic Theory* 12(3): 472–482.

Miller, Gary J. 2005. "The Political Evolution of Principal–Agent Models." *Annual Review of Political Science* 8(1): 203–225.

Mitnick, Barry M. 1973. "Fiduciary Rationality and Public Policy: The Theory of Agency and Some Consequences." Paper presented at the annual meeting of the American Political Science Association. New Orleans. September 4–8.

Mitnick, Barry M. 1975. "The Theory of Agency: The Policing 'Paradox' and Regulatory Behavior." *Public Choice* 24(1): 27–42.

Mitnick, Barry M. 1980. *The Political Economy of Regulation.* New York: Columbia University Press.

Mitnick, Barry M. 1986. "The Theory of Agency and Organizational Analysis." Unpublished working paper, University of Pittsburgh.

Moe, Terry M. 1982. "Regulatory Performance and Presidential Administration." *American Journal of Political Science* 26(2): 197–224.

Moe, Terry M. 1984. "The New Economics of Organization." *American Journal of Political Science* 28(4): 739–777.

Moe, Terry M. 1985. "Control and Feedback in Economic Regulation: The Case of the NLRB." *American Political Science Review* 79(4): 1094–117.

Nielson, Daniel L. and Michael J. Tierney. 2003. "Delegation to International Organizations: Agency Theory and World Bank Environmental Reform." *International Organization* 57(2): 241–276.

Perrow, Charles. 1986. *Complex Organizations: A Critical Essay.* New York: Random House.

Pollack, Mark A. 1997. "Delegation, Agency, and Agenda Setting in the European Community." *International Organization* 51(1): 99–134.

Pratt, John W. and Richard J. Zeckhauser. 1985. "Principals and Agents: An Overview." In *Principals and Agents: The Structure of Business*, eds. John W. Pratt and Richard J. Zeckhauser. Boston: Harvard Business School Press, 1–35.

Rauchhaus, Robert W. 2009. "Principal–Agent Problems in Humanitarian Intervention: Moral Hazard, Adverse Selection, and the Commitment Dilemma." *International Studies Quarterly* 53(4): 871–884.

Riker, William H. 1980. "Implications from the Disequilibrium of Majority Rule for the Study of Institutions." *American Political Science Review* 74(2): 432–446.

Ross, Stephen A. 1973. "The Economic Theory of Agency: The Principal's Problem." *The American Economic Review* 62(2): 134–139.

Salehyan, Idean. 2010. "The Delegation of War to Rebel Organizations." *Journal of Conflict Resolution* 54(3): 493–515.

Sappington, David E. M. 1991. "Incentives in Principal–Agent Relationship." *Journal of Economic Perspectives* 5(2): 45–66.

Scholz, John T. and Feng Heng Wei. 1986. "Regulatory Enforcement in a Federalist System." *American Political Science Review* 80(4): 1249–1270.

Shavell, Steven. 1979. "Risk Sharing and Incentives in the Principal and Agent Relationship." *Bell Journal of Economics* 10(1): 55–73.

Spence, Michael and Richard Zeckhauser. 1971. "Insurance, Information, and Individual Action." *The American Economic Review* 61(2): 380–387.

Valentino, Benjamin. 2004. *Final Solutions: Mass Killing and Genocide in the Twentieth Century.* Ithaca: Cornell University Press.

Von Stackelberg, Heinrich. 1934. *Marktform und Gleichgewicht.* Springer: Wien.

Waterman, Richard W. and Kenneth J. Meier. 1998. "Principal–Agent Models: An Expansion?" *Journal of Public Administration Research and Theory* 8(2): 173–202.

Wood, B. Dan and Richard W. Waterman. 1991. "The Dynamics of Political Control of the Bureaucracy." *American Political Science Review* 85(3): 801–828.

Wood, B. Dan and Richard W. Waterman. 1993. "The Dynamics of Political-Bureaucratic Adaption." *American Journal of Political Science* 37(2): 497–528.

Wood, B. Dan and Richard W. Waterman. 1994. *Bureaucratic Dynamics: The Role of Bureaucracy in a Democracy.* Boulder: Westview Press.

Zegart, Amy B. 1999. *Flawed by Design: The Evolution of the CIA, JCS, and NSC.* Stanford: Stanford University Press.

2   The problem of adverse selection

In the formal literature the two aspects of the agency problem, information asymmetry and preference asymmetry, are cited as the problem of adverse selection and the problem of moral hazard (Eisenhardt 1989: 61). Like most concepts of the principal–agent theory, both problems emerged from early applied work on insurances and were incorporated into the modern work on information and organization in recognition of their much broader theoretical significance (Moe 1984). It is important to distinguish the two problems because they are caused by different causal mechanisms but also because each problem has specific solutions (Rauchhaus 2009). This chapter especially focuses on the problem of adverse selection.[1]

Hidden information: adverse selection

The first potential pitfall for delegation is the problem of adverse selection or hidden information. This problem typically arises as the result of asymmetric information prior to entering into a contract. The principal does not have complete information about true capabilities and intentions of a given applicant. She, for example, does not know whether the agent is hardworking or lazy, talented or untalented, risk-averse or risk-acceptant (Rauchhaus 2009). In other words, the principal cannot observe the type of any given agent, or at least the law (as is often the case) forbids her to use non-anonymous process that would discriminate between types (Salanié 2005). She can only observe the agent's actual performance after the commitment to hire him is made. Potential agents, similarly, do not know whether the principal is honestly portraying the job until they start working. This problem is compounded by the fact that both potential principals and potential agents frequently have an incentive to misrepresent their abilities and preferences (Kiewiet and McCubbins 1991). Even though the principal and the "good" agent share a common interest – the principal wants to hire the best and the best wants to be hired – this does not ease the problem, for the asymmetry remains (Moe 1984). "Good" agents cannot credibly claim that they are, in fact, superbly qualified because all agents have incentives to make the same sorts of claims in order to get the job (Moe 1984).

One of the most often used examples of adverse selection is that of the insurance market. The population being insured is heterogeneous with respect to risk;

some have a higher probability of needing insurance than others. In some cases, the insured have better knowledge of this probability than the insurance company, which is unable to differentiate between those that are more at risk and those that are not (Rothchild and Stiglitz 1976; Arrow 1985). Other examples of the problem of adverse selection include the used car market in which sellers have more information about their vehicle's reliability than prospective buyers (Akerlof 1970); employers that must determine if an applicant is able to perform a job (Rauchhaus 2009); or armed groups that have to attract the right kind of members. Leggett (1981: 188) for example, noted that a Cheka official was complaining about this problem when recruiting potential members for his unit: "often unworthy elements, sometimes even counterrevolutionaries attached themselves to the Vecheka."

However, principals are not helpless in the face of this agency loss. They have and can design ex-ante tools that help to minimize the risk of these losses. In the case of adverse selection, that means they have to design screening and selection mechanisms that increase the probability of attracting those agents that are capable and whose preferences are similar to those of the principal. In other words, they have to select "principled agents" (Brehm and Gates 1994).

Note that closely related to the issue of screening is the issue of signaling (Kreps 1990; Mas-Colell *et al.* 1995). Instead of focusing on what principals can do to screen out unwanted agents, the focus then becomes what agents can do to signal their type. Some of these signals are beyond the agents' control, such as race, age, or gender. Over other signals, however, the applicant has at least partial control (Kiewiet and McCubbins 1991). One of the earliest discussions on screening and signaling issues that arise in delegation relationship was made by Akerlof (1970), who examines the used cars market and discusses some of the ways that individuals can signal the value of their used car. Once the principal "knows" the type of the agent, she is able to predict his behavior with greater confidence (Feaver 2005). However, this knowledge depends to a great extent on the signaling capabilities of the agent, i.e., in obtaining accurate information about the agents.

Incentives

To overcome the problem of adverse selection, principals have to attract the right recruits, i.e., "principled" agents that follow obedient orders. Attracting and selecting the right recruits is then also vital for every armed movement: their very existence depends on whether the group can muster troops (Gill 2007). It is then also of interest to understand how armed group recruit their members. What kind of incentives do they offer? What overcomes the risk of injury or death that members face for participating in combat? It is said that the "right" incentives attract the "right" agents with the ability to excel in certain tasks and as such create efficiency (Laffont and Martimort 2002). The only task for the principal is then also to compose a "good" contract with the "right" incentives. This is already a complicated task when constructing contracts in the legal environment.

However, when talking about attracting agents for organizations that engage in illegal activities, such as armed groups, this task of the principal is immensely challenging: in these kinds of environments, agents are even more risk averse than in normal settings.

The literature on mobilization and recruitment that deal with these questions, has exploded since 1970, when Ted Robert Gurr (1970) formulated his famous question – "why men rebel?" Several recent studies have also sought to explain why some people join armed groups (e.g., Weinstein 2007; Humphreys and Weinstein 2006, Lichbach 1995; Peters and Richards 1998; Gutiérrez Sanín 2004) and why others collaborate with such groups short of joining as full-time combatants (e.g., Wood 2003; Petersen 2001; Popkin 1979; Scott 1976). Initially, it was psychopathological studies that dominated the discussion. They assumed that compulsion to join a non-state militant organization, or the vulnerability to recruitment, was inherent in those who engaged in militancy (Gill 2012: 566). In other words, their argument was that members of armed groups (terrorist or not) are born and not made by the surrounding social and political conditions and group processes (Gill 2007: 151). For example, Hacker's (1976) classification of individual terrorists included one classification, deemed "Crazies," who were propelled to engage in terrorist violence because of mental illness. For Pearce (1977), militants were sociopaths. His analysis centered on convicted terrorists' tattoos. Cooper (1978) and Tanay (1987) also argued that terrorists possess either psychopathic or sociopathic personalities and that the acts of terrorists are merely psychopathic tendencies hidden behind political rhetoric to provide the militant with an excuse (see Gill 2012 for an excellent and more detailed overview on the linkage between personality traits and terrorist recruitment).

Studies of this nature usually contained no empirical data, neither primary nor secondary, and were often condemnatory in nature (Gill 2007). More recent studies have, therefore, failed to uncover these initial pathological traits (e.g., Della Porta 1995) and although not addressing directly the questions of insurgent or terrorist recruitment and collaboration, they have primarily relied, explicitly or implicitly, on the literature that explains the onset of civil war (e.g., Collier and Hoeffler 2004; Fearon and Laitin 2003; Arjona and Kalyvas 2009: 2). Starting from this literature, it is possible to formulate two general categories of individual theoretical conjectures for why people join armed organizations: the greed and grievance theory.[2]

Before explaining these two theories more in detail, note that I am aware of the fact that motivations for joining armed struggles and armed movements go far beyond the simplistic greed versus grievance debate (Herbst 2000). An important feature of many armed groups, although seldom discussed and studied scientifically, is coercion or abduction. Groups such as the Lord's Resistance Army (LRA) or the Sendero Luminoso (SL) in Peru are known for this forceful way of attracting recruits. This lack of attention to the influence of abduction on combatants' behavior is partly due to the fact that many models of rebellion are derived from market analogies, which emphasize the use of positive incentives.

However, armed groups that rely on abduction use often so-called negative incentives, once abducted they threaten to kill the combatants or their family if they consider to leave (Wood 2008). However, in this study, I venture that just because people make choices under some level of coercion – not an uncommon occurrence in any society – this does not remove their agency and their ability to evaluate alternative coping strategies. I, therefore, premise the analysis on the conviction that people have agency, and are not merely victims of circumstances and structures that they do not understand and did not create (Bøås and Hatløy 2008: 36).

A conventional approach for understanding the motivations of armed groups is the so-called grievance theory. This theory has its origins in early models of Ted Robert Gurr (1970) and James Davies (1962) that focuses on the relationship between levels of inequality and deprivation on the one hand, and the onset of internal conflict on the other (Sambanis 2002: 223). Gurr (1970) argued that the potential for collective violence depends on the level of discontent of members of society. This discontent stems from a perceived relative deprivation gap between men's value expectations and their value capabilities. Value expectations are those goods and conditions of life to which people believe they are rightfully entitled and value capabilities are defined as those goods and conditions they think they are capable of attaining or maintaining, given the social means available to them. As such, relative deprivation is the term used to denote the frustration that develops from a discrepancy between the "ought" and the "is" of collective value satisfaction. This discrepancy is subjective, in the sense that people may be subjectively deprived with reference to their expectations even though an objective observer might judge otherwise (Gurr 1970: 24). In other words, the value standards are set by reference to some group or status with which an individual does or is thought to identify. Relative deprivation might produce variations in collective discontent and provides the motive for violence through the psychological "frustration-aggression" mechanism (Brush 1996; Snyder 1978). As Ted Gurr (1970: 33) remarks "the disposition to respond aggressively when frustrated is part of man's biologically inherent tendency, in men and animals, to attack the frustrating agent." It is this mechanism that provides the motivational link between relative deprivation and the potential for collective political violence.

Although, Gurr (1970) was one of the first scholars that clarified the causal mechanism between relative deprivation and political violence, the concept of relative deprivation was already widely used by social scientists (see among others Geschwender 1964). The idea that instability in the form of revolutions follows modernization and that protest followed apparent progress, revived in the 1950s and 1960s (Brush 1996). The phrase "revolution of rising expectations" became a cliché that endures to this day. This idea was visually summarized in the so-called J-curve posed by Davies (1962: 6). In this curve, see also Figure 2.1, Davies (1962) combined the notion that revolutions need both a period of rising expectations and a succeeding period in which people become frustrated. This idea qualifies substantially with the main Marxian notion that

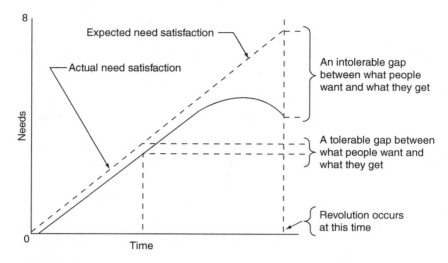

Figure 2.1 Davies' J-curve.

revolutions occur after progressive degradation and with the Tocqueville notion that they occur when conditions are improving. As Davies (1962: 17) states: "by putting Tocqueville before Marx but without abandoning either theory, we are better able to plot the antecedents of at least the disturbances here described." The main difference between the so-called J-curve and Gurr's concept of relative deprivation is that the former emphasizes the importance of a time dimension.

The grievance theory, based on the idea of relative deprivation, argues that factors of discontent are major causal elements that differentiate participants in armed conflict from non-participants. There have been innumerable attempts to identify and categorize these factors of "discontent" or "values" for purposes of psychological, sociological, and political analysis. Gurr (1970: 25) himself, has emphasized a three-fold categorization that included welfare values, power values, and interpersonal values. Scholars, like Paul Collier and Anke Hoeffler (2004) have reformulated (and in some cases – added another category) these values in a more feasible and testable categorization of discontent.

The first category of discontent factors are those related to ethnic or religious differences. This group of discontent factors are to some extent similar to the interpersonal discontent values, as is mentioned by Gurr (1970: 26). For some people, religious or ethnic differences between groups, sometimes as the result of a history of animosity, are believed to make conflict more likely (Horowitz 1985). For example, the conflicts in former Yugoslavia could be explained as the commutation of ongoing animosity between the Serb, Croat, and Bosniak ethnic groups. By extension, the specific actions of armed groups in this area, such as those of the Serb militias in Kosovo, could be seen as being motivated by a desire to redress these "ancient hatreds" (Vinci 2006; Collier 2000a). Not only might identification with a particular ethnicity be a source of conflict, but also, for example, religious or national differences (Esteban and Schneider 2008). For example, a 14-year-old boy residing in the Irish Republic, who identified himself as an Irish Catholic during an interview, clearly exemplified this when answering the question why he thinks that people join paramilitary organizations: "I think that most young people join the groups of their religion as they want to stand up for their country and for what they believe in" (Muldoon *et al.* 2008: 687).

A second important factor that might cause grievances and discontent is focused on economic inequality or welfare values. This source of grievance does not only refer to unequal income between people and the unequal ownership of assets, but also to the economic mismanagement of national governments (Collier 2000a). If a government is seen to inflict sufficient economic misery on its population, it may face an uprising. The successful National Resistance Movement (NRM) rebellion in Uganda in the early 1980s is often seen as an uprising due to despair at gross economic mismanagement by successive regimes (Collier 2000a: 96). The idea of the "rage of the poor" is a rather old argument that can also be found in the work of Karl Marx and Friedrich Engels (1998 [1872]). Economic inequality also plays an important role in attracting recruits for armed movements. The Communist Party of Nepal-Maoist (CPN-M) for example, is primarily based on class, in accordance with its Maoist ideology, but the conflict also has ethnic and caste overtones (Bray *et al.* 2003: 111). Nepal's highly diverse society is dominated by the elite Bahun-Chetri-Newari peoples centered on the Kathmandu valley. The Maoists have proved skilled in exploiting discontent among less privileged ethnic groups primarily based outside this valley, such as the Magars of Midwestern Nepal (Bray *et al.* 2003: 111).[3]

A third narrative of grievance is focused on the lack of political rights or power values as Gurr (1970: 25) calls it (Collier and Hoeffler 2002). Political oppression occurs either through generalized repression or because there is a relative difference in policy influencing capabilities, i.e., some individuals become frustrated because they are unable to express their opinion or concerns via "normal" non-violent political channels. For example, the 1989 uprising in Romania is usually considered to be an example falling into this category of discontent factors (Collier 2000a: 96). As such, violence may meet an individual's basic need when they experience social exclusion (Keen 1998). The birth, for example, of the O'odua Peoples Congress (OPC) in Nigeria in 1994, was connected with a feeling of alienation of the Yoruba group. This ethnicity has been at the sideline of mainstream of Nigerian politics since the 1950s (Akinyele 2001).

Some other scholars emphasize the importance of another important grievance factor, the one of vengeance. Or as Keen (2000: 23) states: "participation in armed groups may also offer excitement and a chance to revenge past wrongdoings." For example, revenge is said to be a common motivations for Tamils joining the Liberation Tigers of Tamil Eelam (LTTE) voluntarily, and other Tamils join rival groups or state forces to avenge violence by the LTTE (Wood 2008: 548). Also in African rebellions revenge plays an important role. When Peters and Richards (1998: 192) asked a child soldier in Sierra Leone why she joined the national army, she replied "when the government soldiers came I wanted to join to get revenge."

Although the examples show that it is possible to find rebellions that are primarily caused by grievances, the grievance theory of conflict finds surprisingly little robust empirical support (Collier 2000a: 98). This has led many scholars to believe that it is unlikely that grievances alone are sufficient for organizing internal conflict and collective mobilization (e.g., Tilly 1978; Tarrow 1994). Most of these scholars have argued that factors such as inequality or other relative deprivation type of factors are always present and that the free rider, coordination, and time-consistency problems together pose formidable obstacles to rebellions motivated purely by grievances (e.g., Lichbach 1994; Olson 1965; Tilly 1978; Collier 2000a).

Although the popular descriptive literature on the impetus for civil conflict and the conduct of armed groups has primarily focused on group grievance, real or imagined, the analytic economic literature, sees grievances as being ubiquitous across most at-risk countries (Regan and Norton 2005). According to this literature, three related models of collective action challenge the thesis that relative deprivation eventually leads to violence (Lichbach 1994: 386). First, public good models maintain that most protest and conflict is about public goods. Armed groups typically claim secession, autonomy, democratization, and redistribution of goods, as their public goods (Kalyvas and Kocher 2007: 181). Public goods are distinguished from private goods by virtue of their jointness of supply and nonrivalness of consumption (Samuelson 1954; Head 1962). Jointness of supply (also referred to as the principal of nonexclusion) refers to the condition whereby such goods cannot be withheld from one member of the group once they are made available to others (Mason 1984). Nonrivalness of consumption, on the other hand, means that one person's consumption of the good does not diminish the amount available to others to consume (Mason 1984). Political goods like democracy, the rule of law, or collective defense, are classic examples of public goods. Note that there are only a few "pure" public goods; most of the goods that we call public goods exhibit these two characteristics to a greater or lesser degree (Mason 1984: 1041).

According to Olson (1965) and applied specifically to the case of politically rebellious behavior by Tullock (1971), by the collective nature of the good, noncombatants will enjoy the benefits of these goods regardless of whether they contribute toward its supply or not. As a result, they have an incentive to withhold their resources (such as time and energy) hoping that the efforts of others will suffice to provide the good. On the other hand, they have much to lose – rebellious behavior may be quite costly (the physical adversity and risk of death inherent to joining an armed group) (Muller and Opp 1986). At the same time, the successful outcome of a revolt by the armed group is a low-probability event (Kalyvas and Kocher 2007). Why, therefore, should agents pay a cost rather than free ride? Such a "free rider" tendency can jeopardize the supply of collective goods and people are likely to obtain a less preferred outcome than if they all behave irrationally and participate (Muller and Opp 1986; Frohlich and Oppenheimer 1970: 105).

Second, expected utility models maintain that the probability of one combatant making a difference to the outcome of a rebellion is quite small. If a single combatant will not affect the result, why should he or she engage in violence rather than pursue private interests? Prisoner's dilemma models combine both perspectives (Lichbach 1994: 386). According to these models, the cards seem stacked against rebellion. Members of armed groups confront possibly disastrous private costs and uncertain public benefits. Moreover, the benefits provide no incentive to act, since they will receive them anyway without participating. In addition, their resources will not make any difference. As such, the individual costs provide every incentive not to act. Olsen (1965) stated that this kind of collective action problem is especially apparent in large groups. The larger the group, the more problematic it is to promote collective action. However, some scholars are of the opinion that the factors that determine whether these problems will be overcome are present in large as well as small groups. Buchanan (1968: 91), for example, states: "During periods of extreme stress, such as was apparently evidenced by the British during World War II, behavior characteristic of small groups may have extended over almost the whole population."

Intertwined with these models, is a third problem that goes under the general heading of time inconsistency; combatants must undergo hardships immediately but the rewards of the new order are only in the future (Herbst 2000: 272). Even if a principal promises her agents rewards for risking their lives, there is no guarantee that they will be able to collect when victory is finally achieved. Or as Collier (2000b: 99) puts it: "the rebel leader has a much stronger incentive to promise things than he has subsequently to deliver them." Because potential recruits recognize this problem, they might not trust the leader and decide not to join the rebellion even though it promises relief from grievances (Collier 2000a). The literature on the problem of time consistency has been an important addition to the rational debate on the calculations and motivations of individual rebels (Herbst 2000). It poses an enormous challenge to the traditional literature that assumes that the motivations to join an armed group are obvious. Moreover, the literature highlights the potential for a clear disjuncture between the interests of leaders and that of followers (Herbst 2000: 273).

If rebellious collective action is stipulated by definition to refer to behavior by nonelites that deviates from legal norms regarding acceptable forms of political participation, and has broad political objectives in the form of providing public goods, the rational models described above are unable to predict the existence of any armed group (Mueller and Opp 1986: 471–472). No average citizen would ever participate in an armed group. History reveals, however, that average citizens choose sometimes to participate in armed groups. The question then is, as Lichbach (1994: 387) asks: "what explains the logic of collective action (rather than 'collective inaction'); that is, 'why so much cooperation' (rather than defection) or 'why free riders are spurned' (rather than taken)?" In other words, the functioning of any armed organization must be based on some circumvention of the above mentioned models (Frohlich and Oppenheimer 1970).

The attempt to explain why rational people would participate in collective rebellion has already produced over two dozen different types of solutions (Lichbach 1994). Most of them are surrounding the idea of making the public good somewhat private by offering material or tangible selective incentive for those who join the armed group, such as direct payment or proceeds of looting.[4] These kinds of incentives are private in the sense that they are exclusive and rival. Participation, in short, is a necessary and sufficient condition for receiving this good (Lichbach 1994: 389). Or as Olsen (1965: 51) states: "group action can be obtained only through an incentive that operates, not indiscriminately, like the collective good, upon the group as a whole, but rather selectively toward the individuals in the group." In other words, while the rebel leadership might be interested in providing public goods, rebel soldiers will only demand adequate provisions that provide for conditions associated with their physical quality of life (Regan and Norton 2005: 323). Critics of Olsen state that this view is overly narrow and too materialist focused. They argue that Olsen ignores the influence of soft incentives, such as citizen duty, a feeling of adventure, a feeling of belongingness, social pressure, and norms. Oots (1989: 144), for instance, states that: "The chance to participate in an adventure, to be a hero, and to be accepted by a peer group can be strong motivations as well. In a few cases, the chance to experience danger can motivate individuals to become terrorists." The argument most often used for explaining this neglect is that these soft incentives are more difficult to measure than the hard ones (Opp 1986: 88–89). In addition, Tullock (1971) argues that although a particular kind of nonmaterial selective incentive is an important motive of "pseudo-rebellious" behavior, engaged in by students in advanced democracies, the entertainment motive is not an important incentive in "serious" rebellion (Muller and Opp 1986: 485).

It is also important to note that most scholars, like Olsen, emphasize positive selective incentives that can be given to individuals who participate – the so-called "pull factors." However, the theory surrounding the use of selective incentives only requires that the private benefits of joining outweigh the private benefits of not joining. This idea then also gives rise to the use of negative selective incentives, i.e., "push" factors, which are generally based on the desire to escape repression and suffering. True, seeking protection does in a way belong to the category of selective incentives and such motives do not refute the general hypotheses discussed here, but they are rarely mentioned in the literature, in spite of the fact that they are often quite important in determining people's behavior (Buijtenhuijs 1996: 18).

It is then also no surprise that this economic approach led scholars to focus on the economic aspect of conflicts (Vinci 2006). As Keen (2000: 27) succinctly commented, "war may be a continuation of economics by other means." This observation was also partly prompted by an observable increase in the self-financing nature of combatant activities. For example, in the conflicts such as those in Angola and Sierra Leone, attacks were not only directed towards the capital and military installations but it was also focused on capturing or protecting natural resource endowments, diverting humanitarian aids, and controlling trade routes (Ballentine and Sherman 2003). These observations led some scholars to believe that the pursuit of war may be economically rational for some of those individuals who participate in it, notwithstanding its cumulative societal destructiveness (Ballentine and Sherman 2003: 3). Economic incentives as such might not only reveal how internal conflicts are being fought but also that the conduct and continuation of the war is determined by economic incentives (Vinci 2006: 30; Ballentine and Sherman 2003). This observation led to the so-called "greed theory" of civil war. This theory contains that individuals join rebel groups because they are primarily motivated by the expectation of material rewards; it states that people choose to become combatants only if there are direct, individual (or selective) material benefits that exceed the expected costs of fighting (Arjona and Kalyvas 2009).

Revolutionary leaders are often aware that these material rewards and benefits are considered to be important incentives for people to support an insurgent movement. Amilcar Cabrai, for example, in a confidential memorandum written in 1965, instructed his fellow Partido Africano da Independência de Guiné e Cabo Verde (PAIGC) members to

> Keep always in mind that the people are not fighting for ideas, for the things in anyone's head. They are fighting for material benefits, to live better and in peace, to see their lives go forward, to guarantee the future of their children. National liberation, war on colonialism, building of peace and progress – independence – all that will remain meaningless for the people unless it brings a real improvement in conditions of life.
>
> (Quoted in Buijtenhuijs 1996: 21)

The same words were echoed by those of Zimbabwe People's Revolutionary Army (ZIPRA) political commissar Colin Matutu, who said about his mobilizing tasks in the rural areas of Zimbabwe: "We didn't only talk political theory, for people did not understand all that political jargon (...). You don't talk about the capitalist or the socialist state to them" (Frederikse 1982: 60–61; Buijtenhuijs 1996: 21). The idea that material benefits enters into the decision process of potential recruits of armed groups is not just an idea of leaders. There are many examples that shows that this idea also prevail in the mind of combatants. Collier *et al.* (2003: 69) for instance, gives the illustration of the Russian civil war of 1919–1920 in which both the Red and the White armies had troubles with recruitment and desertion, especially during summer times. The reason for this was that both armies were composed of peasants, and during the summer peasants had much higher income-earning opportunities, notably the harvest, than in the winter. As such, during the winter peasants became soldiers, while in the summer soldiers became peasants – all based on the provided economic opportunities.

It is obvious that direct material benefits can come from many sources. It can come from direct payment such as wage, from indirect compensation such as food or cattle, but also from external support and by looting. The "greed" thesis does not specify which source it should be, as long as the utility from joining outreach alternative income-earning opportunities. However, many scholars working with the greed-thesis emphasize that soldiers are employees working for a wage, and the source of revenue to pay the soldiers is the looting associated with the conflict. In modern times, massive looting has taken place in the Central African Republic in 1996, the DRC since independence in 1960, and parts of Eastern Europe after the collapse of communism (Keen 1998). As a result, some scholars see combatants as nothing more than individuals that wants to earn some extra money and are active in criminal activities or as Grossman (1999: 269) puts it: "insurgents are indistinguishable from bandits or pirates." He argues that the "romantic notions of idealists notwithstanding, this characterization of revolutions as manifestations of kleptocratic rivalry seems historically accurate." Also Brito and Intriligator (1992) model rebels as suppliers of protected land to drug barons. Hirshleifer (1991) shows that it will generally be rational for the poor to engage in a power struggle against the rich to achieve a transfer of resources. Hence, the analysis of rebellion, as if it were motivated by predation, is the most common form of the greed thesis (Collier 2000: 839).

Different versions of this greed approach have been proposed by students of agrarian revolutions and authors researching civil wars more generally. The former include authors such as Popkin (1979) and Lichbach (1994), who stress not only the importance of materialist selective incentives but also emphasize the relevance of political entrepreneurs who trigger and sustain collective action. However, within the broader literature on civil wars Collier (1999) and Collier and Hoeffler (2004) are the quintessential exponents of the greed theory. Drawing on statistical data of civil wars since the mid-sixties, Collier (1999) concluded that "grievance-based explanations of civil wars" were seriously wrong. He argued instead that the key to understand why such wars erupt lay in greed and the quest for loot by rebel actors and that it was not to be found in self-serving "narratives of grievance" or in any claim on the part of insurgents to be fighting for justice (Berdal 2005). The likelihood of greed-driven wars break-ing out was particularly high, Collier (1999) suggested further, in countries that relied heavily on primary commodity exports, had a surfeit of young, unem-ployed, and poorly educated men and were experiencing a period of rapid eco-nomic decline (Berdal 2005). In contrast to what the grievance theory suggested, ethnic heterogeneity, the level of political rights, economic mismanagement, and regime type had no statistical bearing in the incidence or outbreak of civil wars.

These statistical findings have been subjected to varying interpretations. In their initial strong formulation of the "greed theory" of rebellion, Collier *et al.* (2003) offered a rational actor account that focused on the motives of rebel actors, arguing that greed or loot-seeking rather than grievance or justice-seeking was the key factor in the onset of violent rebellion (Ballentine and Sherman 2003). This suggested that economic resources are not simply pursued to sustain war, but rather that war is pursued in order to capture resources. This is particu-larly the case of warlords. As Berdal (2003: 491) notes, there is a "popular and much published image of modern warlords as concerned exclusively with plunder for personal enrichment and conspicuous displays of wealth." It is true, prima facie, that many warlords do make large profits from their organizations. Moreover, these "businessmen of war" rely "on violence as the main instrument of their economic activity" (Vinci 2006: 30).

The assertion that contemporary armed conflicts are predominantly caused by greed rather than grievance, and in the ways postulated by some of its proponents, has provoked an ongoing, sometimes heated debate and raised a number of important analytical and normative questions (Ballentine and Sherman 2003: 4). First, there are many counterexamples that indicate that the material requirement to sustain a rebellion may be very low: the Mayi Mayi in the DRC provides one example of a low-tech, low-cost but long-lasting rebel movement (Humphreys 2003: 11–12). Also the existence of the Fuerzas Armadas Revolucionarias de Colombia (FARC) in Colombia provides a very strong counterexample. A crucial moment in the formation of this armed group was its decision to disavow individual appropriation of goods (Gutiérrez Sanín 2004: 269). Even admitting the possibility that a handful of individuals actually get rich with the Colombian war, which until now has not been proven, the vast majority of the FARC consist of nonpaid combatants that participate in a conflict in which they do not benefit from looting and in which becoming rich is not a realistic perspective (Gutiérrez Sanín 2004: 269–271).

Another criticism has been directed to the usage of greed versus grievance as a dichotomy. Using this as theories that exclude each other overlooks that in reality a highly diverse and complex set of incentives and opportunity structures are at work. For example, Herbst (2000) states that lootable resources may sometimes be critical and sometimes relatively unimportant in a particular rebellion. Therefore, while scholars and policy makers are correct to recognize economic agendas as one aspect of civil wars in Africa (and elsewhere in the world), it is simply not persuasive to suggest that economic agendas are the only or even the primary driving force behind rebellion (Herbst 2000: 271). In addition, he argues that the relationship between looting and conflict might simply reflect the fact that lootable resources may be necessary, or at least useful, for a conflict to continue (in order for rebels to, among other things, feed themselves) but are not the drivers of the conflict per se (Herbst 2000: 271). This idea is also reflected in a weaker formulation of the greed-thesis offered by Collier *et al.* (2003) that signals a definite shift away from the earlier emphasis on the "motives of rebel actors" to the "opportunity for organized violence" and the "feasibility of rebellion" regardless of motivation (Ballentine and Sherman 2003). In this version, the assumption is that all societies experience grievances, but only where there are opportunities for rebellion do societies experience civil war. Consequently, grievance and greed may have symbiotic relationship in rebellion: "to get started, rebellion needs grievance, whereas to be sustained, it needs greed" (Collier 1999: 9). This idea is confirmed by Herbst (2000: 277) who did a review of the case study literature on rebellions in Africa. His review suggests that there are very few pure cases where only one type of incentive to rebel is present. For instance, there were very few revolutions that were ideologically driven, which did not have a clear economic aspect. More specially, in even the revolts celebrated for their ideological commitment there is a clear looting element (Herbst 2000: 277).

To sum up the argument, although the greed versus grievance debate remains contested, perhaps intractably so, it has nevertheless proved important in pushing forward the research agenda on armed groups and civil war. Moreover, the greed-grievance debate has re-asserted the centrality of empirical research in conceptualizing and understanding the central issue of why fighters fight (Jennings 2007: 16). Deduced from the two strands of literature is that most recruits are recruited with the help of social endowments (i.e., they join out of grievance reasons), like democracy or equal rights or they are recruited with the help of economic endowments (i.e., they join out of material reasons), such as the possibility for looting, food, or wage.

Different types of recruits are attracted by different kinds of endowments (Weinstein 2007). Gutiérrez Sanín (2004), for example, argues that promoting wars on economic incentives is a poor strategy, because mercenaries are disloyal and greedy soldiers make bad fighters (Gutiérrez Sanín 2004: 279). Constant (1997), in his critique of Napoleonic wars, spelled out in detail the reasons of the technical inferiority of greedy soldiers. He stipulates that these types of soldiers have extremely short time horizons and very high levels of risk-taking, which are the worst possible conditions for the evolution of cooperation. Luxury and looting corrupts them; pecking orders divide them. They defend very poorly, because they first look after their own lives. In synthesis, they do not have "pity in success" but lack coordination in defeat (Gutiérrez Sanín 2004: 279). Consequently, self-interested agents are difficult to control because of the direct temptations that they face, and because they will attempt to preserve their information advantages over the principal to realize their own goals (Mitchell 2004: 47). Weinstein (2007) formulates it a bit differently by arguing that those individuals who join groups which offer economic incentives tend to be opportunistic "consumers" who are motivated primarily by private gains, while those who join movements because of grievances are considered to be more committed "investors" (Weinstein 2007).

Attracting and selecting those agents who demonstrate a greater interest in accomplishing the interest of the commander, rather than fulfilling their own short-term private needs, lies in the interest of the principal. She will have more control over agents attracted by social endowments and they are more likely to faithfully execute the given orders of civilian victimization. However, note that attracting recruits on the basis of social and/or economic endowments is not only related to what kind of recruits the principal wants, but also to the endowments available to her. Resource wealth at the country level, for instance, is a necessary condition or the emergence of groups that employ economic endowments to motivate participation in insurgency (although not a sufficient condition) (Weinstein 2007). In contrast, those armed group that arise in resource-poor contexts have no other choice than to rely solely on social endowments to attract recruits. An armed group's initial stock of economic and social endowments and its decisions about how to utilize them may be themselves then also be a function of the leadership and the leader's initial strategy.

The idea that social endowments attract the "better" type of agents for the armed group stands in contrast to the argument offered by Humphreys and Weinstein (2006). They argue that warring factions recruiting combatants with the promise of private benefits are more likely to exhibit high levels of civilian abuse. However, these authors assume that civilian abuse produces private rewards, but at a social cost of the armed group (Humphreys and Weinstein 2006: 433). Consequently, they assume that mechanisms of discipline and group solidarity restrain, rather than enable, the abuse of noncombatant populations. In other words, they do not assume the strategic advantage that civilian abuse can have. Hypothesis 1 summarizes the reverse logic. As explained in the introduction, every hypothesis is formulated on two levels; on the level of the armed groups (meso-level) and on the level of the individual combatant (micro-level).

Hypothesis 1_{meso}: Armed groups composed out of combatants that are recruited on the basis of social endowments are more likely to exhibit higher level of civilian abuse.

Hypothesis 1_{micro}: Combatants that are recruited on the basis of social endowments are more likely to perpetrate higher levels of civilian abuse.

Social density

Besides the prominent role that incentives play in overcoming the adverse selection problem of imperfect information, literature has also emphasized that agents have a desire to follow prevalent behavioral patterns of relevant others (e.g., Lindenberg 1986). It is often argued that these ties between agents are important for collective action. For example, it is widely agreed that participants in social movement organizations are usually recruited through preexisting social ties and that mobilization is more likely when the members of the beneficiary population are linked by social ties than when they are not (e.g., Tilly 1978; Oberschall 1973; Marwell *et al.* 1988: 502; Gill 2007: 153). For example, familial ties aid recruitment in the IRA (Toolis 1995), and the recruitment of female Euskadi Ta Askatasuna (ETA) members (Reinares 2004). Friendship ties were important for enrolling Italian and German left-wing militants (Della Porta 1992), and a mixtures of both are important to the recruitment process of Palestinian groups (Post *et al.* 2005), global jihadists (Sageman 2005), and Colombian armed groups (Florez-Morris 2007).

In addition, game theoretical studies have pointed to the power of correctly categorizing interacting agents as a way to facilitate collective action (Humphreys *et al.* 2002: 6–7). Recent work by Chwe (2001) for example, has reinforced this point by demonstrating the importance of "common knowledge" among agents for the achievement of outcomes. Chwe's (2001: 9–10) research suggests that a social agent may need to have information not simply about the identities of others but also about the information that others have about him, and so on (Humphreys *et al.* 2002: 6–7).

All the above examples show that focusing only on individual incentives is incomplete without accounting for community-level features (Humphreys and Weinstein 2008: 441). These features offer important information on the type and behavior of agents. Taylor (1988) goes as far as stating that attracting agents from one particular social network or community affects the behavior of the group – it determines not only *what* agents want, but also *how* they acquire it. How network features facilitate collective action is still poorly understood. In their impressive book on the salience of ethnicity, Habyarimana *et al.* (2009) describe three broad families of mechanisms that connect these community-level features to collective action and mobilization. Although, they focus on ethnicity as the primary feature of networks, their arguments can be generalized to all kinds of networks based on other features than ethnicity.[5]

The first way in which community-level features can facilitate collective action is by structuring the preferences of agents over social outcomes. In other words, the social network in which agents are embedded can determine what they want. Theorists in social networks emphasize that a sense of belongingness to a particular group, no matter how you define the group, leads agents to demonstrate an in-group bias (e.g., Tajfel *et al.* 1971). Agents value the welfare members of their own group positively and members of other groups negatively. This is primarily due to the fact that they anticipate future interaction with their own kind. In addition, research have shown that members of the same social network are more likely to have preferences in common over different public goods (Habyarimana *et al.* 2009: 9). Miguel and Gugerty (2005), for instance, found out in their model on educational choice that individual preferences over the type of education they receive are correlated across co-ethnics. The differences in preferences over outcomes may ultimately lead to more coordination among members from one and the same network.

Second, some scholars have emphasized that community or social network features affect the set of strategies available to agents (Habyarimana *et al.* 2009: 9). They see these features as a kind of "technology" for collective action. Bates (1983), for instance, maintains that because social networks are often marked by shared language, shared culture, and a shared understanding about modes of social interaction, agents of the same network can coordinate their actions easier (see also Humphreys *et al.* 2002: 9–10; Laitin 2000; Gubler and Selway 2012). This in turn, can enhance in-group communications, a precursor necessary for group mobilization and group coordination. Hardin (1997), for instance, describes in detail how these shared norms provide what he calls the "epistemological comforts of home" and allow for communication and coordination at high levels within each group.

Habyarimana *et al.* (2009: 10) also add to this, that agents from the same group are better able to (or believe they are better able to) read cues about the positions or intentions of potential partners. As a consequence, an agent may be able to select a strategy conditional on information that is not available to an agent from another network (Habyarimana *et al.* 2009: 10). This is partly due to the fact that agents often find themselves contemplating collective activities with the others on a regular basis in the future (Habyarimana *et al.* 2009: 10). In addition, social networks are used to collect information about a potential cooperating agent's unobservable skills or experience (or deficiencies) or to facilitate the sanctioning of an agent who reneges on his agreement (for example, by spreading information about the agent's untrustworthiness so that others will know to be wary of him or her in the future) (Habyarimana *et al.* 2009: 10). For a discussion of the role of networks in sanctioning, see for example Richman (2006), Kandori (1992), Greif (1993), and Fafchamps (2003). Greif (1993) for instance, talks about a coalition of Maghribi traders that enabled the eleventh-century Mediterranean traders to govern trade and enforce contracts between them.

Lastly, attracting agents belonging to the same social network also facilitates reciprocity. The social network often provides a set of informal institutions or norms, allocating the responsibilities that members of a group hold to other members of that group. Within social groups, agents who exploit the trust of others can be identified and sanctioned with relative ease by the response of the community. In game-theoretical terms, collective action is facilitated within the group by punishment strategies that are conditioned on individual behavior, because the cost of obtaining information about an individual's past is low (Fearon and Laitin 1996: 719). Gubler and Selway (2012) for instance, state that ethnicity facilitates social control by the group and their principal. Since membership of an ethnicity is often marked by skin color, language, family ties, or cultural heritage, which are not easily changed or hidden. As a result, individual movement between armed groups based on ethnicity is problematic. This might benefit the principal in a few ways. Perhaps, most importantly, it enhances her ability to control coethnics agents who would dissent from or actively oppose the cause by greatly complicating their ability to exercise the "exit" option from the armed group (Gubler and Selway 2012: 210). In other words, attracting recruits from the same network, might increase the principal's "social control" capabilities. Humphreys and Weinstein (2008: 439) note, for example, that the power of social control in Sierra Leone facilitated also mobilization: "social pressures ... changed how individuals evaluated the costs and benefits of joining the movement." It is also a major point in the work of Kalyvas (2006). He provides a detailed account of how entire communities would be controlled by one side in a civil war, simply through the use of the dense networks that characterizes ethnic groups.

It is important to note that the influence of these three broad ways in which community-level features influence preferences and strategies of a particular group is especially examined in relation to ethnicity and how ethnicity relates to conflict onset. However, especially in the early studies, results were mixed and whether and how ethnicity affected civil war remained a puzzle (Gubler and Selway 2012). Stronger consensus has emerged more recently, as the literature has moved away from one-dimensional measures of the structure of ethnicity, such as fractionalization and the ethnic group size, and how this structure influence grievances that can fuel war (Gubler and Selway 2012: 208). Two strands have emerged in recent literature: the first strand examines the role of ethnicity at the macro-level or meso-level and investigate how ethnicity creates power structures that generate ethnic grievances among groups who are not in power, which then serve as the motivation behind the onset of civil war (Wimmer *et al.* 2009). This strand includes work such as Cederman and Girardin's (2007), who look at the patterns of interactions between ethnic groups in power and marginalized ethnic groups; Fearon *et al.*'s (2007) study on ethnic minority groups holding power; Wucherpfennig *et al.* (2012) research on the influence of past state policies of ethnic exclusion on civil war duration; Wimmer *et al.*'s (2009) who introduced the influential "Ethnic Power Relations" dataset, and Cederman *et al.* (2010), who analyze the influence of ethnic groups on the likelihood of having a conflict with the government. They show that conflict with the government is more likely to erupt when many people of an ethnic group are excluded from state power, when these groups have a high mobilization capacity, and when they have experienced conflict in the past.

The second camp continues the focus of earlier work regarding the structure of ethnicity in engendering grievances, but now reaches down to the micro-level in discussing the facilitation of rebel group mobilization (Gubler and Selway 2012: 208). Overlap between ethnicity and religion, geographic region, and socioeconomic class have all been linked to higher grievances that can fuel civil war (Weidmann *et al.* 2010; Seul 1999). For instance, Gubler and Selway (2012) show that civil war onset is on average twelve times less probably in societies where ethnicity is crosscut by socioeconomic class, geographic region, and religion. In addition, some accounts point to the enhanced mobilization capacities in countries where ethnic groups are regionally clustered and horizontally unequal (e.g., Østby 2008).

To summarize, there are three broad ways in which community-level features might influence preferences and strategies. In examining such potential features, most researchers have focused on the role of ethnicity, as the primary feature of networks. However, their arguments can be generalized to all kinds of networks based on other features than ethnicity. To make the above mentioned arguments more general, we can assume that agents with interpersonal ties (whether this is on the basis of ethnicity, religion or any other ties) recruited for an armed group raises the likelihood of within-group coordination and hence increase the group's ability to engage in collective action. It is this within-group coordination that decreases the likelihood of behavior that goes against the interest of the principal. Especially, considering the fact that they are more likely to share the principal's preference, or at least be perceived to do so (Salehyan 2010: 13). Practically, that means that it might increase the probability of civilian abuse perpetrated by the agents. This idea is captured in the second hypothesis. Again, two hypotheses are formulated, one for on the armed group level and another for the individual level:

Hypothesis 2_{meso}: More socially dense armed movements are more likely to exhibit a higher level of civilian abuse.

Hypothesis 2_{micro}: Combatants active in more socially dense armed movements are likely to perpetrate a higher level of civilian abuse.

In the next chapter, the problem of moral hazard is discussed. This problem is again linked to potential strategies that the principal might employ to overcome the problem and as such increase her control. Consequently, it is hypothesized that this has an influence of the expected level of civilian abuse perpetrated not only by the armed groups but also by the individual combatants.

Notes

1 Note that parts of the theory are already published in the form of an article: Haer, Roos. 2012. "The Organization of Political Violence by Insurgencies." PEPS 18(3).
2 Besides these individual theoretical conjectures, group level conjectures point also to some structural conditions that make individual enlistment more likely. Two leading arguments in this conjecture can be identified: low state capacity encourages the emergence and development of rebellion (Fearon and Laitin 2003; Skocpol 1979), and having a youth bulge (in particular a male bulge), which increases the likelihood for conflict (Utas 2003; Abdullah 1998; 2005). See for more information Arjona and Kalyvas (2009) and Jennings (2007).
3 It is important to note that grievance factors such as economic inequality is often related or enforced by a particular ideology. For example, the Fuerzas Armadas Revolucionarias de Colombia (FARC) is based on communism. They, for example, do not pay their members any salary, and gifts from family members are passed through the hands of the guerilla authorities and at least in theory can be redistributed (Gutiérrez Sanín 2008: 22–24).
4 Besides the use of selective incentives, there are also other factors offered that pose a solution to the collective action problem, i.e., the probability of winning, patronage, or tit-for-tat strategy (Lichbach 1994).
5 It is important to note, however, that these three families of explanations may interact in complex ways and are not that easy to distinguish from each other. There is, for example, a fine line between reciprocity and sanctioning.

References

Abdullah, Ibrahim. 1998. "Bush Path to Destruction: The Origin and Character of the Revolutionary United Front." *Journal of Modern African Studies* 36(2): 203–235.
Abdullah, Ibrahim. 2005. "'I am a Rebel': Youth Culture and Violence in Sierra Leone." In *Makers and Breakers: Children and Youth in Postcolonial Africa*, eds. Alcinda Honwana and Filip de Boeck. Oxford: James Currey, 172–187.
Akerlof, George A. 1970. "The Market for 'Lemons': Quality Uncertainty and the Market Mechanism." *Quarterly Journal of Economics* 84(3): 488–500.
Akinyele, R. T. 2001. "Ethnic Militancy and National Stability in Nigeria: A Case Study of the Oodua People's Congress." *African Affairs* 100(401): 623–640.
Arjona, Ana M. and Stathis N. Kalyvas. 2009. "Rebelling Against Rebellion: Comparing Insurgent and Counterinsurgent Recruitment." Presented at the CRISE Workshop, March 17–18.
Arrow, Kenneth J. 1985. "The Economics of Agency." In *Principals and Agents: The Structure of Business*, eds. John W. Pratt and Richard J. Zeckhauser. Boston: Harvard Business School Press, 1–37.
Ballentine, Karen and Jake Sherman. 2003. "Introduction." In *The Political Economy of Armed Conflict: Beyond Greed and Grievance*, eds. Karen Ballentine and Jake Sherman. London: Lynne Rienner Publishers, 1–15.

Bates, Robert H. 1983. "Modernization, Ethnic Competition, and the Rationality of Politics in Contemporary Africa." *In State versus Ethnic Claims: African Policy Dilemmas*, eds. Donald Rothchild and Victor A. Olunsorola. Boulder: Westview Press,
152–171.

Berdal, Mats. 2003. "How 'New' are 'New Wars'? Global Economic Change and the
Study of Civil War." *Global Governance* 9(4): 477–502.

Berdal, Mats. 2005. "Beyond greed and grievance – and not too soon…" *Review of International Studies* 31(4): 687–698.

Bøås, Morton and Anne Hatløy. 2008. " 'Getting in, getting out': militia membership and
prospects for re-integration in post-war Liberia." *Journal of Modern African Studies*
46(1): 33–55.

Bray, John, Leiv Lunde, and S. Mansoob Murshed. 2003. "Nepal: Economic Drivers of
the Maoist Insurgency." In *The Political Economy of Armed Conflict: Beyond Greed
and Grievance*, eds. Karen Ballentine and Jake Sherman. London: Lynne Rienner Publishers, 107–132.

Brehm, John and Scott Gates. 1994. *Working, Shirking, and Sabotage. Bureaucratic
Response to a Democratic Public*. Ann Arbor: The University of Michigan Press.

Brito, Dagobert L., and Michael D. Intriligator. 1992. "Narco-Traffic and Guerrilla
Warfare: A New Symbiosis." *Defense Economics* 3(4): 263–274.

Brush, Stephen G. 1996. "Dynamics of Theory Change in the Social Sciences: Relative
Deprivation and Collective Violence." *Journal of Conflict Resolution* 40(4): 523–545.

Buchananan, James M. 1986. *The Demand and Supply of Public Goods*. Indianapolis:
Liberty Fund.

Buijtenhuijs, Rob. 1996. "The Rational Rebel: How Rational, How Rebellious? Some
African Examples." *Afrika Focus* 12(1): 3–25.

Cederman, Lars-Erik and Luc Girardin. 2007. "Beyond Fractionalization: Mapping Ethnicity onto Nationalist Insurgencies." *American Political Science Review* 101(1):
173–185.

Cederman, Lars-Erik, Andreas Wimmer, and Brian Min. 2010. "Why Do Ethnic Group
Rebel? New Data and Analysis." *World Politics* 62(1): 87–119.

Chwe, Michael S. 2001. *Rational Ritual: Culture, Coordination, and Common Knowledge*. Princeton: Princeton University Press.

Collier, Paul. 1999. "Doing Well Out of War." Presented at the Conference on Economic
Agendas in Civil Wars, London, April 26–27.

Collier, Paul. 2000. "Rebellion as a Quasi-Criminal Activity." *Journal of Conflict Resolution* 44(6): 839–853.

Collier, Paul. 2000a. "Doing Well out of War: An Economic Perspective." In *Greed and
Grievance: Economic Agendas in Civil Wars*, eds. Mats Berdal and David M. Malone.
Boulder: Lynne Rienner Publishers, 91–111.

Collier, Paul and Anke Hoeffler. 2002. "Greed and Grievance in Civil War." CSAE
WPS/2002–01.

Collier, Paul and Anke Hoeffler. 2004. "Greed and grievance in civil war." *Oxford Economic Papers* 56(4): 563–595.

Collier, Paul, Lani Elliott, Håvard Hegre, Anke Hoeffler, Marta Reynal-Querol, and
Nicholas Sambanis. 2003. *Breaking the Conflict Trap. Civil War and Development
Policy*. Washington: World Bank.

Constant, Benjamin. 1997. *Ecrits politiques*. Paris: Gallimard.

Cooper, H. H. A. 1978. "Psychopaths as Terrorists." *Legal Medical Quarterly* 2(4):
253–262.

Davies, James C. 1962. "Toward a theory of Revolution." *American Sociological Review* 27(1): 5–19.

Della Porta, Donatella. 1992. "Political Socialization in Left-wing Under-ground Organizations: Biographies of Italian and German Militants." In *Social Movements and Violence: Participation in Underground Organizations*, ed. Donatella della Porta. Greenwich: JAI-Press, 259–290.

Della Porta, Donatella. 1995. *Social Movements, Political Violence, and the State: A Comparative Analysis of Italy and Germany*. Cambridge: Cambridge University Press.

Eisenhardt, Kathleen M. 1989. "Agency Theory: An Assessment and Review." *The Academy of Management Review* 14(1): 57–74.

Esteban, Joan and Gerald Schneider. 2008. "Polarization and Conflict: Theoretical and Empirical Issues." *Journal of Peace Research* 45(2): 131–141.

Fafchamps, Marcel. 2003. "Ethnicity and Networks in African Trade." *Contributions to Economic Analysis & Policy* 2(1): 1–51.

Fearon, James D. and David D. Laitin. 1996. "Explaining Interethnic Cooperation." *American Political Science Review* 90(4): 715–735.

Fearon, James D. and David D. Laitin. 2003 "Ethnicity, Insurgency, and Civil War." *American Political Science Review* 97(1): 75–90.

Fearon, James D., Kimuli Kasara, and David Laitin. 2007. "Ethnic Minority Rule and Civil War Onset." *American Political Science Review* 101(1): 187–193.

Feaver, Peter D. 2005. *Armed Servants. Agency, Oversight, and Civil-Military Relations*. Harvard: Harvard University Press.

Florez-Morris, Mauricio. 2007. "Joining Guerrilla Groups in Colombia: Individual Motivations and Processes for Entering a Violent Organization." *Studies in Conflict and Terrorism* 30(7): 615–634.

Frederikse, Julie. 1982. *None but Ourselves: Masses vs Media in the Making of Zimbabwe*. London: Heinemann.

Frohlich, Norman and Joe A. Oppenheimer. 1970. "I Get By With a Little Help From My Friends." *World Politics* 23(1): 104–120.

Geschwender, James A. 1964. "Social Structure and the Negro Revolt: An Examination of Some Hypotheses." *Social Forces* 43(2): 248–256.

Gill, Paul. 2007. "A Multi-Dimensional Approach to Suicide Bombing." *International Journal of Conflict and Violence* 1(2): 142–159.

Gill, Paul. 2012. "Terrorist Violence and the Contextual, Facilitative and Causal Qualities of Group-based Behaviors." *Aggression and Violent Behavior* 17(6): 565–574.

Greif, Anver. 1993. "Contract Enforceability and Economic Institutions in Early Trade: The Maghribi Traders' Coalition." *American Economic Review* 83(3): 525–547.

Grossman, Herschel I. 1999. "Kleptocracy and Revolution." *Oxford Economic Papers* 51(2): 267–283.

Gubler, Joshua R. and Joel Sawat Selway. 2012. "Horizontal Inequalities, Crosscutting Cleavages, and Civil War." *Journal of Conflict Resolution* 56(2): 206–232.

Gurr, Ted R. 1970. *Why men rebel*. Princeton, NJ: Princeton University Press.

Gutiérrez Sanín, Francisco. 2004. "Criminal Rebels? A Discussion of Civil War and Criminality from the Colombian Experience." *Politics and Society* 32(2): 257–285.

Gutiérrez Sanín, Francisco. 2008. "Telling the Difference: Guerrillas and Paramilitaries in the Colombian War." Politics & Society 36(1): 3–34.

Habyarimana, James, Macartan Humphreys, Daniel N. Posner, and Jeremy M. Weinstein. 2009. *Coethnicity: Diversity and the Dilemmas of Collective Action*. New York: Russell Sage Foundation.

Hacker, Frederick J. 1976. *Crusaders, Criminals, Crazies: Terror and terrorism in our time*. New York: Norton.

Haer, Roos. 2012. "The Organization of Political Violence by Insurgencies." *Peace Economics, Peace Science and Public Policy* 18(3): 1–11.

Hardin, Russell. 1997. *One for All: The Logic of Group Conflict*. Princeton: Princeton University Press.

Head, John G. 1962. "Public Goods and Public Policy." *Public Finance* 17(3): 197–219.

Herbst, Jeffrey. 2000. "Economic Incentives, Natural resources and Conflict in Africa." *Journal of African Economies* 9(3): 270–294.

Hirshleider, Jack. 1991. "The Paradox of Power." *Economics and Politics* 3(3): 177–200.

Horowitz, Donald. 1985. *Ethnic Groups in Conflict*. Berkeley: University of California Press.

Humphreys, Macartan. 2003. "Economics and Violent Conflict." Unpublished manuscript, Cambridge: Harvard University.

Humphreys, Macartan and Jeremy M. Weinstein. 2006. "Handling and Manhandling Civilian in Civil War." *American Political Science Review* 100(3): 429–447.

Humphreys, Macartan and Jeremy M. Weinstein. 2008 "Who Fights? The Determinants of Participation in Civil War." *American Journal of Political Science* 52(2): 436–455.

Humphreys, Macartan, Daniel N. Posner, and Jeremy M. Weinstein. 2002. "Ethnic Identity, Collective Action, and Conflict: An Experimental Approach." Presented as the Annual Meeting of the American Political Science Association, Boston, August 29–September 1.

Jennings, Kathleen M. 2007. *"The War Zone as Social Space: Social Research in Conflict Zones."* Fafo report 08 Oslo: Fafo.

Kalyvas, Stathis N. 2006. *The Logic of Violence in Civil War*. Cambridge: Cambridge University Press.

Kalyvas, Stathis N. and Matthew A. Kocher. 2007. "How 'Free' is Free Riding in Civil Wars? Violence, Insurgency, and the Collective Action Problem." *World Politics* 59(2): 177–216.

Kandori, Michihiro. 1992. "Social Norms and Community Enforcement." *Review of Economic Studies* 59(1): 63–80.

Keen, David. 1998. *The Economic Functions of Violence in Civil Wars*. Oxford: Oxford University Press.

Keen, David. 2000. "Incentives and Disincentives for Violence." In *Greed and Grievance: Economic Agendas in Civil Wars*, eds. Mats Berdal, and David M. Malone. Boulder: Lynne Rienner Publishers, 19–41.

Kiewiet, D. Roderick and Mathew D. McCubbins. 1991. *The Logic of Delegation. Congressional Parties and the Appropriations Process*. Chicago: The University of Chicago Press.

Kreps, David M. 1990. *A Course in Microeconomic Theory*. Princeton: Princeton University Press.

Laffont, Jean-Jacques and David Martimort. 2002. *The Theory of Incentives: The Principal–Agent Model*. Princeton: Princeton University Press.

Laitin, David D. 2000. "What is a Language Community?" *American Journal of Political Science* 44(1): 142–155.

Leggett, George. 1981. *The Cheka: Lenin's Political Police*. Oxford: Clarendon Press.

Lichbach, Mark I. 1994. "What makes Rational Peasants Revolutionary?: Dilemma, Paradox, and Irony in Peasant Collective Action." *World Politics* 46(3): 383–418.

Lichbach, Mark I. 1995. *The Rebel's Dilemma*. Ann Arbor: University of Michigan Press.

Lindenberg, Siegwart. 1986. "The Paradox of Privatization in Consumption." In *Paradoxical Effects of Social Behavior. Essays in Honor of Anatol Rapports*, eds. A. Diekmann and P. Mitter. Heidelberg: Physica-Verlag, 297–310.

Marwell, Gerald, Pamela E. Oliver and Ralph Prahl. 1988. "Social Networks and Collective Action: A Theory of the Critical Mass. III." *American Journal of Sociology* 94(3): 502–534.

Marx, Karl and Friedrich Engels. 1998[1872]. *Het Communistisch Manifest*. Amsterdam: Pegasus.

Mas-Colell, Andreu, Michael D. Whinston, and Jerry R. Green. 1995. *Microeconomic Theory*. New York: Oxford University Press.

Mason, T. David. 1984. "Individual participation in Collective Racial Violence: A Rational Choice Synthesis." *American Political Science Review* 78(4): 1040–1056.

Miguel, Edward and Mary K. Gugerty. 2005. "Ethnic Diversity, Social Sanctions, and Public Goods in Kenya." *Journal of Public Economics* 89(11): 2325–2368.

Mitchell, Neil J. 2004. *Agents of Atrocity. Leaders, Followers, and the Violation of Human Rights in Civil War*. New York: Palgrave Macmillan.

Moe, Terry M. 1984. "The New Economics of Organization." *American Journal of Political Science* 28(4): 739–777.

Muldoon, Orla T., Katrina Mclaughlin, Nathalie Rougier, and Karen Trew. 2008. "Adolescents' Explanations for Paramilitary Involvement." *Journal of Peace Research* 45(5): 681–695.

Muller, Edward N. and Karl-Dieter Opp. 1986. "Rational Choice and Rebellious Collective Action." *American Political Science Review* 80(2): 471–488.

Oberschall, Anthony. 1973. *Social Conflict and Social Movements*. Englewood Cliffs: Prentice-Hall.

Olsen, Mancur. 1965. *The Logic of Collective Action*. Cambridge: Harvard University Press.

Oots, Kent Layne. 1989. "Organizational Perspectives on the Formation and Disintegration of Terrorist Groups." *Terrorism* 12(3): 139–152.

Opp, Karl-Dieter. 1986. "Soft Incentives and Collective Action: Participation in the Anti-Nuclear Movement." *British Journal of Political Science* 16: 87–112.

Østby, Gudrun. 2008. "Horizontal Inequalities, Political Environment and Civil Conflict: Evidence from 55 Developing Countries." In *Horizontal Inequalities and Conflict: Understanding Group Violence in Multiethnic Societies*. Basingstoke: PalgraveMacmillan.

Pearce, K. I. 1977. "Police Negotiations. A new role for the community psychiatrist." *Canadian Psychiatric Association Journal* 22(4): 171–175.

Peters, Krijn and Paul Richards. 1998. " 'Why we fight': Voices of Youth Combatants in Sierra Leone. *Africa* 68(2): 183–210.

Petersen, Roger. 2001. *Resistance and rebellion: lessons from Eastern Europe*. Cambridge: Cambridge University Press.

Popkin, Samuel. 1979. *The Rational Peasant: The Political Economy of Rural Society in Vietnam*. Berkeley: University of California Press.

Post, Jerrold, Ehud Sprinzak, and Laurita Denny. 2005. "The Terrorists in Their Own Words: Interviews with 35 Incarcerated Middle Eastern Terrorists." *Terrorism and Political Violence* 15(1): 171–184.

Rauchhaus, Robert W. 2009. "Principal–Agent Problems in Humanitarian Intervention: Moral Hazard, Adverse Selection, and the Commitment Dilemma." *International Studies Quarterly* 53(4): 871–884.

Regan, Patrick M. and Daniel Norton. 2005. "Greed, Grievance, and Mobilization in Civil Wars." *Journal of Conflict Resolution* 49(3): 319–336.

Reinares, Fernando. 2004. "Who are the Terrorists? Analyzing Changes in the Sociological Profile among Members of ETA." *Studies in Conflict and Terrorism* 27(6): 465–488.

Richman, Barak D. 2006. "How Community Institutions Create Economic Advantage: Jewish Diamond Merchants in New York." *Law & Social Inquiry* 31(2): 383–420.

Rothchild, Michael and Joseph Stiglitz. 1976. "Equilibrium in Competitive Insurance markets: An Essay on the Economics of Imperfect Information." *Quarterly Journal of Economics* 90(4): 629–649.

Sageman, Marc. 2005. *Understanding Terror Networks*. Pennsylvania: University of Pennsylvania Press.

Salanié, Bernard. 2005. *The Economics of Contracts. A Primer*. Cambridge: MIT Press.

Salehyan, Idean. 2010. "The Delegation of War to Rebel Organizations." *Journal of Conflict Resolution* 54(3): 493–515.

Sambanis, Nicholas. 2002. "A Review of Recent Advances and Future Directions in the Quantitative Literature on Civil War." *Defence and Peace Economics* 13(3): 215–243.

Samuelson, Paul A. 1954. "The Pure Theory of Public Expenditure." *Review of Economics and Statistics* 36(4): 387–389.

Scott, James C. 1976. *Moral Economy of the Peasant: Rebellion and Subsistence in South East Asia*. New Haven: Yale University Press.

Seul, Jeffery. 1999. "Ours is the Way of God: Religion, Identity, and Intergroup Conflict." *Journal of Peace Research* 36(5): 553–569.

Skocpol, Theda. 1979. *States and Social Revolutions: a Comparative Analysis of France, Russia and China*. Cambridge: Cambridge University Press.

Snyder, David. 1978. "Collective Violence. A Research Agenda and Some Strategic Considerations." *Journal of Conflict Resolution* 22(3): 499–534.

Tajfel, Henri, M. G. Billig, R. P. Bundy, and Claude Flament. 1971. "Social Categorization and Intergroup Behavior." *European Journal of Social Psychology* 1(2): 149–178.

Tanay, Emmanuel. 1987. "Pseudo-Political Terrorism." *Journal of Forensic Science* 32(1): 192–200.

Tarrow, Sidney. 1994. *Power in Movement. Social Movements, Collective Action and Politics*. Cambridge: Cambridge University Press.

Taylor, Michael. 1988. "Rationality and revolutionary collective action." In *Rationality and Revolution*, ed. Michael Taylor. Cambridge: Cambridge University Press, 63–97.

Tilly, Charles. 1978. *From Mobilization to Revolution*. Reading: Addison-Wesley.

Toolis, Kevin. 1995. *Rebel Hearts: Journeys within the IRA's Soul*. London: Picador.

Tullock, Gordon. 1971. "The Paradox of Revolutions." *Public Choice* 11(1): 89–99.

Utas, Mats. 2003. "Sweet Battlefields: Youth and the Liberian Civil War." Doctoral dissertation in Cultural Anthropology, Uppsala University, Sweden.

Vinci, Anthony. 2006. "Greed-Grievance reconsidered: the Role of Power and Survival in the Motivation of Armed Groups." *Civil Wars* 8(1): 25–45.

Weidmann, Nils, Jan Ketil Rød, and Lars-Erik Cederman. 2010. "Representing ethnic groups in space: A new dataset." Journal of Peace Research 47(4): 491–499.

Weinstein, Jeremy M. 2007. *Inside Rebellion: The Politics of Insurgent Violence*. Cambridge: Cambridge University Press.

Wimmer, Andreas, Lars-Erik Cederman, and Brian Min. 2009. "Ethnic Politics and Armed Conflict: A Configurational Analysis of a New Global Dataset." *American Sociological Review* 74(2): 316–337.

Wood, Elisabeth J. 2003. *Insurgent collective action and civil war in El Salvador*. Cambridge: Cambridge University Press.

Wood, Elisabeth J. 2008. "The Social Process of Civil War: The Wartime Transformation of Social Networks." *Annual Review of Political Science* 11(1): 539–561.

Wucherpfennig, Julian, Nils. W. Metternich, Lars-Erik Cederman, and Kristia Skrede Gleditsch. 2012. "Ethnicity, the State, and the Duration of Civil War." *World Politics* 64(1): 79–115.

3   The problem of moral hazard

Selecting "principled" agents for armed groups is, however, not as simple as is portrayed. Agents are likely to endure severe costs in their work (getting harmed or even killed) while great uncertainty surrounds the possible benefits of the principal's preferred outcome, which is often subjected to a very long time horizon (Kalyvas and Kocher 2007). In other words, despite the fact that the principal wants to select and screen her future agents in order to avoid the problem of adverse selection, she might not be able to become selective. Selection and screening is, therefore, not a panacea for political control (Whitford 2002).

Even if the selection of the right type of agents is possible, the joint forcing contract that principal–agent theory recommends can be subverted when agents in an organization form attachments to the goals of their unit, rather than of the general organization (see Warwick 1975). In other words, the selection and screening power is limited when agents can form diverse policy preferences and hold private information (Whitford 2002). This is especially the case when authority is delegated to several agents. In these team production settings, individual agents' actions only partially determine the outcome and it is difficult to determine or define each agent's contribution to this output (Alchian and Demsetz 1972; Holmström 1979). A 16-year-old Kamajo fighter in Sierra Leone explains this idea when answering the question whether he has killed somebody:

> I am not sure if I have killed somebody, because it is group fighting. So maybe you are pointing at one man and your neighbor also [is aiming] at the same man. So after the operation there will be a lot of dead bodies. But you will not be able to identify [which ones you killed] because there were many in action.
>
> (Peters and Richards 1998: 198)

Consequently, the team is trapped in what is essentially a prisoner's dilemma, which can reduce the total effort supplied by subordinates. Although, there is a substantial literature in economics on the design of incentive systems for motivating groups of individuals (see Miller 1992 for an excellent and accessible introduction to this literature), there is still a problem that can plague these incentive systems: the principal has her own kind of shirking, which entails manipulating the subordinates (e.g., Miller 1992). Even if selecting "principled" agents is effective, properly motivating the boss herself remains a serious problem (Bendor *et al.* 2001: 246).

Hidden action: moral hazard

Once she has hired agents and established a contract, another problem arises that underpins every delegation situation, the problem of moral hazard. This problem stems from the inability of the principal to observe an agent's behavior and action once a contract is in place (Rauchhaus 2009). The agent's marginal product does not literally need to be unobservable or hidden. It may well be that while it is possible for the principal to observe the actions in theory, monitoring may in reality be difficult or impossible because of a complex environment or because of high costs or legal restrictions (privacy laws) (Rauchhaus 2009). These hidden actions and related shirking manifest in a variety of situations. Stockholders cannot observe whether the actions that firm managers take are in the best interest; voters cannot observe whether the actions of elected representatives – their agents – are in their best interest; car theft insurance may increase the chance that policyholders will park on the street rather than purchase off-street parking; fire insurance may decrease a home owner's incentive to upgrade a wood shingled roof to fire-retardant tiles; International Monetary Fund bailouts may cause third world countries to have less responsible economic policies; and unemployment insurance might decrease the urgency for the jobless to find work (Arrow 1985; Kiewiet and McCubbins 1991; Rauchhaus 2009).

Unfortunately, however, while the concept of moral hazard is broadly applied in economics, finance, and the insurance industry, it has only received limited attention in political science, especially within the subfield of internationals security (Rauchhaus 2009). However, also the problem of moral hazard pervades in this field. For example, how do we know that the national army is doing what it is supposed to be doing? How do we know that it is serving the interest of the country and not parochial interests, either of individual officers or of some larger group (such as a service or branch)? It is hard enough to monitor the activities of an armed group when the movement is bivouacking, for example, near the capital. However, when it is deployed on a distant battlefield in the fog of war, communications difficulties could render monitoring impossible for even the most attentive military leader (Feaver 2005: 68). The information asymmetries are even worse when talking about the unobservable actions of agents in non-state armed groups that operate selectively (Byman and Kreps 2010).

The most straightforward way to eliminate the conditions of hidden action and information would seem to institute procedures requiring agents to report whatever relevant information they have obtained and whatever actions they have taken. After all, hidden information is no longer hidden if you make the agent reveal it. However, agents have no incentive to reveal their individual actions. On the contrary, because of the existence of a preference asymmetry they have all reasons not to reveal their actions. Consequently, to counter the effects of the moral hazard problem, the principal has to design ex-post mechanisms that allow her to control her agents once they are hired.

These ex-post oversight falls into two broad categories: the imposition of sanctions, where principals attempt to control agency loss through budgetary restrictions, appointments or revising the agent's mandate through legislative or regulatory means; and monitoring, whereby an attempt is made to rebalance the asymmetry of information by surveillance of agents' behavior (Pollack 1997). McCubbins and Schwartz (1984) famously distinguish two of such surveillance strategies: "police patrol" oversight, where the principal engages in continuous and detailed vigilance of agent action; and "fire alarm" oversight, where the principal relies on third parties to alert it to agency transgressions. Although, the second strategy is less costly and imposes fewer demands on the principal than the first, this option is less viable when talking about constraining the behavior of members of armed groups. Unlike delegation relationships in the domestic arena or in international organizations – where principals have established legal channels for enforcing contracts – enforcement problems are particularly difficult in conflict settings, as many armed groups operate outside the law. Consequently, they do not have recourse to normal contract enforcement and control must be endogenized (Collier *et al.* 2003; Salehyan 2010; Gates 2002; McCubbins *et al.* 1987). As such, the principal can only rely primarily on direct methods of monitoring. However, the term monitoring connotes several activities in addition to its oversight connotation. It means not only measuring output performance, apportioning rewards, observing the input behavior of agents as means of detecting or estimating their marginal productivity and giving assignments or instructions in what to do and how to do it. More importantly, it also includes authority to terminate or revise contracts or to sanction individual agents in any other way (Alchian and Demsetz 1972). In other words, monitoring should be coupled with credible threats – sanctions that will be applied if the agency loss becomes problematic.

Organizational structure

Although traditional principal–agent theory minimizes the value of organizational structure, structure and decentralization are fundamental concerns in both traditional organizational theory and political science in general (Whitford 2002). These two fields are especially focused on political institutions' monitoring and oversight mechanisms in practice. They assume that organizational structure, especially under extreme circumstances, matters because it determines the rules of the game and coordinates the choices of agents under these rules (Miller 1992). Whitford (2002: 172) states in his study to the effect of decentralization that "structure [in bureaucracies] both limits the choices members confront and regularizes information flows among members. As a result, structure shapes the outcome of collective choice processes within and sets the bounds of political control [over bureaucracies]." Institutional structure, by establishing rules of jurisdiction and agenda control, strongly limits the outcome of collective choice process.

Armed groups cannot survive merely on motivation and incentives alone; they also need an organizational structure that is capable of translating goals into action (De Zeeuw 2008: 8). The problem for a principal is then also to create an organizational model that allows her to command and control her agents and that is sufficiently robust to stand up to opponents, but flexible enough to change with new circumstance (Tarrow 1994: 136). This of course, depends partly on the initial strategies and capabilities of the leading principal: it is very hard to re-organize an armed group once the structure is in place. Notable exceptions do however exist: the Provisional Irish Republican Army (PIRA) in Ireland for example re-organized their entire armed group around the 1980s (Gill *et al.* 2013; Coogan 2000).

Armed groups differ widely in degree of organization and design of their structures. Some movements like the National Resistance Army (NRA) in Uganda and the Eritrean People's Liberation Front (EPLF) constitutes disciplined centralized organization that at some point during the war stage resembled effective "bush bureaucracies" (De Zeeuw 2008: 8–9). Other movements, such as El Salvador's Farabundo Martí National Liberation Front (FMLN), which served as the command structure of five separate guerilla organizations, and Peru's SL, which made use of a scattered cell structure, had more limited, decentralized organizational structures (De Zeeuw 2008: 9). However, most organizational structures are a mixture of these two extremes; vertical or hierarchical organizations on the one end, and flat or network-like organizations on the other (Pagels 1989: 51; La Porta 1975). Note that, I neglect the category of "anarchy" mentioned by Lake (1999) because I assume that every armed group need some kind of organizational threshold necessary for conducting operations (Heger *et al.* 2008: 5).

The term hierarchy immediately brings up the idea of bureaucratic processes and operations. This involves the progressive breaking down of complex tasks into a discrete number of sub-tasks, which are then carefully recorded so that coordination between them can take place. Hierarchy is related to bureaucracy in the sense that it "involves the overt operation of relations of super ordination and subordination in the process of coordination" (Frances *et al.* 1991: 10). As such, it refers to the distribution of legal authority in an organization, i.e., the right to make decisions, given direction, and reward and punish others. However, authority in hierarchical organizations is strictly a matter of position, so when members leave their position, their authority remains behind to be taken up by the next job incumbent (Hatch and Cunliffe 2006).

The amount of authority an individual agent has in a hierarchical organization depends on his position. Each position in the organization is made subordinate to some other position and consists of clearly defined roles and responsibilities that are standardized and formalized in the form of written rules and procedures (Beetham 1991). When each position in an organization is made subordinate to some other position, authority permits the most highly placed individuals to gather information from and to direct and control the performance of all agents throughout the organization (Hatch and Cunliffe 2006: 104). Carelessness and neglectful actions of individual members can be relatively easily detected and punished (Frances *et al.* 1991: 11). As Gill *et al.* (2014) formulates it: "within such structures one may monitor behavior and compliance more easily – all members know other members and can quickly share information about bad, and good, behavior" (see also Burt 2005). Principals can, for instance, withhold resources as a signal to the agent, but punishment may also take the form of removal of a particular agent, a fairly common mechanism of control in armed groups (Byman and Kreps 2010). For example, the Japanese Sekigun (Red Army) is known to have executed through exposure in the snow, fourteen of its own members who were seen as less than totally committed (through such "crimes" as wearing lipstick or having sex) (Demaris 1977: 20–29).

The command and control chain in hierarchical organizations follows a formal vertical communication network; downward (directing subordinates) and upward (reporting to management) (Gibson *et al.* 1973; Hatch and Cunliffe 2006: 104). Vertical communication makes it therefore relatively easy for the leadership to gather information from and to command and control the performance of all agents. As a result, hierarchical organizations have a strong agenda-setting capacity in which the principal is the so-called focal point. From her flows of information and the agenda originate, with few additional connections that would distort or challenge the agenda-setting capacity (Heger *et al.* 2008). Choices are, as such, made most exclusively at high levels and unquestioning acceptance of top-level decisions is expected (Hutch and Cunliffe 2006: 114). The leadership is then also clearly defined and lower-level members hardly participate in the decision-making procedure. This reduces the amount of arbitrariness and discretion in decision-making. Especially, because formally all agents' decisions are treated the same according to a set of clear and formalized rules (Frances *et al.* 1991: 11). Due to this high level of centralizations and formalization, the organization can quickly respond to the dictates of the leader and enables the employment of large numbers of people and yet preserve unambiguous accountability for the work they do (Jaques 1991: 109; Hutch and Cunliffe 2006: 114). However, when the centralized group becomes too large, decision bottlenecks can undermine the performance by slowing down the organizational response to environmental pressures (Hutch and Cunliffe 2006: 114).

Hierarchical organizations are the most vertically-organized (see Figure 3.1, for an example of an organizational chart of such a structured organization). These organizations allows also for functional differentiation and specialization of units. Functionally-differentiated groups are able to specialize in a way that less hierarchical groups cannot. At the micro-level this implies that within certain sections of the organization, individuals execute very specific goals. On a broader level, however, true functional differentiation implies that the hierarchical organization should generate a variety of goods. This means that hierarchical armed groups will often tend to concentrate efforts into specialized sections,

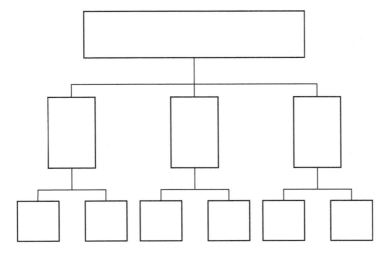

Figure 3.1 Traditional hierarchical structured organization.

whereby some subsection specialize in the production of one sort of goods while others are focusing on other goods (Heger *et al.* 2008; Mayntz 2004). For example, in some armed groups the main distinction is between a military and a support branch, in other cases various units distinguished by functions such as finances, procurement, propaganda, education or health care (Mayntz 2004). An example of an armed group that is known for producing other goods besides violence is the HAMAS. The organizational structure of this armed group is divided in several units, with different functions; internal security, military activities, political activities (protests, demonstrations, etc.) and Islamic preaching (da'wa). All four units have separate regional headquarters in the Gaza strip and the West Bank (Mishal 2003: 582). Also African rebellions are recognized by such a differentiation. The Liberians United for Reconciliation and Democracy (LURD), for instance, had committees compromising 35 members to look after diverse matters including defense, national security, foreign affairs, finance and investment, public relations and propaganda, logistics and health, social welfare and civil administration (Brabazon 2003: 11).

Networks, on the other hand, are often being opposed to hierarchies in a political science perspective. While a more hierarchical organization can be thought of as approximating a unitary actor, network organizations are more likely to be characterized by cell-like structures with varying degrees of connectedness (Heger *et al.* 2008: 6). In general, there are three broad variants: the chain network, where units of the organization link sequentially in a single line, the hub and spoke network, where links to all units radiate outward from a single node, and the all-channel network where all units connect to all others within the organization (Jackson 2006: 245; Arquilla and Ronfeldt 2001) (see also Figure 3.2).

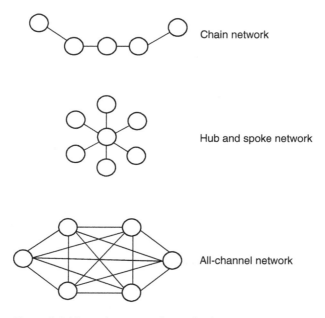

Chain network

Hub and spoke network

All-channel network

Figure 3.2 Network structured organizations

Cells start to look like organizations that, when summed, do not add up to one unitary actor, but rather a collection of different veto-points that replicate similar actions. A typical example of an armed movement that has a cellular structure is the Jemaah Islamiya (JI) active in South East Asia. It consists of at least four cells that have different (and sometimes overlapping) functions. For instance, the Malaysian cell is responsible for recruiting and education and keeping in contact with Al Qaida. The Philippine cell on the other hand is responsible for the logistics – acquiring explosives, guns, and other equipment). The Singapore cell is in charge for the operational locus of the network and the Indonesian unit is accountable for the training) (Abuza 2003).

Network organizations lack a rigid command and control structure: information has multiple sources and multiple directions to flow. As a result, coordination between the nodes or cells in the organization becomes more difficult, as there is not a "party line" to follow and many options and ideas receive the same level of credence and support (Heger *et al.* 2008: 10). This makes the agenda-setting capacities of the principal within networks then also weak; she has no monopoly on information. The operative units, or nodes, enjoy then also a considerable degree of autonomy in planning their day-to-day actions and in the execution of the principal's objectives (Heger *et al.* 2008; Mayntz 2004). Of course, cells may collaborate in their efforts. However, they are more likely to do so on a short-term, rather than on a long-term basis. This is partly due to the

fact the cellular structure of these kinds of organizations does not allow for spe-
cializations, there is a great likelihood for duplication of skills and efforts. This
results in problems for coordination, as units do not necessarily have specific
tasks to perform (Heger *et al.* 2008: 7).

Since there is no clear "party line" to follow, units in a network organizations
have substantial influence on the decision-making process. The decentralization
of decision-making is then also more driven by interaction among many local
informed members of the organizations than by formal authority and control
what is prevalent in hierarchical organizations (Burns and Stalker 1961; Hutch
and Cunliffe 2006). Consequently, network organizations are featured by a high
degree of integration; formal categories or groups such as formal position, geographical location, and market focus are not significant barriers to interaction
(Barker 1993). The lack of strict communication patterns and formalization
makes network-like armed movements attractive from a security perspective;
they are very robust to penetration and compromise since individual units
possess only minimal information about the identity and whereabouts of other
units (Chai 1993: 102). Moreover, even if there is a "leadership" of the movement, such weak connections cannot be "followed upward" (Jackson 2006; Chai
1993). For example, when the ETA in Spain was founded, they opted for an ato-
mistic cellular structure of unconnected local groups of a few individuals acting
autonomously or on orders from a single contact from above (Douglass and
Zulaika 1990). This made it extremely difficult for the Spanish police to pene-
trate the organization and also assured damage control by restricting the amount
of information a captured activist could provide, even under duress of the torture
which had become commonplace during interrogation sessions (Douglass and
Zulaika 1990: 245). Nevertheless, lacking a strict and formal communication
pattern makes it more likely that network forms of armed movements fracture
and split (Jackson 2006: 248). As a result, an end-game settlement of conflict
(e.g., negotiations among adversaries) is very difficult if not impossible (Jackson
2006: 248).

Having a lack of formalization has the advantage that this type of organization is designed to handle tasks and environments that demands flexibility and
adaptability. It can construct a unique set of internal and external linkages for
each demand by stimulating tactical level innovation. Unlike more hierarchical
organizations, which have a fixed set of relationships for processing all problems, the network organization molds itself to each problem (Barker 1993). The
result of this adaptability and flexibility is that tasks and responsibilities of individual members are redefined depending on the situation that has to be encoun-
tered. Consequently, this ideal type of organization has a relatively open and
fluent boundary. New cells are continuously created, and dissolve and as a result
the organization is based on members with different grades of identification with
the organization (Mayntz 2004). For example, the armed group Janatha Vimuk-
thi Peramuna (JVP) in Sri Lanka used a large peripheral body of people
employed on specific limited contracts both for highly specialized operations
and for unskilled tasks for which labor requirements are unstable. For instance,

many young people were only hired occasionally or temporarily for specific and relatively routine tasks, such as pasting up posters (a major channel of communication and propaganda), delivering messages calling particular institutions to participate in strikes or other actions, and monitoring compliance with such calls (Moore 1993: 622).

The differences in the above sketched internal structures have important implications for the agents' behavior and whether they are more likely to be obedient to the principal's directives or not. When a group is loosely structured, when the membership is fluid and norms of conduct underdeveloped, it becomes more difficult for principals alike to enforce standards of conduct and to develop enforcement mechanisms (Zahar 2001: 55). Put differently, cells within network-like organizations have a potential for conducting independent operations (Chai 1993). In contrast, hierarchical groups are recognized by a central core determining the directives and agenda for the rest of the group. It is in these groups then also that principals have more tools available to promote compliance and control agents. At the same time, they have more avenues for punishing indiscipline (Hechter 1987; Whitford 2002).

The extent to which agents perpetrate violence against the civilian population depends greatly on these organizational attributes; it depends on the signals they receive from the principal and the degree to which they believe they can escape punishment (Keen 1998: 52).[1] Lamb (2001: 37) for example, stated that human right abuses perpetrated in Namibia and Angola had sometimes structural origins; "those directly responsible for human right abuses often found themselves elevated within the belligerent's organizational structure." Since it is assumed that the intentional killing and harming of civilians is the result of a strategic order of the principal (e.g., Valentino 2004), it is possible to deduce that agents active in more hierarchical organizations know that disobeying this order is likely to be discovered and punished. Consequently, they are more likely to follow this order of the principal than those agents active in network-like armed movements. Such considerations motivate the formulation of the third hypothesis that is again formulated for the two separate levels of analyses:

Hypothesis 3_{meso}: More hierarchical armed movements are more likely to exhibit a higher level of civilian abuse.

Hypothesis 3_{micro}: Combatants active in more hierarchical armed movements are likely to perpetrate a higher level of civilian abuse.

Commitment

In collective action, every agent would prefer a team in which no other agent shirks. The true marginal costs and values could then be equated to achieve more preferred positions (Alchian and Desetz 1972: 790). Besides the mentioned "hard" instruments to induce control, principal–agent scholars have slowly begun to recognize the importance of "cultural" and "softer" instruments of control. For example, economist Anthony Downs (1967), although focusing on the selfish motives of agents, entertains the possibility that such motives as professional pride and commitment to the public interest are important to some elected officials (Mitchell 2004: 52–53). Also Alchian and Desetz (1972: 790) mention the possibility that nonshirking can be enhanced by a common interest in the guise of a team loyalty or team spirit. These so-called "softer" instruments of control are of special importance when considering that in real-life economic relationships agents and principals face each other for extended time periods. The recognition that contracts have a time dimension has spawned a very abundant literature in recent years (Salanié 2005: 143). However, the idea that team spirit and team loyalty have a positive influence on the performance and productivity of teams is in the field of economic management long established. Organizational commitment is often positively linked to features such as job satisfaction, performance, attendance, and tenure (Hackett *et al.* 1994; Meyer *et al.* 2002). It is then also no wonder that the principal of an armed group might want to invest time, energy and money in the creation of it.

Although there seems to be a minimal shared understanding of what commitment means, ambiguity exists on its exact nature. In canonical principal–agent literature, commitment refers to the ability of agents to restrict their future actions in advance by pledging that they will stick to the contract until some predetermined date (Salanié 2005: 144). In less formal terms, organizational commitment refers to the attachment to the employing organization, including its goals and values. Most often, these goals complement the existing norm and value systems of the agent. However, commitment is more than passive loyalty. Committed members give something (or sometimes even sacrifice something) from themselves (i.e., they have an active relationship based on the exchange of expectations) in order to contribute to the organization's well-being.[2] Hence, affective organizational committed combatants are fighters, who strongly believe in and accept the goals and values of the armed group and are prepared to exert considerable effort on the behalf of the group. They remain with the armed group because they want to, not because they need to or they ought to (also called continuance commitment and normative commitment) (Porter *et al.* 1974; DeCotiis and Summers 1987; Mowday and Steers 1979; Meyer and Allen 1991). Committed members are then also bound to the personal conviction that they have to sustain their activities and their involvement, even when the payoffs are not obvious and the outcomes are uncertain (Salancik 1977: 62–63). As such, group identity overrides individual identity upon the acquisition of group norms (Gill 2007: 154).

It is important to note, that commitment and obedience are two different modes of compliance. While obedience is the main pillar on which the whole superstructure of discipline rests, commitment is the cornerstone in the wall of moral behavior and conscience (Gal 1985: 554). Obedience is then also a sense of duty that originates from an outside authority, initially generated by sanctions and punishments, and further motivated by fear of possible consequences of disobedience (Gal 1985: 556). As soon as agents become less committed to the organizational goals, obedience becomes more necessary and may substitute for commitment (Gal 1985: 562).

Organizational commitment is not only important in public and private firms but it is also the backbone of the military profession. Military activities involve high risk, extreme demands, and severe stress. Under these kinds of circumstances, in which the life of one agent depends on the actions or non-actions of another, compliance with orders and commands becomes the key to organizational functioning (Gal 1985: 553). Or as King (2006: 493) formulates it: "In combat, the armed forces are able to sustain themselves only so long as individual members commit themselves to collective goals even at the cost of personal inquiry or death."

When the level of commitment is too low and when combatants fail to rely on obedient behavior to overcome the discrepancy between his own personal belief system and the demand of the military organization and its leaders, it can have consequences for the functioning of the armed group and the faithful execution of the principal's orders. Regis Debray (1967: 73–74), for instance, notes that this can lead to a situation of an artillery gunner who has not been told in which direction to fire, or a line of attack without a principal direction of attack: the attackers are lost on the field, they shoot at random and die in vain. A lack of commitment can not only lead to individual shirking, but it can also lead to mutiny, fractionalization, or even splits in entire armed groups (Oots 1989). The most striking example involved 20,000 American troops in Manila, who protested their continuing deployment despite the war's end in January 1946 (Gal 1985). Likewise, a hard line commander of the Moro Islamic Liberation Front (MILF) led a mutiny. Opposing peace talks between the government and his armed group, he and his followers attacked un-authorized, Christian communities and formed their own armed group (Gomez 2011).

However, the exact nature of these consequences depends on what the agent is committed to (Salancik 1977: 63). In the case of the Moro Islamic Liberation Front (MILF), low commitment led to a societal abominable outcome (Gould-Williams 2004). However, high commitment can also have negative societal consequences. This is the case when the principal of an armed group orders actions that stand in contrast with personal and moral boundaries, like the killing and harming of civilians. Because commitment allows agents to sacrifice much of their own to fulfill the demands of the organization, highly committed agents are more inclined to overstep these boundaries when ordered and are thus likely to kill and harm more civilians. This idea is captured by the following hypothesis:

Hypothesis 4_{meso}: Armed groups composed of primarily highly committed combatants are more likely to exhibit a higher level of civilian abuse.

Hypothesis 4_{micro}: High committed combatants active are more likely to perpetrate a higher level of civilian abuse.

The origins of commitment[3]

Depending on the goals of the principal, commitment or a lack thereof might have positive or negative societal consequences. However, a lack of commitment leads in most cases to negative consequences for the existence of the armed group. It is then also no surprise that military commanders in their role as principals, apply varying instruments as quasi-management tools that help the agent to identify with the need and goals of the armed movement. But how do these principals ensure the loyalty of their agents? Which mechanisms do they employ to make sure that orders are followed and defection is deterred under circumstances demanding extreme personal sacrifices?

Despite its obvious relevance, organizational commitment has received scant examination within military research and research on armed groups (Allen 2003). The few scholars that approached the topic found out that committed combatants perform better and are more likely to stay with the group (Gade *et al.* 2003). Also Siebold (2006: 186) and Oliver *et al.* (1999), although not examining directly the effect of affective organizational commitment, emphasize that cohesion within armies enhances unit performance and decreases discipline problems. In addition to the relatively few studies on the military and commitment, there are also few that have actually investigated what organizations and their leaders can do to enhance commitment (e.g., Whitener 2001).

Those studies that have been conducted, however, do provide some evidence to suggest that organizations can influence employees' commitment through their economic Human Resource Management (HRM) practices (Meyer and Smith 2000; Haer *et al.* 2011). HRM is an approach that involves all management decision and practices that directly affects or influences the people, or human resources, who work for a particular organization or firm (Shahnawaz and Juyal 2006). Besides influencing the overall competence of employees, the cost effectiveness and the congruence between the employee and the organization's goals, organizational commitment is regarded as an immediate and, perhaps, the most critical outcome of these HRM practices (Beer *et al.* 1984).

Reasoning from the principal–agent theory, HRM practices are considered to be determined by proactive, strategically intended decisions from the side of the principal. These practices are then also the means through which firms are able to align employee behavior with the strategic goals of the principal once an agent is hired. However, due to the applied nature of these practices, there has been little scholarly attention devoted to the linkages between principal–agent theory and HRM practices as a solution in overcoming the problem of adverse selection and of moral hazard underlying every delegation relationship (Wright and McMahan 1992). Jones and Wright (1992) are one of the few scholars that approached the HRM practices from a principal–agent perspective. Using an analysis based on marginal cost and benefit curves, they noted that HRM decision making can be made to have specified solutions that will maximize profitability. Although the purpose of these authors was not to present a model of HRM, the principal–agent theory is quite useful for describing the underlying theoretical rationale for human resource practice (Wright and McMahan 1992: 309). Also Eisenhardt (1988) is an exception. She relies on agency theory as one of the many explanations for the determinants of compensation systems, examining how agency theory variables such as span of control, were related to whether or not retail stores used commission pay systems.

Like the solutions offered by the principal–agent theory to overcome the problem of adverse selection and of moral hazard, HRM practices promote, reinforce and influence commitment through four strategies that the principal can employ to enhance affective organizational commitment: a careful recruitment and selection procedures of employees ex-ante, the training and socialization process, the possibility of promotion and the assessment of employees and the amount of compensation and benefits they receive ex-post (Meyer and Allen 1997; Meyer and Smith 2000).[4] It is important to note that the employment of these four strategies by the principal might be partly determined by the availability of resources. Military training, for instance, is costly (energy and money wise) and time consuming. In contrast, giving a particular combatant a promotion does not cost the principal a lot of money and might be, therefore, more available as a strategy for enhancing commitment for those armed groups which have little to no money to support their activities. In other words, leaders of armed groups that operate in a resource-rich environment and who have a lot of money available are able to implement more of these commitment strategies than those who operate in a resource-poor environment.

Recruitment and selection

In the development of organizational commitment, the recruitment and selection of fighters for the armed group is an important strategy to overcome the problem of adverse selection. A careful recruitment process, in which recruits are selected with, in essence, the same norms and values as promoted by the armed group, secures those potential combatants that the group needs. Other recruits, those who for example join for private gains or who have a high propensity for turnover can be identified early and turned down.

There are different strategies to identify the recruits that fit the organization. However, the key of every strategy should be the exchange of trustworthy information between the recruit and the armed group. Studies like Cable and Judge (1996) and Judge and Cable (1997), revealed for example, that if the organization provides potential applicants with information on both positive and negative aspects of the job, the candidate will not only develop a higher level of organizational commitment, a higher level of job satisfaction and a higher level of trust in the organization and will therefore be better able to cope with the demands of the job (Meyer and Allen 1997).

Strategies to identify the right recruit for an armed group are different in nature than those general used in legal public and private firms. Perhaps with the exception of the FARC in Colombia, hardly any armed group has official "job talks" in which they give the recruit a realistic job preview (Gutiérrez Sanín

2008). However, while some people make the conscious decision to join the armed group and are likely to have at least an idea what to expect, others are simply abducted and forced to fight against their will. By abducting their recruits, leaders deny potential members of making consciously the decision to join or not. Hence, it can be expected that those recruits are less committed than those that joined on a voluntarily basis. This is summarized in the following hypothesis:

Hypothesis 5_{micro}: Combatants who join the armed group voluntarily are more likely to show a high level of affective organizational commitment.

Socialization

Another important strategy for leaders to create organizational commitment among combatants is through the process of socialization that occurs after the agent is hired. This HRM practice is one of the many strategies intended to resolve the problem of moral hazard. In this socialization process, new recruits acquire the social knowledge and skills necessary to assume a specific role in the armed group (Van Maanen and Schein 1979). It is important to note, however, that this acquirement of knowledge and skills is really a process. As Horgan (2008: 85) note: "for any given individual, becoming involved in terrorism will reflect a dynamic, through highly personalized, process of incremental assimilation and accommodation." This incremental assimilation and accommodation is mostly done through the provision of various forms of training (Ahmad and Bakar 2003). During the Cold War, for example, the United States and Soviet Union developed special military training facilities for various proxy insurgent groups (Salehyan 2010: 13). Also armed movements like the Eritrean Peoples' Liberation Army (EPLA), the Front de Libération Nationale (FLN) in Algeria, the Pan Africanist Congress (PAC) in South Africa, and the Zimbabwe African National Union (ZANU) and the Zimbabwe African People's Union (ZAPU) in Zimbabwe are known to have made similar costly investments in the political indoctrination of their fighters (Herbst 2000: 279; Pateman 1998: 126). Training is designed to create cohesion and solidarity through nurturing the group and fighting spirit of the individual as well as to produce an adequate level of expertise (Keegan *et al.* 1985). Hence, it is one of the cornerstones of any armed group; they can hardly be effective without it.

In addition to training, the socialization process involves the usage of internal mechanisms that promote discipline such as avenues for punishment. Punishment practices in armed groups vary according to the influences of national character, citizenry and leaders of the organization (Hamby 2002). Although distinctive, its primary purpose is to socialize each combatant by guiding him or her to the daily routine of working in an armed group by punishing what is regarded in the group as "bad" behavior. Hence, the combatant gains more awareness of what is expected of him or her. However, the effect of punishment on commitment is not straightforward. Too much punishment can be counterproductive. However, to test the influence of these two traditional associated socialization elements on the creation of organizational commitment, two hypotheses are formulated:

Hypothesis 6.1_{micro}: The more training the combatants receive, the higher their level of affective organizational commitment.

Hypothesis 6.2_{micro}: The more punishment the combatant receive, the higher their level of affective organizational commitment.

Compensation and benefits

A third strategy to enhance the level of organizational commitment among troops is to give the individual combatant a kind of benefit or compensation for their participation in group's activities. This idea of providing rewards for particular behavior is nothing new in the principal–agent theory. This theory, as is described in previous sections, is to a large extent a matter of incentives: incentives to work hard, incentives to produce good quality products, incentives to study, incentives to invest, incentives to save, etc. (Laffont and Martimort 2002). Incentives and rewards also play a role in battles. For hundreds of years, soldiers stood to profit from their efforts in battle. In the Middle Ages, for instance, wealthy prisoners could be ransomed and their horses and armor sold by their captors (Keegan *et al.* 1985: 53). Armed groups which provide their members with benefits are perceived by the combatants as showing greater care, concern, and as being fair (i.e., they feel supported by their organization). This in turn, enhances affective organizational commitment on the side of the employee (Paul and Anantharaman 2004).

Benefits and compensation can come in many different forms. Loscocco (1990) for example, has focused in her research solely on the effect of financial rewards and conclude that: "women and men who reported that they are well-rewarded financially were also more likely to be committed to their companies" (Loscocco 1990: 170). Although Loscocco (1990) has focused on legal public organizations, receiving a wage or extra money for participation might also play a crucial role in establishing organizational commitment in armed groups. However, these groups can also provide other tangible rewards, such as drugs, traditional medicine, extra food and/or male or female sex slaves. In addition to these tangible forms of compensation, some scholars have emphasized the positive effect of intrinsic rewards, such as self-image re-enforcement on organizational commitment (e.g., Angle and Perry 1983; Meyer and Allen 1997). The effect of compensation and benefit on the level of organizational commitment shown by combatants can be summarized by the following hypothesis:

Hypothesis 7_{micro}: The more rewards combatants receive, the higher their level of effective organizational commitment.

Promotion and assessment

The last strategy that the HRM theory offers to enhance organizational commitment consists of policies and practices concerning the upward movements of employees (Meyer and Allen 1997). Again this HRM practice plays a role after the agent is hired. Policies concerning promotion are perceived as evidence that the organization, whether an armed group or other kind, is committed to the individual employee, which leads them to reciprocate. Young *et al.* (1998) for example, show that employees who believe that they have internal career opportunities are more committed. These career opportunities in armed groups consist often in the form of receiving a different military rank or a different task within the operative unit. In the LRA in Uganda, for example, most children are initially load carriers – a hard and exhausting job. When they gain the trust of their commander, some children are promoted to guards or watchmen, responsibilities that are easier to carry out and which are considered as prestigious tasks (Haer *et al.* 2011).

However, the seemingly simple positive relationship between promotion and the level of affective organizational commitment is complicated by the fact that too much promotion might work counterproductive. As Kaplin and Ferris (2001) pointed out, promotion has to be perceived as "fair" and "deserved." Receiving too often promotion or seeing that too many people receive promotion can lead to a subsequent reduction of the value of intrinsic rewards (Deci 1971; Pfeffer and Lawler 1980). Hence, promotion does not always lead to an increase in affective organizational commitment. Similar to punishment, promotion is not necessarily about direct personal experience. Seeing others being promoted as a reward for a well-done job can be sufficient to make individuals believe that their own chances for promotions are also high if they behave in the right way. Experiencing an inflation of promotion in the unit, on the other hand, makes promotion less valuable and desirable to the individual combatant.[5] To test the influence of promotion on the level of commitment, the following two contrasting hypotheses are formulated:

Hypothesis 8.1$_{micro}$: The more promotion combatants receive, the higher their level of affective organizational commitment.

Hypothesis 8.2$_{micro}$: The less promotion combatants receive, the higher their level of affective organizational commitment.

Figure 3.3 shows all the above-mentioned linkages in one picture. The first four hypotheses concern those that examine the influence of particular organizational characteristics of armed groups and combatants on the level of perpetrated civilian abuse. The other four hypotheses look at the origins of commitment. As the picture shows, the hypotheses are not always independent from each other. For example, the way in which combatants are recruited has influence on their level of perpetrated civilian abuse, but it is also hypothesized that it influences the level of commitment.

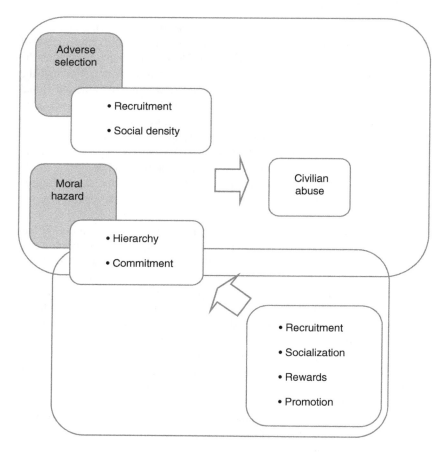

Figure 3.3 Visual presentation of the hypotheses.

In the next chapter, I explain the research design necessary to test the formulated hypotheses on the armed group level. Not only will I devote attention to how I have measured the main independent and dependent variables, but also to how I have collected all the information necessary to test the formulated hypotheses.

Notes

1 It is important to note that I do not examine the tactics of armed groups. To be more precise, I have not discussed or set up any hypothesis that examines whether the tactics used to kill the civilian population (i.e., do they use for instance suicide bombers, car bombs, or just knives to kill the noncombatant population) are related in any sense to the organizational structure of the armed group. This particular topic falls outside the scope of this book. However, currently some very interesting research examines tactical

changes (of especially terrorist organizations) and how this is related to group structures (e.g., see for an impressive overview Gill *et al.* 2013; Bloom and Horgan 2008).

2 Notice that commitment is different than job satisfaction, since the latter emphasizes the specific task environment where an employee performs his or her duties (Mowday and Steer 1979). As such, commitment is often seen as a more stable aspect of the organizational life.

3 Note that parts of this section are already published in Haer (2011).

4 There is some confusion over which practices are considered to be part of the HRM strategy (Gould-Williams 2004). However, most of the practices mentioned in the literature fall into one of these four general categories.

5 It might also be the case that there is a curve-linear relationship between receiving promotion and the level of organizational commitment of the combatant. However, due to the data limitations, it is not possible to test this relationship.

References

Abuza, Zachary. 2003. *Militant Islam in Southeast Asia. Crucible of Terror.* Boulder: Lynne Rienner Publishers.

Ahmad, Kamarul Zaman and Raida Abu Bakar. 2003. "The association between training and organizational commitment among white-collar workers in Malaysia." *International Journal of Training and Development* 7(3): 166–185.

Alchian, Armen and Harold Demsetz. 1972. "Production, Information Costs, and Economic Organization." *American Economic Review* 62(5): 777–795.

Allen, Natalie J. 2003. "Organizational Commitment in the Military: A Discussion of Theory and Practice." *Military Psychology* 15(3): 237–253.

Angle, Harold L. and James L. Perry. 1983. "Organizational Commitment: Individual and Organizational Influences." *Work and Occupations* 10(2): 123–146.

Arquilla, John and David Ronfeldt. 2001. *Networks and Netwars: the future of terror, crime, and militancy.* Santa Monica: RAND Corporation.

Arrow, Kenneth J. 1985. "The Economics of Agency." In *Principals and Agents: The Structure of Business*, eds. John W. Pratt and Richard J. Zeckhauser. Boston: Harvard Business School Press, 1–37.

Barker, James R. 1993. "Tightening the iron cage: Concretive control in self-managing teams." *Administrative Science Quarterly* 38(3): 408–437.

Beer, Michael, Richard E. Walton, and Bert A. Spector. 1984. *Managing Human Assets.* New York: Free Press.

Beetham, David. 1991. "Models of Bureaucracy." In *Markets, Hierarchies and Networks. The Coordination of Social Life*, eds. Grahame Thompson, Jennifer Frances, Rosalind Levačić, and Jeremy Mitchell. London: Sage Publications, 128–140.

Bendor, Jonathan, Amihai Glazer, and Thomas Hammond. 2001. "Theories of Delegation." *Annual Review of Political Science* 4(1): 235–269.

Bloom, Mia and John Horgan. 2008. "Missing Their Mark: The IRAs Proxy Bomb Campaign." *Social Research* 75(2): 579–614.

Brabazon, James. 2003. "Liberia: Liberians United for Reconciliation and Democracy (LURD)." Armed Non-State Actors Project Briefing Paper No. 1, February, 1–13.

Burns, Tom and George M. Stalker. 1961. *The management of innovation.* London: Tavistock Publisher.

Burt, Ronald S. 2005. *Brokerage and Closure: An Introduction to Social Capital.* Oxford: Oxford University Press.

Byman, Daniel and Sarah E. Kreps. 2010. "Agents of Destruction? Applying Principal–Agent Analysis to State-Sponsored Terrorism." *International Studies Perspectives* 11(1): 1–18.

Cable, Daniel M. and Timothy A. Judge. 1996. "Person-organization fit, job choice decisions and organizational entry." *Organizational Behavior and Human Decision Processes* 67(3): 294–311.

Chai, Sun-Ki. 1993. "An Organizational Economics Theory of Antigovernment Violence." *Comparative Politics* 26(1): 99–110.

Coogan. Tim Pat 2000. *The IRA*. New York: Palgrave.

Collier, Paul, Lani Elliott, Håvard Hegre, Anke Hoeffler, Marta Reynal-Querol, and Nicholas Sambanis. 2003. *Breaking the Conflict Trap. Civil War and Development Policy*. Washington: World Bank.

Debray, Regis. 1967. *Revolution in the Revolution?* New York: Grove Press.

Deci, Edward L. 1971. "Effects of Externally Mediated Rewards on Intrinsic Motivation." *Journal of Personality and Social Psychology* 18(1): 105–115.

DeCotiis, Thomas A. and Timothy P. Summers. 1987. "A Path analysis of a model of antecedents and consequences of organizational commitment." *Human Relations* 40(7): 445–470.

Demaris, Ovid. 1977. *Brothers in Blood – the International Terrorist Network*. New York: Verlag Scribner.

De Zeeuw, Jeroen. 2008. "Understanding the Political Transformation of Rebel Movements." In *From Soldiers To Politicians. Transforming Rebel Movements After Civil War*, ed. Jeroen de Zeeuw. Boulder: Lynne Rienner Publishers, 1–32.

Douglass, William A. and Joseba Zulaika. 1990. "On the Interpretation of Terrorist Violence: ETA and the Basque Political Process." *Comparative Studies in Society and History* 32(2): 238–257.

Downs, Anthony. 1967. *Inside Bureaucracy*. Boston: Little Brown.

Eisenhardt, Kathleen M. 1988. "Agency- and institutional-theory explanations: The case of retail sales compensation." *Academy of Management Journal* 31(3): 488–511.

Feaver, Peter D. 2005. *Armed Servants. Agency, Oversight, and Civil-Military Relations*. Harvard: Harvard University Press.

Frances, Jennifer, Rosalin Levačić, Jeremy Mitchell, and Grahame Thompson. 1991. "Introduction." In *Markets, Hierarchies and Networks*, eds. Grahame Thompson, Jennifer Frances, Rosalind Levačić, and Jeremy Mitchell. London: Sage Publication, 1–21.

Gade, Paul A., Ronald B. Tiggle, and Walter R. Schumm. 2003. "The Measurement and Consequences of Military Organizational Commitment in Soldiers and Spouses." *Military Psychology* 15(3): 191–207.

Gal, Reuven. 1985. "Commitment and Obedience in the Military: An Israeli Case Study." *Armed Forces and Society* 11(4): 553–564.

Gates, Scott. 2002. "Recruitment and Allegiance: The Microfoundations of Rebellion." *Journal of Conflict Resolution* 46(1): 111–130.

Gill, Paul. 2007. "A Multi-Dimensional Approach to Suicide Bombing." *International Journal of Conflict and Violence* 1(2): 142–159.

Gill, Paul, John Horgan, Samuel T. Hunter, and Lily D. Cushenbery. 2013. "Malevolent Creativity in Terrorist Organizations." *Journal of Creative Behavior* 47(2): 125–151.

Gill, Paul, Jeongyoon Lee, Karl R. Rethemeyer, John Horgan, and Victor Asal. 2014. "Lethal Connections: The Determinants of Network Connections in the Provisional Irish Republican Army, 1970–1998." *International Interactions* 40(1): 52–78.

Gomez, Jim. 2011. "Muslim rebels order commander to stop mutiny; Manila worries infighting threatens peace talks." The Canadian Press (28 April).

Gould-Williams, Julian. 2004. "The Effects of 'High Commitment' HRM Practices on Employee attitude: the views of public sector Workers." *Public Administration* 82(1): 63–81.

Gutiérrez Sanín, Francisco. 2008. "Telling the Difference: Guerrillas and Paramilitaries in the Colombian War." Politics & Society 36(1): 3–34.

Hackett, Rick D., Peter Bycio, and Peter A. Hausdorf 1994. "Further assessments of Meyer and Allen's (1991) three-component model of organizational commitment." *Journal of Applied Psychology* 79(1): 15–23.

Hatch, Mary J. and Ann L. Cunliffe. 2006. *Organization Theory*. New York: Oxford University Press.

Horgan, John. 2008. "From Profiles to Pathways and Roots to Routes: Perspectives from Psychology on Radicalization into Terrorism." *Annals of the Academy of Political and Social Science* 618(1): 80–94.

Hutch, Mary Jo and Ann L. Cunliffe. 2006. *Organization Theory. Modern, Symbolic, and Postmodern perspectives*. Oxford: Oxford University Press.

Jackson, Brian A. 2006. "Groups, Networks, or Movements: A Command-and-Control-Driven Approach to Classifying Terrorist Organizations and its Application to Al Qaeda." *Studies in Conflict & Terrorism* 29(3): 241–262.

Jaques, Elliot. 1991 "In Praise of Hierarchy." In *Markets, Hierarchies and Networks. The Coordination of Social Life*, eds. Grahame Thompson, Jennifer Frances, Rosalind Levačić, and Jeremy Mitchell. London: Sage Publications, 108–118.

Jones, G. and Patrick Wright. 1992. "An economic approach to conceptualizing the utility of human resource management practices." In *Research in Personnel and Human Resource Management volume 10*, eds. Kendrith Martin Rowland, and Gerald R. Ferris. Greenwich: Jai Press, 271–300.

Judge, Timothy A. and Daniel M. Cable. 1997. "Applicant personality, organizational culture, and organization attraction." *Personnel Psychology* 50(2): 359–394.

Haer, Roos 2011. "Commitment among Fighters: A Research Note." *Peace Economics, Peace Science and Public Policy* 17(1): 1–6.

Haer, Roos, Lilli Banholzer, and Verena Ertl. 2011. "Creating Compliance and Cohesion – How Rebel Organizations Manage to Survive." *Small Wars & Insurgencies* 22(3): 415–434.

Hamby, Joel E. 2002. "The Mutiny Wagon Wheel: A Leadership Model for Mutiny in Combat." *Armed Forces & Society* 28(4): 575–600.

Hechter, Michael. 1987. *Principles of Group Solidarity*. Berkeley: University of California Press.

Heger, Linday, Danielle Jung, and Wendy Wong. 2008. "Organizing for Resistance: How Group Structure Impacts the Character of Violence." Presented at the 49th International Studies Association Annual Conference, San Francisco, March 26–29.

Herbst, Jeffrey. 2000. "Economic Incentives, Natural resources and Conflict in Africa." *Journal of African Economies* 9(3): 270–294.

Holmström, Bengt. 1979. "Moral hazard and Observability." *The Bell Journal of Economics* 10(1): 74–91.

Kalyvas, Stathis N. and Matthew A. Kocher. 2007. "How 'Free' is Free Riding in Civil Wars? Violence, Insurgency, and the Collective Action Problem." *World Politics* 59(2): 177–216.

Kaplin, David M. and Gerald R. Ferris. 2001. "Fairness Perceptions of Employee Promotion

Systems: A Two-Study Investigation of Antecedents and Mediators." *Journal of Applied Social Psychology* 31(6): 1204–1222.

Keegan, John, Richard Holmes, and John Gau. 1985. *Soldiers: A History of Men in Battle*. New York: Elizabeth Sifton.

Keen, David. 1998. *The Economic Functions of Violence in Civil Wars*. Oxford: Oxford University Press.

Kiewiet, D. Roderick and Mathew D. McCubbins. 1991. *The Logic of Delegation. Congressional Parties and the Appropriations Process*. Chicago: The University of Chicago Press.

King, Anthony. 2006. "The Word of Command: Communication and Cohesion in the Military." *Armed Forces & Society* 32(4): 493–512.

Laffont, Jean-Jacques and David Martimort. 2002. *The Theory of Incentives: The Principal–Agent Model*. Princeton: Princeton University Press.

Lake, David A. 1999. *Entangling Relations*. Princeton: Princeton University Press.

Lamb, Guy. 2001. "Putting Belligerents in Context: The Cases of Namibia and Angola." In *Civilians in War*, ed. Simon Chesterman. London: Lynne Rienner Publishers, 25–39.

La Porta, Todd R., ed. 1975. *Organized Social Complexity: Challenge to Politics and Policy*. Princeton: Princeton University Press.

Loscocco, Karyn A. 1990. "Reactions to bluecollar work: A comparison of women and men." *Work and Occupations* 17(2): 152–177.

Mayntz, Renate. 2004. "Organizational Forms of Terrorism. Hierarchy, Network, or a Type sui generis?" MPifG Discussion Paper 04/4. Köln: Max-Planck-Institut für Gesellschaftsforschung.

McCubbins, Mathew D. and Thomas Schwartz. 1984. "Congressional oversight overlooked: Police patrols versus fire alarms." *American Journal of Political Science* 28(1): 165–179.

McCubbins, Mathew D., Roger G. Noll, and Barry R Weingast. 1987. Administrative Procedures as Instruments of Political Control. *Journal of Law, Economics, & Organization* 3(2): 243–277.

Meyer, John P. and Natalie J. Allen. 1991. "A three-component conceptualization of organizational commitment." *Human Resource Management Review* 1(1): 61–89.

Meyer, John. P. and Natalie J. Allen. 1997. *Commitment in the Workplace: Theory, Research, and Application*. Thousand Oaks: Sage.

Meyer, John P. and Catherine A. Smith. 2000. "HRM Practices and Organizational Commitment: Test of a Mediation Model." *Canadian Journal of Administrative Sciences* 17(4): 319–331.

Meyer, John. P., David J. Stanley, Lynne Herscovitch, and Laryssa Topolnytsky. 2002. "Affective, continuance, and normative commitment to the organization: a meta-analysis of antecedents, correlates, and consequences." *Journal of Vocational Behavior* 61(1): 20–52.

Miller, Gary J. 1992. *Managerial Dilemmas. The Political Economy of Hierarchy*. Cambridge: Cambridge University Press.

Mishal, Shaul. 2003. "The Pragmatic Dimension of the Palestinian Hamas: A Network Perspective." *Armed Forces & Society* 29(4): 569–589.

Mitchell, Neil J. 2004. *Agents of Atrocity. Leaders, Followers, and the Violation of Human Rights in Civil War*. New York: Palgrave Macmillan.

Moore, Mick. 1993. "Thoroughly Modern Revolutionaries: The JVP in Sri Lanka." *Modern Asian Studies* 27(3): 593–642.

Mowday, Richard T. and Richard M. Steers. 1979. "The Measurement of Organizational Commitment." *Journal of Vocational Behavior* 14(2): 224–247.

Oliver, Laurel W., Joan Harman, Elizabeth Hoover, Stephanie M. Hayes, and Nancy A. Pandhi. 1999. "A Qualitative Integration of the Military Cohesion Literature." *Military Psychology* 11(1): 57–83.

Oots, Kent Layne. 1989. "Organizational Perspectives on the Formation and Disintegration of Terrorist Groups." *Terrorism* 12(3): 139–152.

Pagels, Heinz R. 1989. *The Dreams of Reason: The Computer and the Rise of the Sciences of Complexity*, New York: Bantam Books.

Pateman, Roy. 1998. *Eritrea: Even the Stones Are Burning*. Lawrenceville: Red Sea.

Paul, A.K. and R.N. Anantharaman. 2004. "Influence of HRM practices on organizational commitment." *Human Resource Development Quarterly* 15(1): 77–88.

Peters, Krijn and Paul Richards. 1998. "'Why we fight': Voices of Youth Combatants in Sierra Leone." *Africa* 68(2): 183–210.

Pfeffer, Jeffrey and John Lawler. 1980. "The effects of job alternatives, extrinsic rewards, and commitment on satisfaction with the organization: A field example of the insufficient justification paradigm." *Administrative Science Quarterly* 25(1): 38–56.

Pollack, Mark A. 1997. "Delegation, Agency, and Agenda Setting in the European Community." *International Organization* 51(1): 99–134.

Porter, Lyman W., Richard M. Steers, Richard T. Mowday, and Paul V. Boulian. 1974. "Organizational commitment, job satisfaction, and turnover among psychiatric technicians." *Journal of Applied Psychology* 59(5): 603–609.

Rauchhaus, Robert W. 2009. "Principal–Agent Problems in Humanitarian Intervention: Moral Hazard, Adverse Selection, and the Commitment Dilemma." *International Studies Quarterly* 53(4): 871–884.

Salancik, Gerald R. 1977. "Commitment is Too Easy!" *Organizational Dynamics* 6: 62–80.

Salanié, Bernard. 2005. *The Economics of Contracts. A Primer*. Cambridge: MIT Press.

Salehyan, Idean. 2010. "The Delegation of War to Rebel Organizations." *Journal of Conflict Resolution* 54(3): 493–515.

Shahnawaz, M. G. and Rakesh C. Juyal. 2006. "Human Resource Management Practices and Organizational Commitment in Different Organizations." *Journal of Indian Academy of Applied Psychology* 32(3): 267–274.

Siebold, Guy L. 2006. "Military Group Cohesion." In *Military Life: The Psychology of Serving in Peace and Combat. Military Performance*, eds. Amy B. Adler, Thomas W. Britt, and Carl A. Castro. Westport: Praeger Security International, 185–201.

Tarrow, Sidney. 1994. *Power in Movement. Social Movements, Collective Action and Politics*. Cambridge: Cambridge University Press

Valentino, Benjamin. 2004. *Final Solutions: Mass Killing and Genocide in the Twentieth Century*. Ithaca: Cornell University Press.

Van Maanen, John and Edgar H. Schein. 1979. "Toward of Theory of Organizational Socialization." *Research in Organizational Behavior* 1: 209–264.

Warwick, Donald P. 1975. *A Theory of Public Bureaucracy: Politics, Personality, and Organization in the State Department*. Cambridge: Harvard University Press.

Whitener, Ellen M. 2001. "Do 'High Commitment' Human Resource Practices Affect Employee Commitment? A Cross-Level Analysis Using Hierarchical Linear Modeling." *Journal of Management* 27(5): 515–535.

Whitford, Andrew B. 2002. "Decentralization and Political Control of the Bureaucracy." *Journal of Theoretical Politics* 14(2): 167–193.

Wright, Patrick M. and Gary C. McMahan. 1992. "Theoretical Perspectives for Strategic Human Resource Management." *Journal for Management* 18(2): 295–320.

Young, Brian S., Stephen Worchel, and David J. Woehr. 1998. "Organizational Commitment among Public Service Employees." *Public Personnel Management* 27(3): 339–348.

Zahar, Marie-Joëlle. 2001. "Protégés, Clients, Cannon Fodder: Civil-Militia Relations in Internal Conflicts." In *Civilians in War*, ed. Simon Chesterman. London: Lynne Rienner Publishers, 43–65.

Part II
The armed groups

4   Web survey design

In this chapter, I explain the research design necessary to test the previously formulated hypotheses. I will first devote attention to the case selection (i.e., which armed groups are included in the dataset) and how I measure civilian killings. Thereafter, I explain in detail how I have collected systematically and empirically information on the internal structure of the different armed groups under scrutiny. In doing so, I explain how I have made the Web survey, who was selected to participate in this survey, and how I have measured the different independent variables.

Measuring one-sided violence

The variable of greatest scientific and normative significance is the dependent variable: the level of civilian abuse perpetrated by different armed groups. Although observers of the state of human rights around the world recognize that actors clearly differ substantially in the amount of respect given to these rights, capturing these perceived variations in a measure that can be feasibly quantified and reliably recorded is an endeavor fraught with many problems (Poe *et al.* 1999: 297). See for example, Lopez and Stohl (1992), Jabine and Claude (1992), and Gibney and Dalton (1997), for criticism on the measurement of human rights abuses.

Nevertheless, organizations such as Amnesty International and the US State Department provide regular estimates on the extent of human rights abuses across the world. These ratings are, however, often not presented in a systematic quantified form, which makes using them for any statistical analyses difficult to say at least (Poe *et al.* 1999: 297). Those datasets that form an exception are mostly limited to genocide or mass killing (Harff 2003; Valentino *et al.* 2004; Rummel 1994), interstate wars (Downes 2004), or rely only on a proxy for violence (Azam and Hoeffler 2002). Only few datasets have focused primarily on recording information on violence against the civilian population.

The Armed Conflict Location Event Dataset (ACLED) is such an exception. This event-based dataset is primarily focused on coding the exact location, dates, and additional characteristics of individual battle evens in states affected by civil war. It includes information on the location of battles, territorial transfers as a result of these battles, and the establishment, strongholds, and presence of rebel movements. For some countries, ACLED reports also events of one-sided violence perpetrated by either government or rebel actors in the period of 1997–2009 (see for more information Raleigh and Hegre 2005). However, this particular data is unsystematically collected. There is, for example, no fixed set of sources that have to be searched through and no fixed definition of one-sided violence. As a result, the coding of one-sided violence events is unreliable and unsystematic across conflicts and coders.

Another dataset on one-sided violence is the Political Instability Task Force (PITF) Worldwide Atrocities dataset.[1] This global event-based dataset describes in quantitative terms the deliberate killing of noncombatants in the context of a wider political conflict. It records all events of civilian killings in which at least five civilians are killed. This threshold merely provides a rule of thumb above which the coders can confidently code all of the reported events given the available resources (Agence France Presse, Associated Press, New York Times, and Reuters). This dataset contains more than 5,400 data observations in the period from 1995 till 2008. These observations are recorded in great detail; the number of victims, perpetrators, and the conditions under which the killing and harming took place are recorded. The PITF dataset overcomes then also some of the problems troubling ACLED – it has a fixed number of sources to be coded, and it uses a fixed definition of what constitutes atrocities against the civilian population. However, like ACLED, the disadvantage of this dataset is that it is an event-based dataset; information on atrocities against civilians is disaggregated and reported over time. Consequently, using this dataset for analyses also requires information on the organizational structure (and its changes) of armed group over time. This information is, however, not readily available and very complicated to collect.

For these reasons, I rely for my dependent variable on a more aggregated dataset with a larger time span, the Uppsala Conflict Data Program (UCDP) One-sided Violence Dataset version 1.3–2010b and version 1.3–2011, 1989–2010. In these two datasets, information is gathered on the occurrence of one-sided violence, i.e., the use of armed force by the government of a state or by a non-state actor (those actors being other than the state and formally organized by having announced a name), against civilians which results in at least 25 deaths (per year and per actor) (Eck *et al.* 2004: 136). This definition excludes criminality and personal violence, as well as fatalities caused by general rioting or other types of unorganized social unrest. Moreover, it excludes extrajudicial killings by the government, the harming of civilians, and most importantly it excludes fatalities as a result of unintentional and indirect use of violence (Eck and Hultman 2007: 235).

Unintentional deaths compromise those killings that result inadvertently from conflict, for example, civilians caught in a cross-fire. These killings are not included in the dataset since the intention of the conflict parties was to kill each other and not the civilian population. Direct killings encompass all deaths caused by the direct use of armed forces by an actor, such as by bombing or shooting

(Eck and Hultman 2007: 235). Intentional starvation, what happened for example in Algeria, is for instance not included in the UCDP One-sided Violence datasets because it is not a direct action (Eck and Hultman 2007: 235; Kalyvas 1999).

The foundation for the data collection is an automated events data search using VRA® technology (Eck and Hultman 2007: 236). This search machine automatically retrieves all articles within specified parameters – in this case, all news reports which contain information about individuals getting killed. The search retrieved news reports from five international new bureaus: Reuters News, British Broadcasting Corporation (BBC) World Monitoring, Agence France Presse, Dow Jones International News and Xinhua News Agency. In addition, EFE News Service was used for Latin America. After retrieving the news articles, every report was individually read and hand coded. Whenever possible, this coding was also supplemented by case-level data (Eck and Hultman 2007: 236) The incidents of one-sided violence are then reported by the yearly estimates of the actual death count of all one-sided violence undertaken by either the government or rebel side. As such, it is more aggregated that the other two mentioned datasets. See Eck and Hultman (2007) for more information on the coding rules and the definition of one-sided violence.

Case selection

The UCDP One-sided Violence datasets report 686 instances of civilian abuse in the period of 1989–2010 around the world. These instances were perpetrated by 198 different actors. From these violent events, 231 accounts were perpetrated by government actors resulting in more than 569,000 civilians getting killed. Figure 4.1 shows the amount of civilians killed per state actor. Especially the governments of Rwanda (511,491), Sudan (10,243), Zaire (9,260), Afghanistan (6,596), and Burundi (4,218) have targeted civilians on a large scale. Although state actors caused more civilian death than all non-state actors together, non-state actors seem to rely more often on this strategy: from the 686 events of one-sided violence, 455 were perpetrated by non-state actors, resulting in more than 130,000 civilians getting killed. Figure 4.2 shows the amount of civilians killed by non-state actors per country. Two countries stand out in the figure: the DRC (55,809), and Bosnia-Herzegovina (12,639). In both countries, non-state actors have killed the largest number of civilians compared to other countries.

Figure 4.3 shows the amount of civilian killings per year of both state as well as non-state actors. The figure displays a very stark rise of civilian killed by state actors in the year 1994, due to the Rwandan genocide. Also in 1997, one can see a rise in the amount of civilians getting killed by state actors, due to the Great African war in Congo. In this war, the Zairian together with the Rwandan government intentionally target civilians on a large scale. Non-state actors were especially active in 1996 and 2002. In 1996, the Alliance des Forces Démocratiques pour la Libération du Congo-Zaïre (AFDL), a rebel group fighting against the Congolese Mubutu government, killed many civilians. In 2002, 46 incidents of one-sided violence occurred, resulting in more than 8,400 killed civilians.

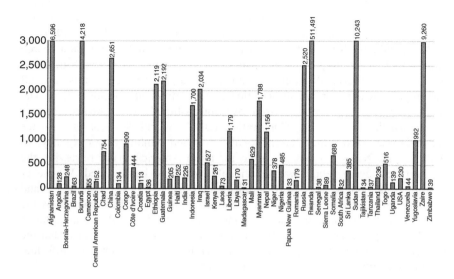

Figure 4.1 Amount of one-sided violence by state actor (source: UCDP One-sided Violence Dataset version 1.3–2010b and 1.3–2011).

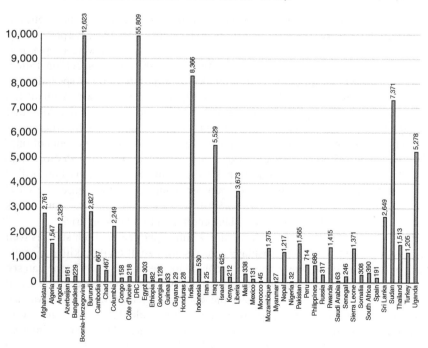

Figure 4.2 Amount of one-sided violence by non-state actors per country (source: UCDP One-sided Violence Dataset version 1.3–2010b and 1.3–2011).

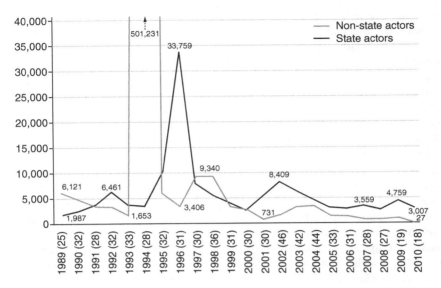

Figure 4.3 Amount of one-sided violence by actor across years (source: UCDP One-
sided Violence Dataset version 1.3–2010b and 1.3–2011).

Most of these killings were perpetrated by two Congolese rebel groups, the
Rassemblement Congolais pour la Démocratie (RCD) and the Union des Patri-
otes Congolais (UPC). The leader of the latter armed group, Thomas Lubanga, is
now prosecuted by the International Criminal Court for the perpetrated atrocities
during this year (Miraglia 2008).

This study is primarily interested in acts of violence against civilians perpetrated by non-state actors. Non-state actors or unconventional belligerents are significantly understudied for reasons ranging from a bias towards legitimate state actors
to the practical constraints on close analysis of non-state groups due to a lack of
reliable data (Eck and Hultman 2007: 234; Jones and Carter 2001: 238). Nonethe-
less, studying the behavior of these actors is an important area for further inquiry,
particularly if the international community wishes to influence the behavior of
these militias in order to protect civilians and resolve conflicts (Jones and Carter
2001: 238). In addition, understanding rebel movements is important because they
pose an armed threat to the functioning of the state, a point surprisingly ignored in
the literature (Herbst 2000: 282). Furthermore, there are also practical reasons why
focusing on non-state actors rather than state actors. It is highly likely that one-
sided violence events perpetrated by state-actors with repressive styles of government are underscored in the two datasets (Claude and Jabine 1992). When these
actors commit wholesale violations of human rights, they probably try to keep the
relevant information from the media in fear of sanctions by the international community. Because the UCDP One-sided Violence datasets largely originate on the

basis of national and international news media, it might be the case that governments' acts are underscored.

However, distinguishing state actors from non-state actors pose problems, also for the UCDP One-sided Violence datasets (Eck and Hultman 2007). For example, it is difficult to determine whether the HAMAS is a state or non-state actor. Originally, this armed group was a non-state actor, yet legally, after winning the 2006 legislative election, those of its members who formed the first Cabinet were state actors. But because Fatah and the international community refuse to recognize HAMAS' cabinet, its members were never treated as such (Gunning 2009).

The difficulties that arise when trying to distinguish state actors from non-state actors is probably due to the interrelated process of globalization and state failure, which opened many doorways for armed groups to arm and fund themselves (Vinci 2006: 50). These factors have radically changes the nature of such groups and allowed them to adapt and evolve into completely new forms (Vinci 2006: 50; Vinci 2006a: 28). The boundary between state and non-state is then also fluid. Capacity wise, they often differ. However, many of the characteristics of a state – such as provision of security and welfare, control over territory, power of taxation, legitimacy – are shared by numerous non-state actors while not all states enjoy all the characteristics they are supported to have in equal measures (Gunning 2009). For instance, Christopher Clapham (1996: 222) has noted when discussing non-state actors that:

> [they] possess armed forces and administrative structures, control varying amounts of territory, extract resources from the populations under their control, and enjoy a level of legitimacy among those populations which certainly varies but which frequently exceeds that of formally constituted governments.

Since they possess so many typical state-like features, armed groups can be thought of as functioning as a single unit which is more than just the sum of the individuals of which it is compromised.

In Appendix 4, all 147 non-state actors are listed that were identified by the UCDP One-sided Violence dataset 2010b and 2011.[2] However, some of these non-state actors are excluded from this case selection. Some identified non-state actors were too unspecified, like the "Serbian Republic of Bosnia and Hercegovina" or "Serbian irregulars." Other listed non-state actors, referred to geographical areas rather than to official recognized armed groups. For instance, "Republic of Abkhazia" or the "Republic of Nagorno-Karabakh." In addition, some identified non-state actors were renamed; they were replaced by the name of their military wing. For example, the African National Congress (ANC) mentioned in the UCDP dataset of 2010b is a political party. However, the party has a military wing responsible for the human rights abuses called the Umkhonto we Sizwe (MK). The ANC is then also replaced by the MK. The same holds for the CPN-M, which has the People's Liberation Army (PLA) as its military wing, the

Communist Party of the Philippines (CPP) that has the New People's Army (NPA) as its military executer, the PAC, which had the Azanian People's Liberation Army (APLA) as its military wing, and the MILF, who has the Bangasamoro Islamic Armed Forces (BIAF) as its military executers.

Expert Web survey

To collect information on concepts such as greed, grievances, social density, hierarchy, and commitment is more challenging than gathering information on civilian abuse and selecting the cases. No comparative dataset exists on armed groups measuring in a systematic and quantitative way these concepts and their importance for different armed groups. This information is also not possible to code on the basis of existing literature on armed groups. Although this literature gives some insights in these concepts, they do not offer this information on a systematic basis, let alone in a comparative format. For instance, Gutiérrez Sanín (2008) gives some insights in the functional difference between the Colombian paramilitary organization and the FARC. He for example states (2008: 16) that

> the paramilitary has generally been a male, paid force, in which the economic ladder and the military hierarchy tend to overlap and delinquent groups and networks are admitted, with a shorter organizational ladder to climb than in the FARC, with much less strict discipline, and with an economic system of selective incentives for both the leadership and the fighters.

However, he does not say anything about the amount of hierarchy of the two groups, how these groups differ relatively to other armed groups around the world, and how hierarchy is measured.

To collect this kind of information in a comparative and systematic format, I decided to design and conduct an expert survey. The use of expert surveys as an instrument to collect data is quite common in political science and, in particular, in studies of the European Union (Dorussen *et al.* 2005). They even play a greater role in the measurement of policy positions of political parties (e.g., Castles and Mair 1984; Laver and Mair 1999; Ray 1999). Surprisingly, in conflict studies, expert surveys are less often used, despite the fact that these surveys allow for estimation of quantities that are difficult or even impossible to observe in reality (Benoit and Laver 2006). In addition, expert surveys allow the researcher to use a single format to ask a common set of questions, i.e., researchers can control the number of dimensions that are central to the comparative research (Hooghe *et al.* 2010). Consequently, expert surveys are often employed when the object of inquiry is complex. They bridge the divide between case studies and the comparison of large number of cases.

There are many modes of expert surveys, such as mail or written surveys, face-to-face surveys, phone surveys, or internet surveys. Each of these survey modes has its advantages and disadvantages over the other modes. For example, experts might feel less pressure to response immediately with mail or written surveys compared to face-to-face interviews, which might increase response rates. Given the nature of the information that need to be collected, the fact that experts are not geographical concentrated, and that their telephone numbers or addresses are not always available, I decided to collect information via an internet survey. To be more precise, via an server-sided Web survey, in which experts complete the survey while connected to the internet through a browser, with the answers being transmitted to the survey on a flow basis (Couper 2008).

The advantages of using internet surveys compared to other survey modes have been extensively documented. Web surveys make it for researchers feasible to collect data from much larger samples, especially considering that the Internet and particularly the World Wide Web has reached widespread penetration in the world (Couper 2008). As a result, sampling error bias is diminished with the use of Web surveys (Schonlau *et al.* 2002). Web-based surveys are also more cost-effective in comparison to other modes of data collection: there is, for instance, no need for postage and printing the surveys or to train interviewers for a face-to-face survey. In addition, Web surveys can deliver rich visual content that allows for interaction with the experts that can work in favor of better completed questionnaires without missing or commission errors (Vincente and Reis 2010).

It is therefore no surprise that the use of Web surveys is proliferating and, in some respects, this development is salutary. However, along with the positive aspects offered by Web surveys, there are important methodological concerns that cannot be ignored if survey quality is to be guaranteed (Vincente and Reis 2010). Data quality is usually measured by the number of respondents who have, intentionally or unintentionally, missed at least one survey item or by the percentage of missed items on respondents' surveys (Schonlau *et al.* 2002). In comparison to other modes, Web surveys are generally connected with a high number of these missing values, i.e., low response rates, which might cause bias in survey estimates (e.g., Couper 2000; Lozar Manfreda *et al.* 2008; Umbach 2004; Vincente and Reis 2010). Accepting that high response rates are generally considered to be desirable, all things equal, much Web survey research has been devoted to the layout of the survey and how to design it so that respondents are more inclined to start and finish the survey. But before I talk about the design of the Web survey, I first discuss the operationalization of the independent variables.

Measuring the independent variables

To measure the four major independent variables; recruitment, social density, hierarchy, and the level of commitment among the fighters, 33 closed-ended questions and 2 open-ended questions are formulated.

Recruitment

Measuring greed and grievances as the basis for recruitment for armed groups is challenging. There is a heated debate going on how to measure these two concepts.

For instance, most grievance models, do not directly measure the perceived discrepancy between one's desired unrealistic goal and one's actual level of attainment (Brush 1996: 530). Rather, they focus on the latter part. In addition, most of the grievances models suffer from the fact that they measure only the respondents' attitudes toward collective violence, not their actual participation. Furthermore, the distinctions between the measures of greed versus grievances are not as exclusive as is often presented. The term "grievance" is generally used to designate political factors such as exclusion and repression, whereas "greed" refers to economic motivations. But "grievance" has also been associated with economic factors such as inequality. Some scholars, for instance, have pointed out that a surfeit of undereducated young men, which Collier (2000) uses as an indicator of greed, may also be read as an indicator of grievance, thereby leaving unclear whether the terms capture mutually exclusive phenomena (Ballentine and Sherman 2003: 14).

Besides the problem of measuring the two concepts on the macro-level, transforming the concepts to a lower level (i.e., to the level of the armed groups) poses extra challenges. Instead of using state-measures like Gross Domestic Product per capita as an indicator of economic motivations, this disaggregating makes it necessary to find indicators that are on the armed group level for these kinds of motivations. The concepts of "greed" and "grievances" are in the final Web survey measured with the help of nine questions. These questions are loosely based on a survey held by Humphreys and Weinstein (2006) in Sierra Leone:

- To your knowledge, does the armed group have clear defined political goals, such as separation of a particular territory, replacing the government, or implementing particular laws?
- To what extent do you think "regular" members are aware of these political goals?
- Some people join an armed group because they experience political repression and/or political exclusion. How important do you think are these political reasons for the recruit's decision to join the armed group?
- Some people join an armed group because they experience inter-ethnic and/ or inter-religious hatred. How important do you think are these ethnic and religious reasons for the recruit's decision to join the armed group?
- Some people join an armed group because they seek to revenge past humiliations and defeats. How important do you think revenge is for the recruit's decision to join the armed group?
- Some people join an armed group because they are discontent about existing economic inequality. How important do you think economic inequality is for the recruit's decision to join the armed group?
- To your knowledge, are recruits offered material benefits such as money, drugs, food, and/or livestock in return for joining the armed group?
- To your knowledge, how often is the armed group engaged in plundering?
- Is plundering promoted by the commanders of the armed group?

The first six questions are designed to measure the different grievance factors that are mentioned in the literature. They measure the presence of political repression, political exclusion, inter-ethnic and religious hatreds, economic inequality, and vengeance as possible discontent factors. Moreover, because I assume that grievance and greed are not mutually exclusive concepts, as also proposed by Collier (2003) in the later versions of his argument, I have formulated the questions in such a way that they allow for measuring the degree in which they are present in the armed group. For example, experts could indicate how important particular grievance factors were in the decision to join and not only indicate that these grievances exist. The use of these "degree-questions" allows for more variance.

The last three questions are focused on the concept of "greed." The questions measure whether combatants receive material rewards for joining and whether they are involved in plundering. This last question is partly based on the idea that greed-driven rebellions are mainly interested in plundering.

Social density

The idea that socially dense networks or socially cohesive networks, whether they consist of people with the same kind of ethnicity or any other kind of connection, can overcome within-group collective action problems is not something new. However, most studies that try to test this idea primarily rely on social network data or on ethnic mobilization data on the state level. Since this part of the study is focused on armed groups, both strands of studies are not useful in the design of questions measuring social density. Additionally, there are many characteristics on which the social network can be based. Identifying the most important ones is very costly; it takes many different questions, which goes at the cost of the limited time that experts have available or are willing to invest in the survey. I, therefore, decided to use only one question:

• Some armed groups try to recruit potential members from specific ethnic and/or religious groups. To what extent does the armed group try to attract recruits with the same ethnic and/or religious backgrounds?

This question measures social density indirectly by asking about the recruitment strategies of the armed group and whether the group tries to attract particular kind of combatants. The question is focused on the role of ethnicity and religion, because these two possible characteristics are the most often mentioned in the literature as determining the density of a group of people.

Hierarchy

Measuring the level of hierarchy of an armed group poses also some difficulties. Not only are there many different definitions of hierarchy, but there are also many different operationalizations and measurements of hierarchy. In political science, most of the definitions refer to the one proposed by Weber (1946 [1925]), which refers to bureaucracy as the ultimate form of hierarchy. However, in order to make a distinction between armed groups that have a more hierarchical structure and those who have a more network-like structure, it is necessary to have several questions measuring this concept.

The questions used in this survey are largely based on Pugh's (2003 [1973]) measurement of organizational structure. He identifies six characteristics of hierarchical structure: high level of specialization, high levels of standardization, high levels of standardization of employment practices, high levels of formalization, and high levels of centralization and configuration. Pugh (2003 [1973]) possesses several questions for the measurement of each characteristic. See Appendix 2 for the exact formulation of the items he proposed. As with the other independent variables, the items proposed by Pugh (2003 [1973]) are mainly developed with legal public and private organizations in mind. Hence, some of these items are changed so that they fit armed organizations and the context in which they arise. In total, 11 questions were asked to experts, measuring different elements of hierarchy:

- In general, how hierarchical do you think the armed group is organized?
- Is the armed group engaged in other activities like providing education and healthcare?
- Is the armed group affiliated with a political party?
- In some armed groups there are rules written down that constrain a recruit's behavior by determining their behavior in particular situations. To your knowledge, do such written rules exist for the armed group that you are an expert on?
- In some armed groups there are standard procedures for hiring new recruits. For instance, recruits are interviewed by one of the commanders or they have a trial period. To your knowledge, does such a standard procedure in the armed group?
- To your knowledge, how are commanders of the armed group generally appointed?
- Does the armed group make use of military language for their ranks, such as "officer," "sergeant," or "general"?
- To what extent do you think that individual members of the armed group can make their own decisions concerning the use of violence?
- To your knowledge, are members of the armed group punished for disobeying orders of their commanders?
- How is the punishment decided upon?
- Who, generally, carries out the punishment?

Again, before actual measuring the different elements of hierarchy, a general question is asked to the experts of the armed groups, measuring the overall level of hierarchy. Thereafter, each element of hierarchy is measured with one or more questions. To measure specialization, two questions are asked about the general behavior of the armed group and to what extent they are specialized in producing violence. To measure the general level of standardization, experts are asked to what extent the armed group has formulated any rules of behavior that are compulsory for every combatant. To examine the level of standardization of employment practices, several questions are developed; questions are asked about whether standard procedures exist for hiring new recruits, how commanders are appointed in the group, and about punishment. The formalization characteristic of hierarchical organizations is measured by asking whether the armed group makes use of military ranks. The level of centralization of the armed group is measured by asking to what extent individual members can make their own decisions concerning the use of violence.

The only characteristic of hierarchy that is not covered by these questions is the degree of configuration. Measuring this concept is problematic since a very detailed overview of the armed group is necessary. For example, one of the indicators measuring configuration, is the percentage of employees in each functional specialization. Determining the percentage of combatants solely active in producing violence is difficult, even for experts. Armed groups are simply too dynamic: new recruits are hired, others members leave the group (or escape), and again other die during combat. Consequently, this element of hierarchy is not measured.

Commitment

To measure the level of commitment among the combatants of an armed group, I make use of the Organizational Commitment Questionnaire (OCQ). This is a standardized questionnaire developed by Porter *et al.* (1974) to measure the level of commitment within an organization. The measure was created with commitment being a generally affective reaction to the organization rather than specifically to the work (Cook *et al.* 1981). Organizational commitment is, therefore, characterized by three important factors: a strong belief in, and acceptance of, the organization's goals and values; a readiness to exert considerable effort on behalf of the organization; and a strong desire to remain a member of the organization (Cook *et al.* 1981).

The OCQ has proven to be reliable and valid over time (Dubin *et al.* 1975; Mowday *et al.* 1974; Porter *et al.* 1976; Porter *et al.* 1974; Steers 1977; Steers and Spencer 1977; Stone and Porter 1975). The Cronbach's alpha coefficient (measuring the internal consistency or reliability) of this measure remains consistently high in these studies, in addition to other people who used the questionnaire years later (Cook *et al.* 1981).

The original OCQ consists of 15 items. However, recently Commeiras and Fournier (2001) showed that although the 15-item version of the OCQ can be a useful tool, the 9-item version has a better overall fit. In addition, they show that one of the items of the OCQ, item number 4 ("I would accept almost any type of job assignment in order to keep working for this organization") is problematic. Without this particular item, the OCQ exhibit better fit properties, in addition to be more parsimonious (Commeiras and Fournier 2001: 243; Mathieu and Zajac 1990; Allen and Meyer 1990). As a result, only eight questions of the OCQ are used as the basis for measuring commitment among the combatants. The exact wording of these items and the different versions of the OCQs can be found in Appendix 1.

There are some problems, however, when applying the OCQ to armed groups. First, the OCQ is developed with the idea that the questions are asked to the actual employees of the organizations. However, this is problematic in my research design, since sampling combatants of every selected armed group is difficult. Consequently, the questions were transformed so that experts were able to answer them. Second, the items are developed by researchers that examine organizational commitment in legal public or private organizations and not in organizations active in illegal practices. Hence, the formulation of some items needed to be changed. Related to this point, is the problem of context and culture. The OCQ has proven to be useful to measure commitment in other cultures than the Western one, most notably the Asian culture (e.g., Suliman and Iles 1999). However, the measure has, to my knowledge, not often been applied to other cultures and continents besides the Asian and Western context. All in all, the eight-item OCQ is only used as the basis of the questions measuring commitment among combatants. In total, the Web survey contained seven items:

- To what extent do you think that the members of the armed group are committed to the organization?
- Some armed groups forbid their members to have contact with their family members, friends, and/or other people that are not part of the group. To what extent do members of the armed group, on which you are an expert, have contact with people from outside the group?
- In general, how hard is it for members to leave the armed group?
- If members have left the armed group, to what extent do you think they still have contact with their former comrades?
- To what extent do members care about the fate of the armed group?
- How proud do you think the members are to be part of the armed group?
- To what extent are members loyal to the armed group?

As with all the other variables, I started the commitment part of the Web survey with a general question concerning the level of commitment. The other questions are based on the eight-item OCQ. The questions concerning being proud and caring about the fate of the armed group are quite literally copied. Other items of the OCQ were not included, not even in a changed format (for example, item numbers 3, 4, 5, and 6). These items were not only very hard to transform into questions but also did not take into account the context of armed groups. Therefore, they were replaced with questions on the difficulties leaving the armed group and the relationship combatants have with people from outside group. These kinds of questions were not included in the OCQ, since employees in legal organizations often do not have to leave their house for a longer period of time to live with the organization. In addition, there are few differences between those who are working for the organization and those who are not.

In addition to these seven questions, two additional questions were added. These questions, although they seem to related at first sight more to recruitment, are closely related to commitment:

* In general, are members of the armed group abducted or did they join voluntarily?
* Some armed groups recruit their members for a lifetime, i.e., once they join they are expected to stay forever with the group. In general, are members of the armed group recruited for life?

Organizational commitment depends in large part on whether recruits join the army voluntarily and consciously; attachment might be a result of a life-time commitment.

For most described questions, I used a five-point Likert-type rating scale. Likert scales are commonly used to measure attitudes, providing a range of possible responses to a given question or statement. As such, Likert scales allow for degrees of opinion, rather than expecting a simple yes/no answer form the respondent. Experimental research has shown that especially the five-point and seven-point scale are appropriate answer scales. The 10-point format, for example, produces slightly lower relative means than either the five- or seven-point scales (Dawes 2008). More finely graded scales do not improve the reliability and validity further (Dawes 2008).

Not surprisingly, I did not use these Likert Scales for the open-ended questions. I included two open questions in the survey: one asking for the names and e-mail addresses of other experts and another question allowing experts to make additional comments on the survey and there given answers.

Identifying experts

To gather reliable data via a Web survey, it is essential to carefully select experts. In this study, "experts" were defined as people with expertise on the internal structure of the armed movements. Experts were primarily selected on the basis of their (academic) publications or policy briefings. Consequently, not all selected experts are academically schooled or working at the university. For example, some experts are working for NGOs like the United Nations, Human Rights Watch, the World Bank, or smaller organizations like the Colombian demobilization NGO Manos por la Paz (Hands for Peace), or the Sudanese organization Human Rights and Advocacy Network for Democracy (HAND) active in the Darfur region.

While it would be better to have a very large pool of experts per armed group, only few persons are privy to the relevant information and have the relevant expertise. This is mainly due to the fact that armed groups work often secretively and outside the legal realm. However, I selected, whenever possible, at least two experts per armed group. See Appendix 4 for the number of experts per armed group.

For some groups it was not possible to find any experts. This is due to several factors. First, some selected armed groups are simply too small or too unknown. For instance, for the Gazotan Murdash – an armed group known for the Moscow subway bombings in 2004 – no experts were found. This terrorist organization was unknown before this attack, and has also not been heard of since these bombings. Second, for some other armed groups, no experts were found because the literature downplayed their role in civil war relative to other groups. For example, no experts could be found for the LURD, a known armed group active in the Liberian civil war from 1999 to 2003. In this particular war many different actors were involved, such as the Movement for Democracy in Liberia (MODEL) and several other groups fighting for Charles Taylor. Due to the number of active actors, the role of the LURD is deemphasized in the literature. Third, in the initial case selection some armed groups' factions were mentioned as separate actors. Although I am aware of the fact that particular factions are very independent and sometimes even hardly in contact with the core of the armed group, finding experts on factions is difficult since they are often relatively small. Hence, armed groups' factions were excluded from the analyses.[3] Lastly, the e-mail addresses of some experts, which are a necessity for conducting a personalized Web survey, were not found. Some experts moved to another university without leaving the new e-mail address, some finished their studies and found a job in the policy sector, and again others did not publish their e-mail addresses online out of security reasons (this occurred especially in the case of experts researching active armed groups, such the Mara Salvatrucha gang (MS-13)). In addition, some NGOs like Amnesty International and Human Rights Watch have a policy of not publishing the contact addresses of their employees online. Consequently, from the initial selection of 147 armed groups, only 88 armed groups were selected for further analyses. See Appendix 4 for the number of experts per selected armed group.

Web survey implementation

The Web survey was implemented using the Unipark program, a survey software that allows users to create Web surveys with minimal effort. It is a commonly used program, allowing for straightforward programming and is in comparison to other providers low priced. The program is rather flexible in the sense that participants can interrupt filling in the questionnaire and continue later, the system records information when participants break off or the time they needed to complete the questionnaire and individual screens. In addition, it allows for integrating sophisticated and non-standardized tools to the questionnaire design (Haer and Meidert 2013). Especially this later feature of Unipark makes the program very attractive for Web surveys. Before the actual Web survey was implemented, several pretests were conducted.

Pretesting

Many things can be done to minimize to deployment of poorly designed Web surveys resulting in low response rates. Careful pretesting is one of them (Couper 2008). Valuable insights can be gained from different pretests in which respondents interact with the survey instrument. Three pretests were conducted, in which experts and non-experts were selected to make methodological, content-related, or technical comments on the questionnaire. Survey researchers have shown a remarkable agreement on the amount of necessary pretesters. Sheatsley (1983: 226) argues that "It usually takes no more than 12–25 cases to reveal the major difficulties and weaknesses in a pretest questionnaire." This judgment is similar to that of another prominent methodologist, who maintained that "20–50 cases is usually sufficient to discover the major flaws in a question-naire" (Sudman 1983: 181).

The first two pretests were participating pretests, in which the respondents were informed of the pretest purpose. The last one, conducted among experts of not selected armed groups was an undeclared one (Presser *et al.* 2004). The first pretest was conducted at the end of February 2011. In total, 17 non-experts were e-mailed, in which they were asked to evaluate the Web survey by filling in the survey while focusing on the lay-out, whether they understood the questions, and whether they thought the answer categories fit the questions. The selected test-persons varied in social demographic characteristics (native language, age, level of education, gender, etc.). In addition, some of these pretesters used different browsers to open the Web survey. This first pretest round was characterized by a response rate of more than 75 percent: from the 17 pretesters, 13 filled in the survey. Some pretesters were primarily looking at the technical side of the survey, while others were more focused on the structure of the survey and the question wording.

At the end of March 2011, a second pretest was conducted in which 14 other non-experts selected where asked to assess the questions. Again this pretest panel showed variation in gender, level of education, and in language. From the 14 people, two were, however, also part of the first pretest round. These two were asked again because of their experience with Web surveys. This pretest round had a response rate of 86 percent. Only two pretesters did not answer to the evaluation request and one broke off prematurely. This pretest round was different than the first one in the sense that besides the evaluation of the ques-tion, also attention was given to the procedures and implementation of the survey. For example, the respondents received a personalized invitation e-mail, in which a fake publication and armed group was mentioned. In addition, a reminder was send to them whenever they did not fill out the survey. Like the first pretest round, the comments on the Web survey varied. However, signifi-cantly fewer comments were made about the survey design and the content of the questions.

The last pretest was conducted mid-April 2011. This undeclared pretest was held among experts of armed groups that were not selected. These experts were not informed about the fact that they were pretesters of the Web survey, since they would then be less inclined to invest time and energy in a survey in which they know that they were just pretests. Consequently, this pretest resembled the actual Web Survey most realistically. This undeclared pretest was held only on a very small scale, since few people are experts on the armed groups that were not selected. In total 41 experts on 32 armed groups were send an e-mail invitation to evaluate the behavior of the armed group on which they are an expert. From the 36 respondents that received the survey request (some request came back because of a wrong e-mail address), 18 experts filled out the survey after one reminder (response rate of 43.90 percent). Only one reminder was sent to avoid irritation.

Two methods are in generally used to evaluate an undeclared pretest. First, one method involves response latency, i.e., the time it takes a respondent to answer a question. Response latency is used to evaluate the accuracy of respondents' answers and indirectly to evaluate the questions themselves (Draisma and Dijkstra 2004). It is based on the assumption, that the longer delays signal respondent uncertainty (Presser *et al.* 2004). To evaluate the response latency, the relative timestamp of the different pages is analyzed. Table 4.1 reports some descriptive statistics about this time span of the Web survey pages. The table reports not only the mean, the standard deviation, the minimum, and maximum time in seconds elapsed since opening of the first page until submission of the respective page, but also reports the number of questions on the respective page and its content. In addition, it is reported in the table whether the questions were introduced with an introduction text or not.

Those pages that have a relatively high time span compared to other pages, are those that have two questions on one page, which have an introduction text on the page, on which open-questions were asked. In other words, when only looking at the response latency, no page stands out and the time necessary to answer the questions on the pages seems rather equally distributed. However, when looking at the breakoff rates of the different pages, a somewhat different picture emerges. From the 18 respondents that filled out the pretest, only 13 completed the Web survey. The five respondents that broke off the survey prematurely did this in the beginning of the survey; two of them broke off after the first question (i.e., whether most combatants were abducted or joined voluntarily); three others broke off after the second question (i.e., whether members were recruited for life time or not). However, it is normal in Web surveys that some respondents do not complete the survey and it is most often the case that they will break off in the beginning of the survey. Break off rates should in general become less, the more questions the respondent has answered. This was also the case for this Web survey. Consequently, the break-off rates did not signal that any changes were necessary.

The second way that this third pretest was evaluated was by looking at the comments made by the experts on the survey. The experts could comment on the survey via two ways: by e-mail or by leaving a comment in the comment and suggestions box at the end of the survey. Both ways were used. Most criticism

Table 4.1 Descriptive statistics of the response latency of the survey pages in seconds

No. page	Content of questions	No. questions	Text	Mean	Sd.	Min.	Max.
55060	Other experts	1	Yes	374.94	281.97	0	766
112840	Contact	1	Yes	443.65	327.80	0	837
58789	Amount of targeting and order	2	No	155.76	232.22	0	602
58785	Targeting intentionally	1	No	333.71	248.86	0	677
112661	Political party	1	No	327.82	245.41	0	667
59221	Branches	1	Yes	315.65	235.30	0	653
62015	Loyalty	1	No	304.18	228.28	0	634
62014	Proud	1	No	299.29	225.18	0	627
62013	Fate	1	No	293.41	220.85	0	620
62012	Contact after	1	No	285.59	215.17	0	611
62011	Leaving	1	No	277.88	210.48	0	603
62010	Contact outside	1	No	268.71	203.06	0	594
62006	Commitment	1	Yes	242.29	178,93	0	516
59282	Decision to punish	1	No	149	173.25	0	457
59257	Punishment	1	No	216.47	158.57	0	435
59255	Decision making	1	No	210.35	154.18	0	418
59254	Rank	1	No	199.06	145.88	0	402
59695	Appointment	1	No	191	140.70	0	382
59224	Hiring	1	No	168.06	122.32	0	324
59223	Rules	1	No	160.47	117.61	0	313
101274	Hierarchy	1	Yes	148.24	107.70	0	288
112822	Encouraging looting	1	No	110.76	102.28	0	261
64461	Looting	1	No	131.71	96.04	0	255
64458	Material benefits	1	No	122.29	89.93	0	245
95524	Inequality and vengeance	2	No	111.88	82.27	0	235
64446	Politics and ethnicity	2	No	96.76	72.95	0	205
112606	Awareness politics	1	No	74.29	57.36	0	169
64435	Political goals	1	No	65.12	50.41	0	155
64434	Social cohesion	1	No	60.29	42.43	0	145
101273	Abduction or joining	1	Yes	30.65	17.75	0	68

and confusion was about the fact that the questions were of a general nature and did not depend on the time. For example, an expert on the Frente Sandinista de Liberación Nacional (FSLN) commented: "Answers refer to the pre-1979 period." These kinds of comments point toward the fact that many experts found it difficult to generalize over a period of time. I solved this problem by empha-sizing on the welcome screen that the experts should only generalize over two decades (the dependent variable of one-sided violence was measured during this period).

Another set of comments was directed to the way I collected the data. Most ethnographers or anthropologists refuse to put their ideas and knowledge into fixed categories. Although I had an open question in which they could write down their comments and suggestions, the fixed format did not encourage them to respond. In reaction to these comments I always send them a personal e-mail explaining that I understood that there is a difference between the disciplines and the way in which we gather data. At the same time, I encourage them to fill out the survey anyway.

Implementation

The first round of the survey started on of April 18, 2011. At that day, 287 experts received an e-mail invitation for participating in the Web survey (see Appendix 3). Not all experts were invited in once because many computer servers are not able to send that many outgoing e-mails at once. Moreover, if too many people try to access the same survey on the same server at once, slowdowns occur that might lead some experts to quit the survey prematurely (Dillman *et al.* 2009: 292).

The e-mail invitation was send from a University of Konstanz e-mail account especially created for the survey, increasing on first sight the professional appearance of the survey. The level of professionalism was also increased by choosing a subject line for the e-mail invitation that was informative. The subject line of this invitation e-mail was "Expert survey on armed groups," which made clear to the respondents why they received the e-mail and why they were chosen. From a nonresponse perspective, however, revealing the subject of the survey at the outset may encourage only those who are interested in the particular topic to proceed (Couper 2008: 312–313; Groves 2006). The e-mail invitation provided the experts with information about the content of the survey, contact information, and the URL to the Web survey. All other information was provided in a very personal way; experts were personally saluted (for instance, Dear Mrs. Banholzer) and their publication was mentioned in the e-mail invitation.

In the e-mail invitation an URL was included that contained an access code. Entering this URL in a browser or clicking on this link, gains respondents' entrance into the survey. I chose this login format over a manual login condition (in which respondents have to enter both a password and access code) since Crawford *et al.* (2001) found that providing an automatic login significantly increased response rates by nearly 5 percentage points. The URL was significant, short, understandable, and easy to transcribe or retry when necessary. Once entered the URL in the browser or once the expert clicked on the link, the welcome screen appeared with some instruction about how to proceed to the survey. It also contained some information on the privacy rights of the respondent.

On April 26, a reminder was sent (see Appendix 3). Reminders increases response rated to Web surveys, contributing up to one-third of the sample size (Vehovar *et al.* 2002). The reminder was developed as a standard professional reminder. I decided to send out the first reminders five days after the e-mail invitation. This is somewhat later than is normally suggested in the field of Web survey research. However, I expected that at least some of the experts are working in countries where there is no instant access to the Internet. The second reminder was sent 14 days after the first one. Like the e-mail invitation, the two reminders were sent before working hour. Trouteaud (2004) showed that this increases the response rates significantly since on this time, the survey request is not in direct competition with the ongoing demand of the day.

Besides the initial 287 experts that were e-mailed, another 169 were e-mailed as the result of the open question in the survey asking about the contact data of possible other experts. This increased the response rate enormously. At the end, the response rate was more than 46 percent. This is a very high response rate, considering the fact that the response rate is normally around 30 percent (Couper 2008).

In the next chapter the responses to the questions are described and the formulated hypotheses on the armed group level are empirically tested.

Notes

1 See for more information http://eventdata.parusanalytics.com/data.dir/atrocities.html.
2 Some more non-state armed groups are included in the Appendix, due to the pretest or the preferences of the experts.
3 In case there was information on the amount of perpetrated level of one-sided violence of these factions, this was added to the level of the general armed group.

References

Allen, Natalie J. and John P. Meyer. 1990. "The measurement and antecedents of affective, continuance and normative commitment to the organization." *Journal of Occupational Psychology* 63(1): 1–18.

Azam, Jean-Paul and Anke Hoeffler. 2002. "Violence Against Civilians in Civil Wars: Looting or Terror?" *Journal of Peace Research* 39(4): 461–485.

Ballentine, Karen and Jake Sherman. 2003. "Introduction." In *The Political Economy of Armed Conflict: Beyond Greed and Grievance*, eds. Karen Ballentine and Jake Sherman. London: Lynne Rienner Publishers, 1–15.

Benoit, Kenneth and Michael Laver. 2006. *Party Policy in Modern Democracies*. London: Routledge.

Brush, Stephen G. 1996. "Dynamics of Theory Change in the Social Sciences: Relative Deprivation and Collective Violence." *Journal of Conflict Resolution* 40(4): 523–545.

Castles, Francis G. and Peter Mair. 1984. "Left-right political scales: Some 'expert' judgments." *European Journal of Political Research* 12(2): 73–88.

Clapham, Christopher. 1996. *Africa and the International System: the Politics of State Survival*. Cambridge: Cambridge University Press.

Claude, Richard P. and Thomas B. Jabine. 1992. "Exploring Human Rights Issues with Statistics." In *Human Rights and Statistics, Getting the Record Straight*, eds. Thomas B. Jabine and Richard P. Claude. Philadelphia: University of Pennsylvania Press, 5–34.

Collier, Paul. 2000. "Doing Well out of War: An Economic Perspective." In *Greed and Grievance: Economic Agendas in Civil Wars*, eds. Mats Berdal and David M. Malone. Boulder: Lynne Rienner Publishers, 91–111.

Collier, Paul, Lani Elliott, Håvard Hegre, Anke Hoeffler, Marta Reynal-Querol, and Nicholas Sambanis. 2003. *Breaking the Conflict Trap. Civil War and Development Policy*. Washington: World Bank.

Commeiras, Nathalie and Christophe Fournier. 2001. "Critical Evaluation of Porter *et al.*'s Organizational Commitment Questionnaire: Implications for Researchers." *Journal of Personal Selling and Sales Management* 21(3): 239–245.

Cook, John D., Sue J. Hepworth, Toby D. Wall, and Peter B. Warr. 1981. *The Experience of Work: A Compendium and review of 249 Measures and their Use*. London: Academic Press Inc.

Couper, Mick P. 2000. "Web Surveys: A Review of Issues and Approaches." *Public Opinion Quarterly* 64(4): 464–494.

Couper, Mick P. 2008. *Designing Effective Web Surveys*. Cambridge: Cambridge University Press.

Crawford, Scott D., Mick P. Couper, and Mark J. Lamias. 2001. "Web Survey: Perceptions of Burden." *Social Science Computer Review* 19(2): 146–162.

Dawes, John. 2008. "Do Data Characteristics Change According to the number of scale points used? An experiment using 5-point, 7-point and 10-point scales." *International Journal of Market Research* 50(1): 61–77.

Dillman, Don A., Jolene D. Smyth, and Leah Melani Christian. 2009. *Internet, Mail, and Mixed-Mode Surveys. The Tailord Design Method*. Hoboken: John Wiley & Sons.

Dorussen, Han, Hartmut Lenz, and Spyros Blavoukos. 2005. "Assessing the Reliability and Validity of Expert interviews." *European Union Politics* 6(3): 315–337.

Downes, Alexander B. 2004. "Targeting Civilians in War." PhD dissertation at the Department of Political Science, University of Chicago.

Draisma, Stasja and Wil Dijkstra. 2004. "Response Latency and (Para)Linguistic Expression As Indicators of Response Error." In *Methods for Testing and Evaluating Survey Questionnaires*, eds. Stanley Presser, Jennifer M. Rothgeb, Mick P. Couper, Jusith T. Lesser, Elizabeth Martin, Jean Martin, and Eleanor Singer. New York: Soringer-Verlag, 131–148.

Dubin, Robert, Joseph E. Champoux, and Lyman W. Porter. 1975. "Central Life Interests and Organizational Commitment of Blue Collar and Clerical Workers." *Administrative Science Quarterly* 20(3): 411–421.

Eck, Kristine and Lisa Hultman. 2007. "One-Sided Violence Against Civilians in War: Insights from New Fatality Data." *Journal of Peace Research* 44(2): 233–246.

Eck, Kristine, Margareta Sollenberg, and Peter Wallensteen. 2004. "One-Sided Violence and Non-State Conflict." In *States in Armed Conflict 2003*, ed. Lotta Harbom. Department of Peace and Conflict Research, Uppsala University, 133–142.

Gibney, Mark and Mathew. Dalton. 1997. "The Political Terror Scale." In *Human Rights and Developing Countries*, ed. David L. Cingranelli. Greenwich: JAI Press, 73–84.

Groves, Robert M. 2006. "Nonresponse rates and nonresponse bias in household surveys." *Public Opinion Quarterly* 70(5): 646–675.

Gunning, Jeroen. 2009. *Hamas in Politics: Democracy, Religion, Violence*. New York: Colombia University Press.

Gutiérrez Sanín, Francisco. 2008. "Telling the Difference: Guerrillas and Paramilitaries in the Colombian War." *Politics & Society* 36(1): 3–34.

Haer, Roos and Nadine Meidert. 2013. "Does the first impression count? The Impact of Web Surveys' Welcome Screen on Response Rates." *Survey Methodology Journal* 39(2): 419–434.

Harff, Barbara. 2003. "No Lessons Learned from the Holocaust? Assessing Risks of Genocide and Political Mass Murder since 1955." *American Political Science Review* 97(1): 57–73.

Herbst, Jeffrey. 2000. "Economic Incentives, Natural resources and Conflict in Africa." *Journal of African Economies* 9(3): 270–294.

Hooghe, Liesbeth, Ryan Bakker, Anna Brigevich, Catherine de Vries, Erica Edwards, Gary Marks, Jan Rovny, Marco Steenbergen, and Milada Vachudova. 2010. "Research Note. Reliability and Validity of the 2002 and 2006 Chapel Hill expert surveys on party positioning." *European Journal of Political Research* 49(5): 687–703.

Humphreys, Macartan and Jeremy M. Weinstein. 2006. "Handling and Manhandling Civilian in Civil War." *American Political Science Review* 100(3): 429–447.

Jabine, Thomas B. and Richard P. Claude, eds. 1992. *Human Rights and Statistics: Getting the Record Straight.* Philadelphia: University of Pennsylvania Press.

Jones, Bruce D. and Charles K. Carter. 2001. "From Chaos to Coherence? Toward a Regime for Protecting Civilians in War?" In *Civilians in War*, ed. Simon Chesterman. London: Lynne Rienner Publishers, 237–262.

Kalyvas, Stathis N. 1999. "Wanton and Senseless? The Logic of Massacres in Algeria." *Rationality and Society* 11(3): 243–285.

Laver, Michael J. and Peter Mair. 1999. "Party policy and cabinet portfolios in the Netherlands, 1998: Results from an expert survey." *Acta Politica* 34(1): 49–66.

Lopez, George A. and Michael Stohl. 1992. "Problems of Concept and Measurement in the Study of Human Rights." In *Human Rights and Statistics: Getting the Record Straight*, eds. T.B. Jabine and R.P. Claude. Pennsylvania: University of Pennsylvania, 216–234.

Lozar Manfreda, Katja, Michael Bosnjak, Jernej Berzelak, Iris Haas, Vasja Vehovar. 2008. "Web Surveys Versus Other Survey Modes: A Meta-Analysis Comparing Response Rates." *International Journal of Market Research* 50(1): 79–104.

Mathieu, John. E. and Dennis M. Zajac. 1990. "A review and meta-analysis of the antecedents, correlates, and consequences of organizational commitment." *Psychological Bulletin* 108(2): 171–194.

Miraglia, Michela. 2008. "Admissibility of Evidence, Standard of Proof, and Nature of the Decision in the ICC Confirmation of Charges in *Lubanga.*" *Journal of International Criminal Justice* 6(3): 489–503.

Mowday, Richard T., Lyman W. Porter, and Robert Dubin. 1974. "Unit performance, situational factors, and employee attitudes in spatially separated work units." *Organizational Behavior and Human Performance* 12(2): 231–248.

Poe, Steven C., Neal Tate, and Linda Camp Keith. 1999. "Repression of the Human Right to Personal Integrity Revisited: A Global Cross-National Study Covering the Years 1976–1993." *International Studies Quarterly* 43(2): 291–313.

Porter, Lyman W., Richard M. Steers, Richard T. Mowday, and Paul V. Boulian. 1974. "Organizational commitment, job satisfaction, and turnover among psychiatric technicians." *Journal of Applied Psychology* 59(5): 603–609.

Porter, Lyman W., William J. Crampon, and Frank J. Smith. 1976. "Organizational commitment and managerial turnovers: A longitudinal study." *Organizational Behavior and Human Performance* 15(1): 87–98.

Presser, Stanley, Mick P. Couper, Judith T. Lesser, Elizabeth Martin, Jean Martin, Jennifer M. Rotgheb, and Eleanor Singer. 2004. "Methods for testing and evaluating survey questions." *Public Opinion Quarterly* 68(1): 109–130.

Pugh, D.S. 2003 [1973]. "The Measurement of Organization structures." In *The Sociology of Organizations*, ed. Michael J. Handel. London: Sage Publications, 66–76.

Raleigh, Clionadh and Håvard Hegre 2005. "Introducing ACLED: An Armed Conflict Location and Event Dataset." Paper presented to the Conference on "Disaggregating the Study of Civil War and Transnational Violence." University of California Institute of Global Conflict and Cooperation, San Diego, 7–8 March 2005.

Ray, Leonard. 1999. "Measuring Party Positions on European Integration: Results from an Expert Survey." *European Journal of Political Research* 36(2): 283–306.

Rummel, Rudolph J. 1994. "Power, Genocide and Mass Murder." *Journal of Peace Research* 31(1): 1–10.

Schonlau, Matthias, Ronald D. Fricker, Jr., and Marc N. Elliott. 2002. *Conducting Research Surveys via E-mail and the Web*. Washington: RAND cooperation.

Sheatsley, Paul B. 1983. "Questionnaire construction and item writing." In *Handbook of Survey Research*, eds. Peter Rossi, James Wright, and Andy Anderson. New York: Academic Press, 195–230.

Steers, Richard M. 1977. "Antecedents and outcomes of organizational commitment." *Administrative Science Quarterly* 22(1): 46–56.

Steers, Richard M. and Daniel G. Spencer. 1977. "The role of achievement motivation in job design." *Journal of Applied Psychology* 62(4): 472–479.

Stone, Eugene F. and Lyman W. Porter. 1975. "Job characteristics and job attitudes: a multivariate study." *Journal of Applied Psychology* 60(1): 57–64.

Sudman, Seymour. 1983. "Applied Sampling." In *Handbook of Survey Research*, eds. Peter Rossi, James Wright, and Andy Anderson. New York: Academic Press, 145–194.

Suliman, Abubakr M. and Paul A. Iles. 1999. "The Multi-Dimensional Nature of Organizational Commitment in a Non-Western Context." *Journal of Management Development* 19(1): 71–82.

Trouteaud, Alex R. 2004. "How You Ask Counts. A Test of Internet-Related Components of Response Rates to a Web-Based Survey." *Social Science Computer Review* 22(3): 385–392.

Umbach, Paul D. 2004. "Web Surveys: Best Practices." In *Overcoming Survey Research Problems. New Directions for Institutional Research*, ed. S. R. Porter. San Francisco: Jossey-Bass, 23–38.

Valentino, Benjamin, Paul Huth, and Dylan Balch-Lindsay. 2004. "'Draining the Sea': Mass Killing and Guerrilla Warfare." *International Organization* 58(1): 375–407.

Vehovar, Vasja, Zaletel Batagelj, Katja Lozar Manfreda, and Metka Zaletel. 2002. "Nonresponse in Web surveys." In *Survey Nonresponse*, eds. Robert M. Groves, Don A. Dillman, John L. Eltinge and Roderick J. A. Little. New York: John Wiley & Sons, 229–242.

Vincente, Paula and Elizabeth Reis. 2010. "Using Questionnaire Design to Fight Nonresponse Bias in Web Surveys." *Social Science Computer Review* 28(2): 251–267.

Vinci, Anthony. 2006. "The 'Problems of Mobilization' and the Analysis of Armed Groups." *Parameters* 36(1): 49–62.

Vinci, Anthony. 2006a. "Greed-Grievance reconsidered: the Role of Power and Survival in the Motivation of Armed Groups." *Civil Wars* 8(1): 25–45.

Weber, Max. 1946 [1925]. *The Theory of Social and Economic Organization*. New York: Oxford University Press.

5   Armed group analyses and results

In total 192 experts filled out the Web survey on 80 different armed groups, with an average of 2.40 experts per armed group (and a standard deviation of 3.30). Table 5.1 shows the expert distribution per armed group (see Appendix 4 for the exact amount of experts for a particular armed group).[1]

The survey was filled in for 32 armed groups by only one expert. For the other 48 armed groups, more than one expert answered; for the LRA, for instance, 14 experts filled in the survey. Also the Sudan People's Liberation Army (SPLA) and the Movement of Democratic Forces in the Casamance (MFDC) from Senegal are covered by many experts: respectively 9 and 7 experts. This is probably due to the fact that these groups are known and were until recently very active. This distribution of experts across the different armed groups raises a validity question; i.e., can we trust the information given by one expert in comparison to the information provided by many more experts. In other words, perhaps these single experts have an extreme view on the structure of the armed group or provide false information which would lead to a biased result.

Of course, one should attempt to get as many experts as possible for each armed group. Moreover, researchers should also be aware of the fact that experts may bring widely varying considerations to bear when answering survey questions

Table 5.1 Number of experts across armed groups

No. of experts	No. of armed movement	Percentage	Cumulative percentage
1	32	16.7	16.7
2	21	21.9	38.6
3	12	18.8	57.4
4	5	10.4	67.8
5	4	10.4	78.2
6	2	6.3	84.5
7	1	3.6	88.1
9	1	4.7	92.8
14	1	7.3	100
Total: 192	80	100	

and that this might bias the results. However, having a good expert survey design will alleviate some of these validity concerns (see for more information, Steenbergen and Marks 2007). I have, for instance, designed the questions to be as easy as possible without relying on too complicated (scientific) terms. For instance, instead of asking whether employment practices are standardized, I have asked about standard procedures to attract recruits and have mentioned an example while doing so. Moreover, I have given precise answer instructions when filling out particular questions and I have carefully selected the experts. Consequently, I presume that the potential bias resulting from relying on the judgement of one expert is minimal. This is also confirmed when comparing the mean and variance on the main independent variables of those groups that have only expert and those who have two or more: there are no important differences between the two groups. However, caution should still be exercised when making conclusions.

For those armed groups that had two or more experts, several coding rules were applied in order to have only one value per armed group per question. First, I deleted those experts that indicated "I do not know" or "I choose not to answer" on all survey questions. These experts were clearly interested in the survey but did not provide any useful information on the internal organizations of the armed group. Consequently, the entries of 11 experts were deleted from the dataset. Due to this removal, several armed groups were deleted from the dataset: the Abu Sayyaf Group (ASG) active in the Philippines, the Egyptian Al-Gama'a al Islamiyya, the Indian Bodo Liberation Tigers Force (BLTF), Jemaah Islamiyya from Indonesia, the National Patriotic Front of Liberia (NPFL), the PAC, and the Tehrik-e-Taliban Pakistan (TTP).

Consequently, this expert removal diminished the coverage of the dataset. Only 71 armed groups are then also included in the dataset, some of which are active on the Asian continent and some in Latin America. Most of the armed groups included in the dataset are, however, active on the African continent. This is not surprising considering the fact that this continent seems more prone to conflict than others (Collier and Hoeffler 2002). Armed groups active in Europe and North America are unfortunately not covered. This is primarily due to the fact that most of these groups are not intentionally targeting civilians (at least not more than 25 a year).

After removing some of the experts, another coding rule was applied in order to deal with the several ordinal and dichotomous questions (no question in the survey has an interval-ratio answer scale). Having ordinal or dichotomous answer categories implies that simply taking an "average" respond of several experts is not possible. Rather, a median or modus answer category has to be considered to be the true value for a particular armed movement. However, selecting the median or modus can only be done with an uneven number of experts. Therefore, in case of an even number of experts, the entries of the expert with the most missing values were deleted from the dataset. For example, two experts filled in the survey for the Iraqi group Ansar al-Islam.

To make the number of experts uneven, I deleted one expert (case_id 55) who has 32 missing values (this expert just clicked through the survey without answering any question). Once I had an uneven number of experts per armed group, the mode of every item was chosen. In case there was no most frequently occurring value for the armed group item, than the median value of that item was chosen. If the median value could not be determined (for example, one expert answered 1, another with 0, and a third did not answer) the value was set to be missing.

Measurement

One-sided violence

As already discussed, for the measurement of the amount of one-sided violence perpetrated by the selected rebel groups, I use the UCDP One-sided Violence Dataset version 1.3–2010b and 1.3–2011 (covering the period 1989–2010) (see Eck and Hultman 2007). According to these datasets there are four armed groups that were selected that did not killed any civilians intentionally: the Forces Armées de la République Démocratique du Congo (FARDC), the Mau Mau, the Mouvement des Nigériens pour la Justice (MNJ), and the Ethiopian rebel group Oromo People's Congress (OPC). These groups were included on the basis of the pretests, during which some experts indicated that they would like me to include particular armed groups. Consequently, they received a value of 0. Note, however, that the experts indicated in the survey that at least two of these groups (the FARDC and the Mau Mau) have often targeted civilians intentionally.

On average, the sampled rebel groups killed more than 1,200 civilians in the period of 1989–2010. Some of the groups are, however, more violent than others. At the extreme, one can find the Congolese AFDL. Although this group was only active for one year, the dataset showed that this particular group killed more than 35,000 civilians. Also the Rassemblement Congolais pour la Démocratie (RCD) and the Rwandan Forces Démocratiques de Libération du Rwanda (FDLR), both active in the Congo, are known for targeting civilians on a large scale. The RCD has targeted close to 6,500 civilians, while the FDLR over 5,000.

Other rebel groups are known to have shown restraint: the South African Afrikaner Weerstandsbeweging (AWB) has killed "only" 26 civilians in there separatist struggle. Also the APLA, and the Burmese Karen National Union (KNU) are now for their human rights abuses against the civilian population. Both groups have "only" killed 27 civilians in their quest.

It is important to note that the information on the number of civilians killed is left-skewed; there are many armed groups that "just" killed a few civilians, and there are just a few armed groups that killed many noncombatants. This is very normal for count data. Consequently, scholars working with this kind of data are often advised to use methods based on the Poisson or the Negative Binominal distribution. However, this variable does not follow these distributions perfectly. There are many armed groups that have perpetrated a low level of civilian killings and few armed groups that have perpetrated an enormous amount of civilian killings. However, there are some groups that perpetrated more killings than expected according to this distribution. This is often the case with count data in the field of international relations, such as battle death rates or the number of terror attacks. In these cases, running a Poisson model or a Negative Binominal model (if the variance is greater than the mean) might result in wrong standard deviations. To avoid this problem, I transformed the count data into a categorical variable with 5 categories, ranging from 0 (low level of civilian killings) to 4 (high level of civilian killings). Although this data transformation results in information loss, I no longer risk the possibility of drawing wrong conclusions. Table 5.2 shows the distribution of this variable.

Incentives

Recruitment incentives are measured by two important concepts: greed and grievances. Because some scholars point out that it is very unlikely that only one type of incentive to rebel is present (Herbst 2000), two variables are constructed.

First, the greed index is constructed on the basis of 3 questions. All questions have a 5 point answer scale measuring the extent to which the recruits joined because of material benefits, the possibility of looting, and whether looting is promoted by the commander. Since none of these questions is assumed to be more important than others, a simple additive index is created, ranging from 0 (low level of greed present) to 15 (high level of greed present). On average, armed groups received the greed value of 7 and a standard deviation of 3.4. See Table 5.3 for more descriptive statistics of this variable. Figure 5.1 shows the number of armed groups per greed value.

As the figure shows, some groups, like the Front Islamique Arabe de l'Azawad (FIAA) active in Mali (greed value of 1) are not motivated by greed.

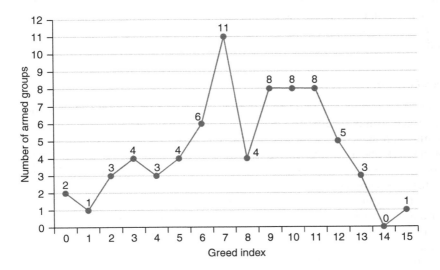

Figure 5.1 Number of armed groups per greed value.

Also the National Liberation Front of Tipura (NLFT), a militant Indian organization, is hardly motivated by these kinds of incentives (the group scored a greed
value of 2). At the other extreme of the greed index, one can find the Sudanese
Janjaweed (value of 15), which coincide with the literature on the Sudanese conflict. Wassara (2010: 276), for example, states that many attacks of the Janjaweed has an economic motivation. Also the FARDC (value of 13 on the greed
index), the Colombian paramilitary organization Autodefensas Unidas de
Colombia (AUC – value of 13 on the greed index) and the communist People's
War Group (PWG – value of 13), are considered to be primarily motivated by
greed. See Table 5.3 for more descriptive information.

Second, I constructed a grievance index based on four questions that measure
the importance of four grievance factors; political repression, inter-ethnic and/or
inter-religious hatreds, revenge for past humiliations, and discontent about existing economic inequality. These questions were selected because they were the
most systematic in measuring this concept; they were formulated in the same
way, they were placed on the same Web screen, and they have the same amount
of answer categories (i.e., they are all measured on a five point scale). The
experts could then also easily indicate the relative importance of these factors.
These four questions were used to construct an additive index ranging from 0
(low level of grievance) to 20 (high level of grievance). On average armed
groups received a grievance index value of 12, indicating that many armed
groups are motivated by grievance factors. As the standard deviation shows,
most sampled armed groups are motivated by grievances, i.e., most armed
groups received a value above 10. There are, however, a few exceptions.
According to the experts, the Interahamwe and the Mozambican Resistência
Nacional Moçambicana (RENAMO) are generally not very much motivated by
grievance factors. On the other hand, there are groups, such as the Pakistani
Lashkar-e-Jhangvi (LeJ) or the Indian Maoist Communist Centre (MCC), which
have a grievance index value of 20. See Table 5.2 for more descriptive statistics
on this variable.

Social density

To measure the amount of social cohesion or social density, only one question
was asked to the experts: to what extent does the armed group try to attract
recruits with the same ethnic and/or religious backgrounds? This question does
not only ask about the importance of the ethnic background of the members but
also about the religious background of the potential members. Table 5.2 shows
the distribution of answers.

For three armed groups, this variable has missing values: the Rwandan Front
Patriotique Rwandais (FPR), the MS-13, and for the United Liberation Front of
Asom (ULFA – a separatist movement from Assam, active in North-East India).
As the table shows, most sampled armed groups attract recruits with a particular
background. For example, the experts on both the HAMAS and the Students
Islamic Movement of India (SIMI) indicated that both groups always tried to

Table 5.2 Frequency distribution of the social cohesion variable

	Frequency	*Percentage*	*Cumulative percentage*
Never	2	2.9	2.9
Rarely	5	7.4	10.3
Occasionally	12	13.2	23.5
Usually	5	48.5	72.1
Always	19	27.9	100
	68	100	

recruit new members with a specific ethnic or religious background, i.e., Muslim background. However, there are also two groups for which the ethnic or religious background of the potential recruit did not play any role: the Revolutionary United Front (RUF) from Sierra Leone and the MK from South Africa. The RUF started as a group with a poorly articulated socialist agenda, in which ethnicity and religion did not play an important role (Restoy 2006). It is then also no surprise that these groups receive a low score. Also for the MK, religion or ethnicity did not play an important role. This armed group was the military wing of the ANC in South Africa and according to their own manifesto it was a body "formed by Africans … it includes in its ranks South Africans of all races" (Umkhonto we Sizwe 1961). Table 5.3 shows more descriptive statistics of this particular independent variable.

Hierarchy

For the measurement of the level of hierarchy per armed group, 10 questions were used. Most of these questions were measured in a dichotomous way. For example, when asking about the standard procedures for hiring new recruits, the experts could only indicate whether these procedures were in place or not. Some other questions were of ordinal or nominal nature. In order to construct a simple additive index, these latter questions were transformed into dichotomous variables. All answer values that indicated a more hierarchical structure received the value of 1, while those answers indicating a looser network structure received the value of 0. For instance, whenever experts indicated that the individual members were never or hardly ever allowed to make their own decision concerning the use of violence, this was considered as an indicator of being a more hierarchical structured armed group. In addition, if the experts indicated that commanders were appointed by superiors, that they also decided on what the punishment would be, and that higher-ranked members were responsible for carrying out the punishment, it was considered to be an indicator of hierarchy. On the basis of all these dichotomous variables, a simple additive index was constructed measuring the amount of hierarchy per armed group.[2] The most hierarchical armed group received then also a value of 10; the more loosely organized armed groups received a value of 0. However, none of the selected armed groups

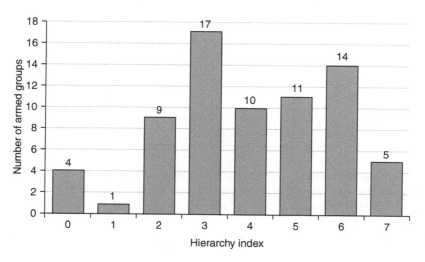

Figure 5.2 Histogram of the number of armed groups per level of hierarchy.

received a value of 10. The constructed hierarchical index ranges from 0 (low level of hierarchy) to 7 (high level of hierarchy). Figure 5.2 shows a histogram picturing the distribution of armed groups per level of hierarchy.

In total, four armed groups received a value of 0, i.e., according to the experts they were not at all hierarchical structured: the APLA active in South Africa, the FIAA, the NLFT, and the Patani United Liberation Organization (PULO) a separatist movement active in Thailand. Those armed groups that received the highest value on the hierarchy index are: the Khmer Rouge (KR), the Liberation Tigers of Tamil Eelam (LTTE), the Indian terrorist group active in Assam National Democratic Front of Bodolan (NDFB), the Dima Halim Daogah (DHD) group active in the Assam area, and the FPR. Especially the FPR and the LTTE are known to be very hierarchical structured. Mayntz (2004) for example, argues that the LTTE is one of the well-structured terrorist organizations that existed. Table 5.3 shows more descriptive statistics of this variable.

Commitment

The last major independent variable is commitment. The commitment index was made on the basis of eight questions, measuring different aspects of this concept. Unlike the measures for hierarchy, all the eight questions were of ordinal nature (5-point scale answer category), making it unnecessary to transform and recode certain variables (except for one question measuring the extent to which combatants have contact to people outside the group). The resulting commitment index should have ranged from 8 to 50. However, for some armed group certain questions were not answered. For example, not all questions were answered for the

Table 5.3 Descriptive statistics of the main dependent and independent variables

Variable	Obs.	Mean	Std. Dev.	Min	Max
One-sided violence	71	1.13	0.65	0	4
Greed	71	7.75	3.41	0	15
Grievance	71	12.46	4.58	0	20
Social cohesion	68	3.91	0.99	1	5
Hierarchy	71	4	1.84	0	7
Commitment	71	21.99	7.29	1	34

Interahamwe and the Chadian armed group Forces Armees pour la Republique Federale (FARF). Due to these missing, the constructed index ranged from 1 (low level of commitment) to 34 (high level of commitment). Examples of those groups that are recognized by low levels of commitment are the APLA, the FIAA, the Cobras that were active in Congo Brazzaville, and the South African right wing separatist movement AWB. Most extreme committed group in the sample are formed by the two Iraqi armed groups: the Ansar al-Islam and the Al Mahdi army. Also in the Nigeria based group OPC is known to have committed members. Table 5.3 shows more descriptive statistics of this particular variable.

Control variables

There are many possible control variables that might influence the behavior of a particular rebel group and shape its interaction with the civilian population. For instance, the social movement literature has long established that resources are the key to the success of organizations (McCarthy and Zald 1977). And the lack of resources has been seen to limit what terrorist organizations can do (Boynes and Ballard 2004). Human capital is often depicted as the key resource (Boynes and Ballard 2004; Asal and Rethemeyer 2008; Asal *et al.* 2013). Barker (1993) and Oots (1989), for instance, point out that as group size increases, it is increasing difficult to sustain a coherent group, making it more difficult for the principal to control her agents. This is partly due to the fact that organizational size is positively associated with the extent of vertical differentiation (more organizational layers), horizontal differentiation (greater division of labor and more functional specialization) and, though the evidence is mixed, with spatial differentiation (more locations) (e.g., Mayhew *et al.* 1972; Blau and Schoenherr 1971; Baker 1993: 403). Oots (1986: 49), for example, argues that small- or medium-sized groups are likely to be deadlier in particular attacks because maintaining large coalitions and organizational structures is particularly challenging and resource intensive. However, it is important to note that this argument is not universally accepted. Asal and Rethemeyer (2008: 439) for example, argue that the larger an organization becomes, the more likely that its membership includes individuals skilled at the methods of death and destruction, capable of raising and managing money, and possessed of access to restricted information, places, and materials.

The best estimate of the size of the rebel armed forces is taken from the Non-State Actor (NSA) dataset (version 3.3; January 24, 2012 – see Cunningham *et al.* 2009), which provides information on the military capabilities and political opportunities available to non-state actors in ongoing wars. This information comes from many different sources, for instance Keesings's Contemporary Archives, New York Times archives, and the Library of Congress Country studies. The NSA data has as the unit of observation conflict dyads between 1946 through 2010. Every dyad consists of a government actor and a non-state actor. If a conflict involves many non-state actors, every non-state actor is linked with the government in a separate dyad. For every non-state actor per dyad, information on the rebel size is provided (see Cunningham *et al.* (2009) for more information on this particular dataset).

Whenever more dyads are existing (because attributes of the conflict changes over time), I have averaged the rebel group size over the amount of dyads. For instance, in the period of 1989 to 2010, four dyads appear involving the rebel group União para a independência total da Angola (UNITA): (1) in the period from 1989–1991; (2) the year of 1992; (3) 1993–1997; and (4) 1998–2002. The rebel group size of UNITA changed in every dyad. In the dataset used in the upcoming analyses, the average rebel group size across 1989–2002 is included. Consequently, I have included the small amount of rebels that initiated the group, the amount of UNITA members that were still active at the end of the group's existence, and those that were members in the period in between. Table 5.4 shows the descriptive statistics of the rebel group size across the 72 armed groups. On average a rebel group has around 1,200 members (with a standard deviation of 20,756). At the extreme, one can find the Mau Mau, an armed group active in Kenya, which has more than 120,000 members. The Indian NDFB has only few members. According to the NSA dataset, they only have 100 active members.

Another important control variable that is included in the analyses in the age of the armed group. Literature on armed group behavior, and in particular on terrorist groups, has argued that organizational age is an important factor in their lethality and effectiveness. Age allows for learning and adaption that can make the armed group more lethal and deadly (Asal and Rethemeyer 2008: 440). Hoffman (1999: 25) has, for example argued, when talking about terrorist organizations, that: "An almost Darwinian principle of natural selection ... seems to affect terrorist organizations, whereby every new terrorist generation learns from its predecessors ... terrorist often analyze the mistakes made by the former comrades who have been

Table 5.4 Descriptive statistics of the control variables

Variable	Obs.	Mean	Std. Dev.	Min	Max
Rebel group size	46	12,302.13	20,756.06	100	120,000
Organizational age	71	18.75	13.10	1	62
No. of actors	52	5.02	8.51	1	40
Battle-related deaths	50	7,382.64	10,424.17	35	57,168

killed or apprehended." This process is also observed in the organizational ecology literature, which emphasize this learning process in the general population of public and private organizations (Hannan and Freeman 1989). Notwithstanding, some other authors (e.g., Gill *et al.* 2013), argue that especially older armed groups have problems in adapting their tactics, to become more "creative," and to embrace new technology. As such, they can become entrenched in their practices, which might in turn decrease their lethality.

Organizational age is coded primarily on the basis of two sources: (1) Revolutionary and Dissident Movement of the World (Szajkowski 2004), and (2): Les Nouveaux Mondes Rebelles: conflicts, terrorism et contestations (Balencie *et al.* 2005). Both sources give basic information on different armed groups in the world. This information is cross-checked with the National Consortium for the Study of Terrorism and Responses to Terrorism (START) database on terrorism, the South Asia Terrorism Portal (SATP) database on Asian armed groups, and academic literature specifically focused on particular armed groups.

For most armed groups these sources could provide exact information on when the armed group was established and whether it was still active in 2010 (and if not, when they stopped). Nevertheless, establishing the year of formation is problematic for some armed groups. For example, the Mayi Mayi group active in the DRC first appeared in 1997. However, this distinctive Congolese formation did exist probably for a much longer period. In addition, it is unclear when exactly the Rwandan Interahamwe was established or when the MS-13 gang was formed. For these cases, an estimated guess was made based on additional sources.

Figure 5.3 shows a semi-survival graph of the armed groups in relationship to their age. On the *y*-axis is the number of armed group displayed. In period $t = 0$, 71 armed groups are sampled. One armed group, the AFDL did exist only for

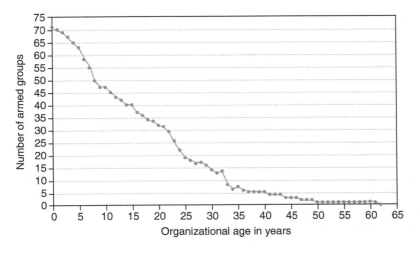

Figure 5.3 Semi-survival graph of the organizational age of armed groups

one year in the covered period (1989–2010). Consequently, at $t = 1$ only 70 armed groups are displayed in the figure. At the other extreme, the KNU is displayed. This particular armed group is already active in Burma for more than 62 years and is the oldest armed group in the sample. The minimum and maximum of this variable can also be found in Table 5.4.

To control for the strategic environment on the battlefield, I included another control variable, measuring the number of groups that are active at the same time and location as the rebel group. This measure is a proxy for the level of competition, which is not unusual among armed groups (government as well as rebel groups) (Oots 1989: 147). Crenshaw (1988: 22), for instance, point out that in Northern Irelands during the 1980s, the IRA competed for members with the Irish National Liberation Army (INLA), while, within the Palestinian resistance movement, Fatah had to compete with the Popular Front of the Liberation of Palestine (PFLP) and a host of other resistance organizations as well.

The level of competition can have serious implications for the dyadic bargaining situation: when several groups are competing with each other, the bargaining process becomes more complicated (Hultman 2007). It is highly likely that competition among groups (especially within the same political movement) is likely to increase the overall level of violent activity within a region (Oots 1989). Not only because each group attempts to obtain the necessary financial resources to supply the incentives needed to keep its membership, but also to demonstrate to its (potential) supporters, the seriousness of the organization's commitment to its goals. In particular, multiple armed groups can create a process of intragroup competition for civilian support, which in turn might affect their use of violence (Hultman 2007: 212). Bloom (2004: 73) states, for instance, when talking about the sense of the use of suicide bombings in the Palestinian–Israeli conflict, that suicide bombing is the result of intragroup competition and outbidding between the different Palestinian armed groups. Also Downes (2006) argues that civilian killings might be the result of intragroup competition about the support of civilians. However, it is important that this increased level of violent activity may, however, prove to be counterproductive if it leads to what Ross and Gurr (1989) refer to as "backlash"; the increased level of violence can cause its public supporters to turn away from the group (Oots 1989: 148).

I used the UCDP Peace Research Institute Oslo (PRIO) Armed Conflict Dataset (version 4–2011; see for more information Gleditsch *et al.* 2002) to construct a variable capturing the possible effect of intragroup competition on civilian killings. On the basis of this dataset, I counted the number of actors (government, as well as, fellow rebel groups) that were active at the same time, in the same location, and in the same conflict, as the armed group under scrutiny. Table 5.4 shows the distribution of this variable. It was only possible to determine for 52 cases the number of actors involved. For example, the Indian Hmar People's Convention (HPC), already struggling for years for an independent Hmar state, are not recognized by the UCDP Armed Conflict Dataset as being involved in a conflict resulting in more than 25 battle-related deaths per year (Gleditsch *et al.* 2002). Consequently, the number of actors involved in fighting is coded as missing. At the other extreme, one can find the Taliban, who was under attack by 40 governmental actors in 2006 and 2007, when a coalition of states (under the US leadership) attempted to ban this armed group. Also the Iraqi armed groups Al Mahdi-Army and the Ansar al-Islam were under attack by many governments in the years around 2005.

One of the most often used explanation of civilian killings is that it has to do with the performance of the parties on the battlefield. Hultman (2007: 205), for example, argues that violence against civilians is used as an alternative conflict strategy aimed at pressuring the government into concessions. When actors are losing battles, they fail in their military strategy (Hultman 2007). Actors who are not willing to give up because of these losses seek to make it costly for the other party to continue fighting. Killing civilians is one of such strategies by which extra costs on the adversary party can be imposed.

To capture the influence of battlefield losses on civilian killings, I counted the number of best estimated battle-related deaths per armed group across the period 1989–2010. For the creation of this variable, I used the UCDP Battle-Related Deaths Dataset (version 5, August 1, 2011 – see for more information on this particular dataset: Bethany and Gleditsch 2005). This conflict-year dataset collects information on the number of battle-related deaths per dyad. Battle-related deaths refer to those deaths caused by the warring parties that can be directly related to the combat. The target of the attacks is either the military forces or rebel actors. In some cases it also includes civilians. However, civilians are only included whenever they are killed due to collateral damage. Consequently, there is hardly any correlation between civilian killings and battle deaths ($r = 0.05$).

The descriptive statistics of the amount of battle-related deaths can be found in Table 5.4. The variable ranges from 35 battle-related deaths in the period of 1989–2010 for the Indian DHD to more than 50,000 for the LTTE. Like the number of fellow actors, this variable is recognized by some missing values. For example, for the MK there is no information available on the amount of battle-related deaths resulting from their fights.

Statistical method

From a sampling perspective, the selected armed groups and experts are the result of a convenience sample since the experts were selected because of their convenience and proximity and not because they are representative for the entire expert population. In addition, the armed groups were selected on the basis of the dependent variable, i.e., there are few armed groups included that have not intentionally targeted civilians. Consequently, it is not allowed to make any inference to the entire population of armed groups on the basis of this sample.

A technique that is able to manage this problem better is the Bayesian approach. Bayesian analysis provides inferences that are conditional on the data and are exact, without reliance on normality approximations based on large sample asymptotes (Congdon 2003). In other words, Bayesian analysis can handle a relative small number of observations. Hence, it is then also ideally suited for making inference to the (random or non-random) sample at hand, rather than making inference to a hypothetical super population as is done by frequentist statisticians (Hangartner *et al.* 2007). This is partly due to the fact that Bayesians have a different interpretation of the concept probability than used by scholars employing "normal" statistical methods (also called the frequentist approach). According to frequentist theory, a probability of an event is the limit of the relative frequency with which it occurs in series of suitably relevant observations in which it could occur. For example, when I toss a (fair) die an infinite number of times, it would result in the numbers one to six arising with equal frequency. The probability of each of these numbers (1/6) is then also the long-run frequency relative to the number of tosses of the die. Strictly speaking, a frequentist only attempts to quantify the probability of an event as a characteristic of a set of similar events, which are at least in principle repeatable copies.

In the Bayesian framework, however, probability simply describes uncertainty, which should be interpreted in its widest sense. An event can be uncertain by virtue of being intrinsically unpredictable, because it is subject to random variability, for example the response of a randomly selected patient to a drug. It can also be uncertain simply because we have imperfect knowledge of it. For example, we do not know the mean level of hierarchy across all armed groups around the world. Only the first kind of uncertainty is acknowledged in frequentist statistics, whereas the Bayesian approach encompasses both kinds of uncertainty (Luce and O'Hagan 2003: 13).

Bayesians consider probability then also as something that is personally defined by the condition under which a person would make a bet or assumes a risk in pursuit of some reward (Gill 2002: 4). Therefore, it is possible, in the Bayesian perspective, to say something about a specific instance with a specific set of data (as is used for this particular study) and a specific null hypothesis, which is a unique event and not a repeatable event. An example of such a unique event is the probability the European Central Bank reduces interest rates (Luce and O'Hagan 2003) or the probability that an armed group does not kill any civilians intentionally.

A good example that shows the difference between the frequentist and the Bayesian approach is mentioned by Carlin and Louis (2000). They give the example of publishing an article: suppose a researcher has submitted his first manuscript to a journal and has assessed the chance of it being accepted for publication. This assessment used information on the journal's acceptance rate or manuscripts like his (let's say around 10 percent), and his evaluation of the manuscript's quality. Subsequently, he is informed that the manuscript has been accepted. If he would be a frequentist, he would estimate the probability that his next submission (on a similar topic) is accepted as being 100 percent (thus far, he had one success in one attempt). However, this assessment might be a bit naïve given what he knows about the journal's overall acceptance rate. If he is a Bayesian, he would probably pick a percentage smaller than 100 percent; he is adjusting his estimate on the basis of prior information (i.e., the overall acceptance rate) (Carlin and Louis 2000: 2).

Since Bayesians are of the opinion that probability is personally defined, there may be as many different probabilities of an event as there are observers. This multiplicity is unsettling to the frequentist, whose worldview dictates a unique probability tied to each event by (in principle) long run repeated sampling. Consequently, they often claim that the whole Bayesian approach is subjective (Luce and O'Hagan 2003: 23). Indeed, Bayesian methods are based on a subjective interpretation of probability. However, the subjective view of probability does not mean that probability is arbitrary. Arbitrary is minimized through basing the probability on defensible evidence and reasoning. More importantly, the probability of the Bayesian is revised in light of new data in a very specific fashion dictated by Bayes' theorem. This theorem states that in the circumstance that we have a long-run series of relevant observations of an event's occurrences and non-occurrences, no matter how spread out the opinions of multiple Bayesian observers are at the beginning of the series, they will update their opinions as each new observation is collected (Luce and O'Hagan 2003). After many observations their opinions will converge on nearly the same numerical value for the probability. Furthermore, since this is an event for which we can define a long-run sequence of observations, a lemma to the theorem says that the numerical value upon which they will converge in the limit is exactly the long-run relative frequency (Luce and O'Hagan 2003: 4). In other words, Bayesians explicitly and openly choose a particular probability distribution and solve differences (and reach a consensus) through the accumulation of new data.

Like other empirical statistical methods, the Bayesian approach begins with a sampling model for the observed data $y = (y_1, \ldots, y_n)$ given a vector of unknown parameters θ. As Bayesians take the view that all unknown parameters have a probability, they suppose that (unlike the frequentists) θ is not a fixed but rather a random quantity having distributional qualities. This is operationalized by adopting a Bayesian probability distribution for θ. This particular distribution is called a prior distribution. This distribution expresses what is known (or believed to be true) before seeing the new data. In other words, it quantifies the uncertainty about θ prior to seeing the data y. And it is especially this prior distribution that is the subject of relentless criticism from frequentist statisticians.[3]

Different types of prior distributions exist, namely informative and non-informative. Uninformative prior distributions (also called flat, diffuse or objective priors) are distributions that have no population basis and play a minimal role in determining the posterior distribution. The idea behind the use of these non-informative prior distributions is to make inferences that are not much affected by external information whenever available. In other words, when using uninformative priors, prior information will more or less get a negligible weight in the synthesis with the data, and the posterior distribution will be in effect based on data information (as expressed in the likelihood function). The uniform distribution is frequently used as such a non-informative prior. Informative priors (or so-called subjective priors), on the other hand, have a stronger influence on the posterior distribution. These priors are typically obtained from past data and represent a blending of the researchers' subjective experience, intuition, and theoretical ideas (Ghosh *et al.* 2006). The influence of the informative prior distribution on the posterior distribution is related to the sample size of the data and the distributional form of the prior. Generally speaking, large sample sizes are required to modify strong priors, where weak priors are overwhelmed by even relatively small sample sizes.

Statistical inference concerning θ is summarized in probability statements in the form of a posterior distribution: the distribution of the unknown parameters after observing the data and updating the model. The posterior distribution $P(\theta|y)$ given Bayes' Law is then also a combination of prior information $P(\theta)$ and sample information from the likelihood function $P(y|\theta)$ (see also Figure 12). To put it more formally: $P(\theta|y) \propto P(\theta)P(y|\theta)$. See Figure 5.4 for an illustration of this mechanism. Even if the prior and the likelihood function are individually quite nice functions whose integrals are well known, this product will almost invariably be sufficiently complex to derive the necessary integrals by mathematical principles (Gill 2002; Luce and O'Hagan 2003: 69). It is then also no surprise that until the 1990s, Bayesian method found little practical application because the necessary computational tools and software (i.e., effective integration algorithms) had not been developed. Anyone who wanted to do serious statistical analysis had no alternative but to use frequentist methods. In little over a decade that position has been dramatically turned around (Luce and O'Hagan 2003: 31). Computing tools have been developed that can tackle the necessary high-dimension integral calculation underlying the Bayesian method.[4]

Now, posterior distributions can be constructed for highly complex problems using Markov Chain Monte Carlo (MCMC) simulation technique. The idea of MCMC is in a sense to bypass the necessary integral calculations rather than to implement them. The Bayesian inference is solved by randomly drawing a very large simulated sample from the posterior distribution. The point is that if we have a sufficiently large sample from this distribution then we effectively have that whole distribution in front of us and anything we want to know about the distribution we can calculate from the sample (Luce and O'Hagan 2003: 32). For instance, if I wish to know the posterior mean I just calculate the mean of this "inferential sample." If the sample is big enough, the sample mean is an

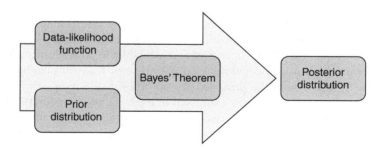

Figure 5.4 The Bayesian approach.

extremely accurate approximation to the true distribution mean, such that I can ignore any discrepancy between the two.

Simple Monte Carlo can be visualized as playing darts – "throwing" points randomly into the space of all possible values of the parameters, with each point independent of the others. This approach is impractical for Bayesian analysis because in a model with many parameters it is extremely difficult to construct an efficient algorithm for randomly "throwing" the points according to the desired posterior distribution (Luce and O'Hagan 2003: 70). Using MCMC, however, solves this problem by having a point wandering around the space of possible parameter values (Luce and O'Hagan 2003: 70). In other words, one uses the previous sample values to generate the next value (with the help of a particular algorithm: the Metropolis-Hastings algorithm, Gibbs' sampling or slice sampling) resulting in a Markov chain. To put it a bit more technical, the basic principle behind stochastic MCMC techniques of posterior simulation is that if an iterative chain of consecutive values, generated computationally, can be set up carefully enough and run long enough, then empirical estimations of integral quantities of interest can be obtained from the later chain values (Gill 2002: 15). As a result, simulations form a central part of many applied Bayesian analyses.

For the models on the level of the armed groups, I extended this Bayesian inference into a Bayesian Ordered Probit (BOP) model in which the sample information is in the format of a maximum likelihood function (see for more information Xie *et al.* 2009). This extension is based on the fact that the dependent variable in these models, i.e., the amount of civilian killings per armed group, is of an ordered nature. To facilitate the implementation of such a model, a data augmentation technique (Cowles 1996) is used such that the latent variable is treated as a unknown parameter to be estimated.

In the analysis that follows, I assume that the predictors have equal prior probabilities, by choosing for an improper prior distribution, given Hoeting *et al.*'s (1999) suggestion that this is a neutral choice when there is little information about the relative plausibility of the models. At the same time, choosing his prior avoids any criticism about subjectivity. It is important to note, however, that when the prior information is very weak (in case of an improper prior distribution), the prior distribution gets so little weight in Bayes' theorem that the posterior distribution is approximating the likelihood function. For the models in this part of the study, three MCMC chains, each of 65,000 iterations (simulations) initiating from randomly chosen starting points, were ran, discarding the first 2,000 iterations (simulations) as burn-in (the part of the iterations that is necessary for the randomly moving point to settle into the chain). It is important to note, that there is no fix rule of how many iterations (and burn-in) is needed. Scholars just have to make sure that the models are converging. Even though MCMCs are guaranteed to converge with an infinite number of iterations, finite iterations require that one should assess (non-) convergence. The first way to assess convergence is with trace and density plots. Figure 5.5 shows an example of these plots for the parameter social cohesion. For every parameter these plots are produced.

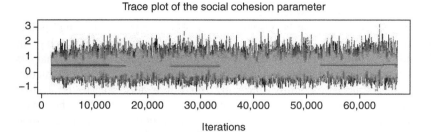

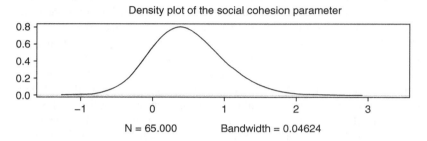

Figure 5.5 Example of a trace and a density plot.

The upper plot is called a trace plot. It shows the values that the parameter takes during the runtime of the chain. The trace can not only tell you whether the chain is mixing well but also whether it has reached its stationary distribution (the distribution of points is not changing as the chain progresses). The above trace plot shows that the social cohesion variable is indeed converging, the mean and variance of this parameter is relatively constant. The plot below is usually called a marginal density plot, or just the posterior density plot. Basically, it is the (smoothened) histogram of the values in the trace plot, i.e., the distribution of the values of the parameter in the chain. In other words, the mean across all iterations as is illustrated by the trace plot is the same mean as in the density plot. These marginal densities, if robust, are considered to be the main output of a Bayesian analysis (they offer a mean and a standard deviation of the estimated parameter).

Besides the visual inspection, there are several statistical diagnostic tests that need to be assessed before convergence can be determined. Note that many diagnostic tools are designed to verify a necessary but not sufficient condition for convergence: there are no conclusive tests. The most often used tests that are also for this study calculated, are Heidelberg and Welch (1983) (this diagnostic tool tests whether the Markov chain is a covariance stationary process), Raftery and Lewis (1992) (this tool evaluates the accuracy of the estimated percentiles), Geweke (1992) (this tool tests whether the mean estimates have converged by comparing means from the early and latter part of the Markov chain), and the version of Gelman and Rubin (1992) (this tool evaluates whether all chains converge to the same target distribution). While the first three tests compare the mean and variance for non-convergence of a single chain, the fourth test compares the mean and variance for all three chains. The results of all these tests indicated convergence.

Besides these conventional tests, I use measures of autocorrelation of all model parameters and cross-correlation between the model parameters in order to determine how fast the chain is mixing through its stationary distribution. Figure 5.6 shows an example of an autocorrelation plot of the social cohesion parameter.

As the figure shows, the social cohesion parameter shows only in the beginning of the chain a high correlation. The longer the chain, the less auto correlation can be established. This indicates that the model can be calculated with a Bayesian approach. In addition, all the models are checked for possible cross-correlation between the parameters. Marginal densities "hide" correlations between parameters and it might be the case that parameter uncertainties appear to be much greater in the marginal densities that they actually are. However, the cross-correlation tests show that this level is satisfactorily low.

Results

Table 5.5 shows the mean, the standard deviation, and the credible interval of every parameter. Both coefficients are to some extent similar in interpretation of the coefficient and standard deviation in standard regression analyses. However, unlike the standard frequentist approach, the results allow for a probabilistic interpretation. Normally, one cannot find any asterisks in any table displaying a Bayesian analyses. However, for space saving reasons, I have used asterisks in the table rather than portraying the credible intervals. Asterisks in the table, do then also not indicate statistical significance, but rather that there is a 95 percent, 90 percent or 85 percent probability that the credible interval contain the mean of the parameter.

In the first ten rows, one can find the parameter coefficients of the independent and control variables, while in the last three rows the coefficients of the cutoff points (e.g., the gammas) are presented. These gamma coefficients show

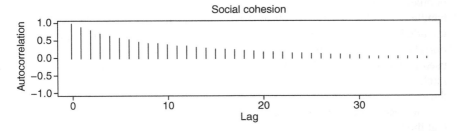

Figure 5.6 Example of an autocorrelation plot.

Table 5.5 Parameter estimation results of the armed group hypotheses

Variables	Model 1	Model 2	Model 3	Model 4	Model 5
Constant	2.1402***	−1.0078	2.0758***	4.2190***	2.1591***
	(0.8495)	(0.0030)	(0.6020)	(1.3470)	(0.9034)
Greed	0.0523	1.4139***			0.0543
	(0.0492)	(0.0389)			(0.0523)
Grievance	−0.0863***	−0.4658***			−0.0792***
	(0.0377)	(0.0136)			(0.0405)
Social cohesion	0.0690	0.4803			0.1011
	(0.1712)	(0.0499)			(0.1757)
Hierarchy			0.1030	0.4189***	0.0844
			(0.1034)	(0.2127)	(0.1107)
Commitment			−0.0356	−0.1406***	−0.0246
			(0.0266)	(0.0061)	(0.0307)
Rebel group size		0.0001***		0.0000	
		(0.000)		(0.0000)	
Organizational age		0.0728**		−0.0003	
		(0.0040)		(0.0022)	
No of actors		0.1387**		−0.0003	
		(0.0078)		(0.0030)	
Battle-related deaths		0.0002***		0.0000**	
		(0.0000)		(0.0000)	
Gamma 2	3.0382***	18.1669***	2.9605***	5.2600***	3.1200***
	(0.3367)	(0.0044)	(0.3181)	(0.9523)	(0.3505)
Gamma 3	3.7259***	18.8287***	3.5671***	5.7380***	3.8134***
	(0.4111)	(0.0044)	(0.3727)	(0.9682)	(0.4239)
Gamma 4	4.1408***	19.3438***	3.9521***	6.1870***	4.2404***
	(0.4754)	(0.0044)	(0.4368)	(1.0000)	(0.4890)
N	72	72	72	72	72

Note
The presented coefficients are produced by Bayesian Ordered Probit, using the using the data augmentation approach of Cowles (1996). * the credible interval of 85% does not include a 0; ** the credible interval of 90% does not include a 0; *** the credible interval of 95% does not include a 0.

that there is not much difference between the coefficients of the cutoff points, which indicates that the categories of the dependent variable are similar and that an ordered probit model can be calculated. Important to note is also the fact that the analysis is done across all 72 observations. Although, this might be a low number of observations in regular statistical analysis, Bayesian analysis can handle a smaller number of observations (especially relative to the number of included variables) due to the fact that it does not rely on normality approximations based on large sample asymptotics (Congdon 2003). However, since I have used informative priors, the posterior distribution is approximating the maximum likelihood function. Consequently, making strong conclusions on the basis of these 72 observations is not possible.

The second column of Table 5.5 shows the effect of the different strategies that the principal can employ before she contracts the agents, without controlling for other possible influential factors. In other words, the first model in the table shows the effect of the two strategies that the principal can employ to overcome the problem of the adverse selection (i.e., strategies to increase the change that she attracts "principled" recruits) on the level of perpetrated civilian killings.

In the theory chapters, I argued that one of the strategies is to offer a specific kind of incentive. Particular incentives will attract particular kind of recruits. Consequently, the principal can determine indirectly what kind of recruits she attracts for her group. Moreover, based on the work of Weinstein (2007), I argued that especially those recruits that are attracted by social endowments (for instance, by the promise of democracy and free elections) are those that are more likely to follow the orders of the principal. Consequently, I hypothesized that armed groups composed out of combatants that are recruited on the basis of these particular endowments (or grievances) are more likely to exhibit higher level of civilian abuse than those groups that are composed out of combatants motivated by greed. To examine the effect of greed and grievances on the level of perpetrated civilian killing, two variables were included in the analysis: grievances and greed.

When looking specifically at the linkage between grievances and civilian killings, the table shows that this assumed positive link (and the negative link between greedy armed groups and civilian abuse) is not confirmed by the Bayesian analysis. Although the coefficients are not directly interpretable, the negative grievance coefficient of -0.0863 indicates a negative effect between the two variables; those armed groups that attract recruits on the basis of social endowments (grievances) are less likely to kill the noncombatant population. This effect is highly reliable at the 95 percent credible interval (this interval does not include a zero). At the same time, the coefficient of 0.0523 shows that there is a positive link between greed and civilian abuse: those armed groups that attract recruits on the basis of material endowment (or greed aspects) are more likely to kill civilians during a conflict. This effect is, however, not very statistical reliable, since the credible interval include a zero. A strong conclusion about the linkage between greed and civilian abuse can therefore not be made.

Altogether these results stand in contrast to the formulated hypothesis in the theory chapters. This negative result might be explained by the fact that armed movements primarily motivated by grievances, such as ethnicity and ideology, have generally long time horizons: it takes time to establish democracy and or a fairer representation in the parliament. It might be that these particular combatants realize that the killing of civilians, although ordered by the principal, might have enormous negative consequences for the survival of any armed group in the long run (Downes 2006). When killing civilians, armed groups might force the civilian population to withdraw their support and start getting involved in the conflict by supporting other groups, i.e., they switch side. Furthermore, due to the killings other states might get involved in the conflict in an attempt to halt these abuses. Additionally, conflict resolution and the process of nation-building are severely affected and get more complicated. Recruits primarily motivated by material rewards, on the other hand, have a short time horizon; their reward comes often immediately and consequently they do not need for gratification. As a result, it might be likely that armed groups attracting these particular recruits do not consider the potential negative long-term consequences of killing civilians and are as such less constraint in their behavior. Another explanation might be the idea that most armed groups that recruit members via material rewards need to provide a steady stream of such rewards to keep their members attached. As a result, it might be the case that these groups allow looting activities. This indiscriminate taking of goods by force might often result in civilian victims. Whatever explanation holds is unclear and should be under scrutiny in future research.

Besides providing the right incentives to recruit a particular type of agent, principals can also overcome the adverse selection problem by hiring her recruits from one particular social network. This strategy makes coordination of action easier by overcoming, for instance, language barriers. In addition it is argued that behavior contrasting the orders of the principal is more easily detected when members of the armed group are all recruited from the same network. To sum up, it is hypothesized that attracting recruits from the same network might overcome the problem of collective action and adverse selection. Consequently, the level of control exercised by the principal might increase, which is hypothesized to increase the level of civilian abuse. The positive coefficient of 0.069 indicates that there is indeed a positive relationship between the two concepts; more socially cohesive groups are more likely to perpetrate civilian killings than armed groups that are less socially cohesive. It is important to note, however, that although there is indeed a positive relationship, this relationship is not statistically reliable. The lack of effect might be partly due to the measurement of social cohesiveness. In this study, social density or cohesiveness is only measured with one question about the ethnic and religious backgrounds of the members. However, density can also be formed on the basis of other characteristics than just ethnicity and religion. It might also be reinforced by race, family structures, and friends. These concepts are, however, not included in the operationalization of this concept.

The third model of column displays the second calculated model. This particular model is just like the previous one, focused on the effect of the strategies that tackles the problem of adverse selection. However, unlike model 1, it includes also the discussed control variables. Generally, it seems that including these variables increases the effect of the main independent variables on the level of perpetrated civilian abuse. For instance, the variable coefficient of grievance increases from −0.0863 to −0.4658; those armed groups that attract recruits on the basis of social endowments are less likely to kill civilians during a conflict. This effect is still significantly reliable in this second model.

Including the control variable also strengthens the impact of the variable greed on civilian killing. This variable was positive but not statistically reliable in the previous model. There is now, however, a statistically reliable relationship between armed groups primarily motivated by material benefits and the level of perpetrated civilian abuse; the greedier the armed group, the more human right abuses they are likely to perpetrate. However, this result is still against my expectations, as was formulated in the first hypothesis.

The second hypothesis that was formulated linked social density to civilian killing. I argued that the more social cohesive an armed group was (the more members are recruited from the same social network – whether this network is based on ethnicity, religion or any other category), the more likely that they would follow the order of the principal to kill civilians during the course of a conflict. The second model in that table shows that there is indeed a positive relationship and that this relationship has become stronger after including the control variable. However, again this effect is not statistically reliable. In other words, although the information given by the armed groups experts show some initial relation, I cannot say for sure whether the found relationship holds in reality. Future research should examine this potential linkage in more detail.

It is important to note, that all the included control variables are statistically reliable, indicating that the environment in which these acts against human rights are perpetrated plays an important role. The positive and highly statistically reliable coefficient of the rebel group size, indicates that the larger the rebel group, the more likely they would kill civilians during a conflict. This confirms the idea formulated by, among others, Asal and Rethemeyer (2008: 439), saying that larger groups are the more lethal ones due to the possibility that members can specialize in "death and destruction." This result stands of course, in contrast to the idea that principals have a better control over small armed groups than larger armed groups, i.e., small armed groups are more effective in killing civilians. However, it might be the case that small armed groups are perhaps perpetrating more one-sided violence events, but that the amount of civilians killed in these actions are lower than those resulting from actions perpetrated by larger groups. This possible linkage between the number of attacks and the resulting amount of killed civilian is outside the scope of this book. However, if one would like to test this potential relationship, new data have to be collected about the number of perpetrated acts against the civilian population of armed groups. Currently, the UCDP One-sided Violence datasets does not include any information about the number of perpetrated attacks (Eck and Hultman 2007). For terrorist groups, however, this information is available.

The last two control variables, which are more related to the environment in which these human rights abuses take place, are both also statistically reliable. I hypothesized that the number of other armed groups has influence on the level of perpetrated civilian killing due to a competition effect over civilian support (Hultman 2007). The positive coefficient of 0.1387 confirms this positive relationship between the variables. Additionally, the variable measuring the influence of battle deaths has also a statistically reliable effect on the amount of perpetrated one-sided violence. It was argued that killing civilians might have a strategic reasons; actors who fail in their military strategy (they are losing many combatants on the battlefield), will try to make it costly for the other actor to continue fighting. Killing civilians is one of such strategies by which extra costs on the adversary party can be imposed. This is statistically confirmed by the analysis: the positive and statistically reliable coefficient of 0.0002 indicates that the more battle deaths occur, the more likely civilians are killed by the armed group during the conflict.

To sum up the results of the first two models; the first hypothesis is rejected. Armed groups that are motivated by grievances are not more likely to kill civilians. On the contrary, they are even more likely to kill civilians. The second hypothesis, however, is partly confirmed. The table shows a positive relationship between social density of an armed group and whether this group is killing more civilians. However, this is only partly confirmed because the coefficients are not statistically reliable.

Model 3 and 4 in the table pictures the effect of the two other strategies that the principal can employ to increase her control over her troop. I argued that in order to overcome the moral hazard problem (i.e., the problem that the leader of an armed group does not know whether the individual combatant does what he is supposed to be doing on the battlefield), two strategies could be employed. First, the principal could try to structure her armed group in a hierarchical way. This vertical structure can make it easier for her to detect those combatants that do not follow her orders. Second, she could spend much time, energy, and money in creating organizational commitment among the members of her armed groups. Increasing this kind of commitment makes it more likely that combatants follow orders, even if these orders are against their own personal beliefs.

Model 3 displays the effect of these two strategies on the level of perpetrated civilian killings, without the effect of any of the control variables. The positive coefficient of the hierarchy variable (0.103), measuring the level of hierarchy of the armed groups, indicates that it is indeed the case, as was hypothesized in the third hypothesis, that the more hierarchically the armed group is structured, the more likely civilians are to be killed over the course of a conflict. Having a hierarchical structure seems then also to strengthen the control of the principal over her troops; they are more likely to follow her orders. However, it is important to note that this effect is not statistically reliable. The data is not good enough to say that this effect is true in all cases.

The last ex-post strategy that the principal can employ to increase her control was creating commitment among her combatants. I hypothesized that armed groups composed of highly committed combatants are more likely to exhibit higher level of civilian abuse than those armed groups that are composed of low-level committed combatants. However, the analyses show a different picture. The negative (not reliable) coefficient of 0.0356 indicates that the more armed groups are composed of highly committed members, the fewer civilians they will kill in their quest. This result stands in contrast with the last formulated hypothesis. A possible explanation of this contradictory result might be the fact that highly organizational committed members, will do whatever it takes to ensure the survival of the armed group, even if this would mean to go against the order from their leader. Since it was argued that targeting civilians can seriously damage the organization, it might be likely that highly committed members are less likely to perpetrate one-sided violence. However, the results are not statistically reliable and are, therefore, not conclusive.

Model 4 of the table depicts these two strategies together with the batch of control variables also used in the second model of the table. Like this previous model, including the control variables strengthen the effect of the independent variables on the level of civilian abuse; the two strategies become statistically reliable on the 95 percent credible interval. The coefficient of the variable measuring the level of hierarchy increases from 0.103 to 0.4189. Moreover, this particular variable has become highly statistically reliable. In other words, the more hierarchically an armed group is structured, the more likely its members will kill civilians during the course of a conflict. This confirms the third hypothesis as is formulated in Chapter 3.

Including the control variables also increases the negative effect of commitment. In other words, the Bayesian analysis now statistically reliable confirms that armed groups composed of many highly organizational committed members are less likely to kill civilians. Not only did the effect of the coefficient rise but the effect is now statistically reliable. A potential explanation might be, as already said before, that organizational committed members are committed to the organization rather than to its leader. However, this potential explanation has to be tested in future research; information should not only be collected on organizational commitment but also on the level of commitment to the leader. Currently, in organizational commitment literature this is often intertwined. However, the above analysis shows that perhaps in more political (rather than business) organizations, it might be two complete different things.

From all of the four control variables, only the effect of the battle-related deaths is statistically reliable. This means that, as is also the case in model 2, the more battle-related deaths occur during a conflict, the more likely civilians will be killed by armed groups. The other three control variables are far from statistical reliable and their effect size has been diminished. It is therefore not possible to say anything at all about the effect of the size of the rebel group the age of the rebel group, or how the number of other actors on the battlefield influences the level of perpetrated civilian killings.

The last column in Table 5.5, displays the effect of all strategies together. This model is primarily used as a robustness check, since model-fit statics cannot be calculated for Bayesian Ordered Probit models. Including all four strategies in one model, decreases the statistical reliable effect of each of the strategies. This is no surprise given the fact that these strategies are theoretically not independent form each other. Notwithstanding, the direction of each strategy remains robust. Armed movements composed of recruited primarily motivated by greed are more inclined to target civilians then those groups in which combatants are motivated by social endowments, social cohesive armed groups are more likely to perpetrate civilian abuse, hierarchical structured armed groups are more deadly, and groups composed of highly committed members are less likely to kill civilians. These results also appear when changing the prior distribution of the parameters. Note that a complete full model, including the four independent variables and the control variables, is not presented in the table. This is due to the fact that this model was unable to converge. Convergence problems with Bayesian analysis is a common problem especially when the variance of each of the variables is so extreme.

In the next chapter, I will test the hypotheses, as were formulated in the theoretical chapters, on the individual level. Before analyzing how these four strategies of the principal influences her control and in turn the level of civilian abuse perpetrated by the individual combatant, I will first devote attention to the research design necessary to gather information of the individual combatants. In doing so, I especially focus on the methodological issues of gathering micro-level information in conflict zones.

Notes

1 Note that parts of the analyses and results are already published by Haer (2012).
2 Also a Rasch index was made. However, this index did not lead to any significantly different result than using an additive index in the analyses.
3 Note, however, that even in frequentist statistics there is subjectivity surrounding probabilities. However, they avoid this subjectivity by relying on, for example, the P-value to test null-hypotheses.
4 It is still true that Bayesian methods are often more complex than frequentist methods and that, although the computational techniques are reasonably well understood in academic circles, there is still a lack of user-friendly software for the general practitioner (Luce and O'Hagan 2003: 31).

References

Asal, Victor and R. Karl Rethemeyer. 2008. "The Nature of the Beast: Organizational Structures and the Lethality of Terrorist Attacks." *Journal of Politics* 70(2): 437–449.

Asal, Victor, Paul Gill, R. Karl Rethemeyer, and John Horgan. 2013. "Killing Range: Explaining Lethality Variance within a Terrorist Organization." *Journal of Conflict Resolution* 00(0): 1–27.

Baker, Wayne E. 1993. "The Network organization in Theory and Practice." In *Networks and Organizations. Structure, Form, and Action*, eds. Nitin Nohria and Robert G. Eccles. Harvard: Harvard Business School Press, 397–405.

Balencie, Jean-Marc, Arnaud de La Grange, and Romain Bertrand. 2005. *Les Nouveaux Mondes Rebelles: conflicts, terrorism et contestations*. Paris: Editions Michalon.

Barker, James R. 1993. "Tightening the iron cage: Concertive control in self-managing teams." *Administrative Science Quarterly* 38(3): 408–437.

Bethany, Lacina and Nils Petter Gleditsch. 2005. "Monitoring Trends in Global Combat: A New Dataset of Battle Deaths." *European Journal of Population* 21(2–3): 145–166.

Blau, Peter M. and Richard A. Schoenherr. 1971. *The Structure of Organizations*. New York: Basic Books.

Bloom, Mia. 2004. "Palestinian Suicide Bombing: Public Support, Market Share, and Outbidding." *Political Science Quarterly* 119(1): 61–88.

Boyns, David and James David Ballard. 2004. "Developing a Sociological Theory for the Empirical Understanding of Terrorism." *American Sociologist* 35(2): 5–25.

Carlin, Bradley P. and Thomas A. Louis. 2000. *Bayes and Empirical Bayes Methods for Data Analysis*. New York: Chapman & Hall.

Collier, Paul and Anke Hoeffler. 2002. "Greed and Grievance in Civil War." CSAE WPS/2002–01.

Congdon, Peter. 2003. *Applied Bayesian Modelling*. Chisester: John Wiley & Sons Ltd.

Cowles, Mary K. 1996. "Accelerating Monte Carlo Markov Chain Convergence for Cumulative-link Generalized Linear Models." *Statistics and Computing* 6(2): 101–110.

Crenshaw, Martha. 1988. "Theories of Terrorism: Instrumental and Organizational Approaches." In *Inside Terrorist Organizations*, ed. Dave C. Rapoport. New York: Columbia University Press, 13–31.

Cunningham, David, Kristian Skrede Gleditsch, and Idean Salehyan. 2009. "It Takes Two: A Dyadic Analysis of Civil War Duration and Outcome." *Journal of Conflict Resolution* 53(4): 570–597.

Downes, Alexander B. 2006. "Desperate Times, Desperate Measures. The Causes of Civilian Victimization in War." *International Security* 30(4): 152–195.

Eck, Kristine and Lisa Hultman. 2007. "One-Sided Violence Against Civilians in War: Insights from New Fatality Data." *Journal of Peace Research* 44(2): 233–246.

Gelman, Andrew and Donald B. Rubin. 1992. "Inference from Iterative Simulation Using Multiple Sequences." *Statistical Science* 7(4): 457–472.

Geweke, John F. 1992. Evaluating the Accuracy of Sampling-Based Approaches to the Calculation of Posterior Moments. In *Bayesian Statistics 4*, eds. José M. Bernardo, James O. Berger, A. Philip Dawid, and Adrian F.M. Smith. Oxford: Oxford University Press, 169–193.

Ghosh, Jayanta Kumar, Mohan Delampady, and Tapas Samanta. 2006. *An introduction to Bayesian analysis: theory and methods*. New York: Springer.

Gill, Jeff. 2002. *Bayesian Methods: A Social and Behavioral Sciences Approach*. Boca Rota: Chapman and Hall.

Gill, Paul, John Horgan, Samuel T. Hunter, and Lily D. Cushenbery. 2013. "Malevolent Creativity in Terrorist Organizations." *Journal of Creative Behavior* 47(2): 125–151.

Gleditsch, Nils Petter, Peter Wallensteen, Mikael Eriksson, Margareta Sollenberg, and Håvard Strand. 2002. "Armed Conflict 1946–2001: A New Dataset." *Journal of Peace Research* 39(5): 615–637.

Haer, Roos. 2012. "The Organization of Political Violence by Insurgencies." *Peace Economics, Peace Science and Public Policy* 18(3): 1–11.

Hangartner, Dominik, André Bächtiger, Rita Grünenfelder, and Marco R. Steenbergen. 2007. "Mixing Habermas with Bayes: Methodological and Theoretical Advances in the Study of Deliberation." *Swiss Political Science Review* 13(4): 607–644.

Hannan, Michael T. and John Freeman. 1989. *Organizational Ecology*. Cambridge: Harvard University Press.

Heidelberg, Philip and Peter D. Welch. 1983. "Simulation Run Length Control in the Presence of an Initial Transient." *Operations Research* 31(6): 1109–1114.

Herbst, Jeffrey. 2000. "Economic Incentives, Natural resources and Conflict in Africa." *Journal of African Economies* 9(3): 270–294.

Hoeting, Jennifer A., David Madigan, Adrian E. Raftery, and Chris T. Volinsky. 1999. "Bayesian Model Averaging: A Tutorial." *Statistical Science* 14(4): 382–417.

Hoffman, Bruce. 1999. "Terrorism Trends and Prospects." In *Countering the New Terrorism*, eds. Ian O. Lesser, Bruce Hoffman, John Arquilla, David Ronfeldt, and Michele Zanini. Santa Monica: Rand, 7–38.

Hultman, Lisa. 2007. "Battle Losses and Rebel Violence: Raising the Costs for Fighting." *Terrorism and Political Violence* 19(2): 205–222.

Luce, Bryan R. and Anthony O'Hagan. 2003. *A Primer on Bayesian Statistics in Health Economics and Outcome Research*. Sheffield: Centre for Bayesian Statistics in Health Economics.

Mayhew, Bruce H., Roger L. Levinger, J. Miller McPherson, and Thomas F. James. 1972. "System Size and Structural Differentiation in Formal Organizations: A Baseline Generator for Two Major Theoretical Propositions." *American Sociological Review* 37(5): 629–633.

Mayntz, Renate. 2004. "Organizational Forms of Terrorism. Hierarchy, Network, or a Type sui generis?" MPifG Discussion Paper 04/4. Köln: Max-Planck-Institut für Gesellschaftsforschung.

McCarthy, John D. and Mayer N. Zald. 1977. "Resource Mobilization and Social Movements: A Partial Theory." *American Journal of Sociology* 82(6): 1212–1241.

Oots, Kent Layne. 1986. *A Political Approach to Transnational Terrorism*. New York: Greenwood Press.

Oots, Kent Layne. 1989. "Organizational Perspectives on the Formation and Disintegration of Terrorist Groups." *Terrorism* 12(3): 139–152.

Raftery, Adrian E. and Steven Lewis. 1992. "How Many Iterations in the Gibbs Sampler?" In *Bayesian Statistics 4*, eds. José M. Bernardo, James O. Berger, A. Philip Dawid, and Adrian F.M. Smith. Oxford: Oxford University Press, 763–773.

Restoy, Enrique. 2006. "Sierra Leone. The Revolutionary United Front (RUF). Trying to influence an army of children." Paper presented on the "Forum on armed groups and the involvement of children in armed conflict." Coalition to Stop the Use of Child Soldiers, Chateau de Bossey, Switzerland, 4–7 July 2006.

Ross, Jeffrey Ian and Ted Robert Gurr. 1989. "Why Terrorism Subsides: A Comparative Study of Trends and Groups in Canada and the United States." *Comparative Politics* 21(4): 405–426.

Steenbergen, Marco R. and Gary Marks. 2007. "Evaluating expert judgments." *European Journal of Political Research* 46(3): 347–366.

Szajkowski, Bogdan, ed. 2004. *Revolutionary and dissident movements of the world*. London: Harper.

Umkhonto we Sizwe. 1961. "Manifesto of Umkhonto we Sizwe. Leaflet issued by the Command of Umkhonto we Sizwe." (February 2012). http://web.archive.org/web/20061217090228/www.anc.org.za/ancdocs/history/manifesto-mk.html.

Wassara, Samson S. 2010. "Rebels, Militias and Government in Sudan." In *Militias, Rebels and Islamist Militants. Human Secuirty and State Crises in Africa*, eds. Wafula Okumu and Augustine Ikelegbe. Tshwane: Institute for Security Studies, 255–286.

Weinstein, Jeremy M. 2007. *Inside Rebellion: The Politics of Insurgent Violence*. Cambridge: Cambridge University Press.

Xie, Yuanchang, Yunlong Zhang, and Faming Liang. 2009. "Crash Injury Severity Analysis Using Bayesian Ordered Probit Models." *Journal of Transportation Engineering* 135(1): 18–25.

Part III
The combatants

6 Quantitative interviews with combatants

Within the field of quantitative conflict studies, most empirical scholars analyze civil conflicts and human rights abuses as being self-contained and homogenous concepts, ignoring the smaller individual level dynamics in which they are embedded (O'Loughlin and Raleigh 2008). Often, they forget that at a fundamental level, these phenomena originate from people's behavior and how people interact with society and their environment. This would not be such a problem if we were able to simply transfer the state or the armed groups' level explanations to the level of the combatant without loss of explanatory power (Buhaug 2010). Many of such attempts, however, suffer from the problem of ecological fallacy. However, the rigorous theoretical and empirical analysis of civil conflict and the occurrence of violence is then also impossible in the absence of close attention to micro-level dynamics. Likewise, it is incorrect to explain behavior of combatants by reference only to the actions of the armed groups.

If we want to uncover much-needed fundamental micro-level dynamics, broaden our research agenda, and develop effective policy interventions, it is necessary to devote attention to the combatants and place them at the center of the analysis. Recognizing this, scholars like Kalyvas (2008) and Buhaug (2010) have pushed for a new micro-level research agenda. This agenda calls for systematic collection of data at the sub-national level. In contrast to the more aggregated level, a focus on the individual level offers the possibility of improving quality, testing micro foundations and causal mechanisms, maximizing the fit between the concepts and data, and controlling for many variables that can be held constant (Kalyvas 2008: 397–398). As such, this rather new research agenda makes space for the individual voices of those who are usually excluded from the academic debate (Gunning 2010).

This new agenda requires researchers to put effort in collecting data at a lower level of analysis. For example, researchers like Raleigh and Urdal (2007) and Buhaug (2010) have spent considerable effort in collecting geographical point data on armed conflict. However, there are almost no studies surveying active or former militia and there are even less studies that employ individual interviews to gather information. A noteworthy exception is Guichaoua's (2009) study among 167 Nigerian militia members. Also a study conducted by Arjona and Kalyvas (2006) used interviews with former combatants. Notwithstanding, this lack of systematic micro-level individual data is due to the conventional wisdom that quantitative research should be limited to post-conflict situations or to situations where hostilities have ceased (Vlassenroot 2005). To put it differently, quantitative researchers and analysts should be prepared to engage in research in conflict situations. Otherwise, knowledge and understandings tend to be stuck at the pre- and postwar level (Goodhand 2000). Consequently, conflict regions and their dynamics will be misunderstood or never identified at all, which in turn might lead to a narrowed research agenda. This can have severe consequences when the international policy community examines the available policies in the decision to intervene or not (Lee *et al.* 2006).

To fill this niche in scientific research, this study extends the above armed-group level research on the variation of civilian abuse to the level of the combatants. In doing so, I have collected systematic data on the individual level by interviewing (former) combatants of the different armed groups active in the DRC. However, before discussing the details of the data collection process, it is necessary to devote attention to the DRC, its history and its current political state. This especially important because the data collection process is to a large extent influenced by these factors.

Case selection: the Democratic Republic of the Congo

The DRC is a country that was (and still is) in a conflict characterized by extreme violence, mass population displacements, widespread rape, and a collapse of public health services. The outcome has been a humanitarian disaster unmatched by any other in recent decades (Coghlan *et al.* 2006: 44). The International Crisis Group (2009), for instance, called it the site of one of the world's worst ongoing humanitarian crises. Also Human Rights Watch (2009), especially focusing on the most vulnerable people, noted: "[it is the] worst place in the world to be a woman or child."

However, it is unclear just how many civilians have been killed or harmed as the result of this war and its aftermath. A recent mortality study conducted by the International Rescue Committee (IRC) (2007) estimated that the conflict and humanitarian crisis in the DRC have taken the lives of an estimated 5.4 million people since 1998 and continue to leave as many as 45,000 dead every month, arguably making the DRC the deadliest humanitarian crisis since World War II. This death tool exceeds those of other recent crises, including those in Bosnia (estimated 250,000 dead), Rwanda (800,000), Kosovo (12,000), and Darfur in Sudan (70,000) (Coghlan 2006: 44).

Although the Second Congo war officially ended in December 2002, it has since then given the way to several smaller conflicts in the five eastern provinces that continue to exact an enormous toll on the lives and livelihoods of the Congolese people (International Rescue Committee 2007). Many warring factions are still straying through large areas of the country, raiding villages and committing severe human rights abuses. The International Rescue Committee estimated in 2007, that 2.1 million deaths have occurred since this formal end of the war

(International Rescue Committee 2007). In addition to killings, thousands of civilians have been abducted and pressed into forced labor to carry weapons, ammunition, or other baggage across the treacherous terrain by government and non-state militias (Human Rights Watch 2009). Furthermore, in the last years, many reports of women and girls (and some reports of men and boys) who have been raped have surfaced. Sexual violence, as a weapon of warfare, has been extremely rampant in Congo (Maedl 2010).

This ongoing conflict, especially in the eastern provinces of the DRC has been marked by a constant shift in alliances between confusing arrays of belligerents. One-time enemies turn into allies and back into enemies again in swift succession, confusing Congolese citizens and political analysts alike. In most cases, these shifting alliances are at the cost of the civilian population. Local populations have been accused of being "collaborators" by one side or by the other and are sometimes deliberately targeted, i.e. so-called "punished" by attackers (Human Rights Watch 2009: 10). These "punishments" cannot be contributed solely to one particular actor. A multitude of rebel and national armies are responsible for these widespread human right abuses of the civilian population. Although these Congolese armed groups operate in a similar setting, they pursue different political or economic goals and have diverse internal structures, which make them interesting for this study.

Short history

In order to understand the dynamics underlying the conflict and the motivations of the political actors it is necessary to analyze the roots of the DRC conflict.

Immediately after its independence from Belgium in 1960, the DRC felt into a state of chaos and disintegration (Olsson and Fors 2004). After many different military coups, Colonel Joseph Mobutu seized power in 1965. This coup was quietly approved by the Western powers, who considered Congo as an important pawn in the Cold war – as an African bastion of anti-communism (Olsson and Fors 2004). The support of the Western world helped Mobutu significantly to hold his gigantic and ethnically divided country together. When rebel movements threatened to overtake parts of the country in 1964 and in 1977–78, Western powers intervened with military support (Schatzberg 1997). Even during the last months of Mobutu's reign in 1997, France allegedly organized the hiring of foreign mercenaries in order to avoid the dictator's fall from power (Callaghy 2001).

Mobutu changed the country's name to Zaire and his own to Mobutu Sese Seko. In the 1970s, Mobutu and his affiliates seriously started to lay their hands on the country's wealth. In a process called "Zairianization," key economic sectors were put under direct state control (Nzongola-Ntalaja 2002). Mobutu's kleptocratic regime was coupled with poor growth rates and mounting public external debt. In the beginning of the 1990s, Mobutu's power was significantly diminished when international donor pressure forced him to abandon the one-party rule. Moreover, his government assumed some of his former powers (Olsson and Fors 2004).

In the events leading to the overthrow of the Mobutu regime, it is necessary to recount earlier developments in the neighboring country Rwanda. Rwanda's two major ethnic groups, the Hutu and the Tutsi, had fought a small-scale civil war since 1990 when the FPR, an army of Tutsi rebels, hosted and supported by Uganda, invaded the country. The Rwandan government led by the Hutu president Juvenal Habyarimana and supported by troops from France, was initially successful in suppressing the rebels but the war weakened Habyarimana's authority which led him to seek peace with the FPR. The resulting cease-fire ended on April 6, 1994, when Habyarimana was killed along with the president of Burundi after their plane was shot down. Although it is still not clear who is responsible for this attack, extremist Hutu groups drew their own conclusions and started a systematic genocide of the civilian Tutsi minority and moderate Hutus in Rwanda. The FPR under leadership of Paul Kagame managed to conquer Kigali and oust the Hutus government by July 18, 1994. Fearing Tutsi revenge, around 1.2 million Hutu fled to the North and South Kivu provinces in neighboring Zaire (Emizet 2000; Olsson and Fors 2004). Among the refugees that poured into North and South Kivu were 20,000 to 25,000 heavily armed soldiers from the defeated Rwandan army and between 30,000 and 40,000 Interahamwe militiamen and several leading figures of the former Rwandan regime, who were responsible for the genocide (Hoffmann 2010).

At this point, Mobutu saw an opportunity to regain his position and powers. He agreed to host these refugees on Congolese soil and thereby becoming a partner to international organizations (Olsson and Fors 2004). However, the presence of over a million highly politicized and well-organized and often armed Rwandan (and Burundian) refugees, fundamentally transformed the ethnic and political atmosphere in the Kivu provinces (Romkema 2007). Once settled in the camps, many Hutu refugees wanted to re-conquer Rwanda and to deal the final blow to their Tutsi enemies. In addition, they became heavily involved with the local conflicts, siding with the Congolese Hutu (Hoffmann 2010).

Mobutu used the change in ethnic composition in the Kivu provinces to instigate hostilities towards the Banyamulenge, a people of Tutsi origin who had lived in Eastern Congo for generations. The Banyamulenge long opposed Mobutu due to his open support for the extreme Rwandan Hutu regime. In desperation of several measures against them, they turned to their Tutsi cousins in Rwanda, who were under sever attack by the Hutu militia (supported by Mobutu) that used the refugee camps in Kivu as a base for attacks (Olsson and Fors 2004). In September 1996, the FPR joined the Banyamulenge and helped them to attack the Hutu refugee camps on Congolese soil. They were soon joined by many small anti-Mobutu rebel groups which engaged in battles against Mobutu's government forces. One such small anti-Mobutu group was the AFDL led by Laurent Kabila, who was living in the mountains of South Kivu where he was leading a state-within-state (Olsson and Fors 2004). These anti-Mobutu forces were heavily supported by the neighboring countries of Uganda, Burundi, and Rwanda.

The AFDL and their Tutsi comrades were immediately successful. This was mainly due to the fact that Mobutu kept his unpaid army weak and divided so that it would not pose a threat. Their resistance melted away as the Tutsi coalition approached. During their march westwards, some 200,000 Hutu refugees were allegedly killed (Emizet 2000). At the same time, the Cold War allies Belgium and the United States declared that they would no longer come to Mobutu's rescue. Only France, frightened by the prospect of an English-speaking new regime, remained Mobutu's friend to the bitter end (Olsson and Fors 2004). On May 17, 1997, Mobutu fled Zaire and Laurent-Désiré Kabila assumed power in the DRC.

After he took office, Kabila reinforced the ethnic basis of the political system by favoring people from his own ethnicity. His government contained many Tutsi (both Rwandan and Congolese) and Banyamulenge in top political and military positions. According to Clark (2001), this placed a strain on Kabila's legitimacy, as most Congolese regarded the Rwandan politicians as foreign occupiers. Kabila, on his turn, was seen by many as a president that was promoting only the strategic interest of Rwanda and Uganda (Ndikumana and Emizet 2005). Rwanda and Uganda on their turn accused Kabila of not recognizing the role they played in toppling the Mobutu regime. They also alleged that he was providing support to remnants of Hutu extremists who survived the attacks of 1996 (Romkema 2007). The troubled relationship collapsed after Kabila announced on July 27, 1998, the end of military cooperation with Rwanda and Uganda and ordered all foreign troops to leave the country. This move was an apparent attempt to pre-empt a coup, and was a direct cause of the rebellions that took place in both Goma and Kinshasa a few days later (Nzongola-Ntalaja 2002).

After the failure of these rebellions, troops from Rwanda and Uganda entered Congo on August 2, 1998. This invasion, less than a week after their departure ordered by Kabila, was the beginning of the so-called Second Congo War. The crisis escalated when Rwandan troops, with some support from Uganda, attempted to seize Kinshasa. At this point, Zimbabwe and Angola intervened on behalf of the Kabila government, saving it from collapse (Clark 2001; Ndikumana and Emizet 2005). Namibia, Chad, and Sudan would later join Kabila's allies, although Chad and Sudan withdrew relatively early (Olsson and Fors 2004). Many Congolese and international actors found that whereas the 1996–1997 rebellion liberated them from Mobutu, the 1998 rebellion only served the interest of Rwanda and Uganda (Ndikumana and Emizet 2005). The war lasted for several years and caused millions of dead and extraordinary human suffering. In part of this suffering, the international community exercised pressure on the warring parties, resulting in a 1999 cease-fire agreement, i.e., the Lusaka agreement, signed in the Zambian capital Lusaka. However, the impact of this agreement was initially limited. While fighting on the front lines diminished considerably, a guerilla war behind the front lines continued until 2002, affecting most of rural Eastern DRC and causing far more casualties than the war on the front line had ever done (Romkema 2007).

The situation changed when Laurent Kabila was assassinated in his own palace by one of his body guards on January 16, 2001. His son was sworn in as his successor 10 days later. Almost immediately after Joseph Kabila became president, agreements focusing on the transition of the Congolese government towards democracy were signed, and foreign troops did largely withdraw from Congolese soil. However, optimism was tempered given the persistent fighting between rebel groups in the Northeastern part of the Congo. This led the United Nations (UN) to adopt Resolution 1493, which authorizes the deployment of UN peacekeepers, i.e., the Mission de l'Organisation des Nations Unies en République Démocratique du Congo (MONUC) (Olsson and Fors 2004; Romkema 2007). Although the presence of MONUC has improved the situation in Congo (Themnér and Wallensteen 2011), the country is still faced with major challenges, among others, rebel groups, human right abuses, economic debt, inflation, unemployment, diseases, natural disasters, and refugee flows.

Political actors in the Kivus

In the DRC, there is a confusing number of armed actors active. Some of these actors change sides, others split into several smaller armed groups or disappear entirely. In the discussion of these actors, I therefore, primarily focus on six groups that were active in the Kivu provinces, the provinces in which the interviews were held, in 2009. Consequently, some armed groups are ignored in this discussion.

The first group that played an important role in the two Kivus provinces, is the Forces Démocratiques pour la Libération du Rwanda (FDLR), which was created in 2003 in the Congolese city of Lubumbashi (Romkema 2007: 7). This armed group is a political-military movement that originates from ex-FAR (Forces Armées Rwandaises) soldiers, ex-Interahamwe militiamen and Hutu civilians who fled the offensive of the FPR in neighboring Rwanda after the genocide in 1994 (Spittaels and Hilgert 2008: 8). Although, FDLR leadership is still dominated by former Rwandan army personal and politicians, it has also integrated several Rwandan and sometimes Congolese combatants from the refugee community in the DRC, who have no personal involvement in the genocide.

The FDLR claims to aim at overthrowing the government of Rwanda and to further democratize this country (Romkema 2007: 7). However, its internal discourse is more extreme and ethnically motivated. In addition, some of the FDLR leaders use the movement to protect themselves. Most of those leaders are seen as the leading masterminds of the Rwandan genocide, and cannot return to Rwanda unless they are prepared to stand trial (Romkema 2007: 7).

In late 2008, the FDLR was estimated to have at least 6,000 combatants, controlling large areas of North and South Kivu, including many key mining areas (Human Rights Watch 2009). From these 6,000 fighters, 200 to 300 are suspects of the Rwandan genocide (Romkema 2007). The FDLR's president and supreme commander is Ignace Murwanashyaka, who is based in Germany. He was arrested on November 17, 2009, on charges of war crimes and crimes against humanity. The group's military commander in Eastern Congo is General Sylvester Mudacumura.

The FDLR presence in especially the two Kivu provinces is a security problem for several reasons: the group has an ongoing history of serious human rights violations and their existence serves as a pretext for Rwanda to interfere in the ongoing conflict on Congolese soil (Spittaels and Hillgert 2008: 11). However, the FDLR is military weakening since most of their fighters seem to prefer disarmament. Moreover, the Congolese national army changed its tolerant attitudes towards this particular movement in early 2009, and launched success-ful military operations against the group (Human Rights Watch 2009: 25). As a result, they are losing control over territory and over the extraction and/or mar-keting of minerals and precious stones (Romkema 2007).

The second group that plays an important role in the conflict is the so-called, Mayi Mayi (or Maï Maï). This group forms the so-called third piece to Eastern Congo's violent puzzle, with the rebels on one side, the government forces on the other, and the Mayi Mayi often terrorizing the uncontrolled areas in between (Gettleman 2008). The Mayi Mayi is in contrast to all other rebel movements, a distinctly Congolese phenomenon. The movement appeared in 1997, when naked Mayi Mayi fighters took over control of the border gate between Goma and Gisenyi (northern Rwanda). This was the first time in their existence that they presented themselves to the outside world (Vlassenroot and Van Acker 2001). The term "Mayi Mayi" refers to maji, the Kiswahili word for water, because many of the Mayi Mayi fighters grease themselves up with a mixture of palm oil and holy water before stepping on the battlefield. Because of this magical mixture, bullets fired at these fighters are said to turn into water (Inves-tor Relations Information Network 2006; Gettleman 2008).

The Mayi Mayi is a traditional community based militia group who claims to defend the marginalized Congolese people, who suffer from the enduring warfare between the different armed groups (Spittaels and Hillgert 2008). Their conviction is that they are fighting a just war to defend the nation from extinc-tion or subjugation. Consequently, the movement tries to create a veritable state within the state in the territories they control. In these territories, official institu-tions like the police and the civil administration are reinvigorated while at the same time local communities are instituted to sensitize the civilian population (Hoffmann 2010).

Although they are often perceived as liberating the Congolese people, inter-national agencies, like the UN, see them rather as a rag-tag organization lacking clear political ambitions but who have the capability of putting any peace process at risk (Hoffmann 2010). This view of international agencies is partly due to the fact that the Mayi Mayi is not just one armed group. Rather, it refers to a broad variety of self-defense groups that have the most tenuous internal cohesion: different Mayi Mayi groups allied themselves with a variety of domes-tic and foreign government and guerilla groups at different times. Since there seem to be little internal cohesion, it is difficult to estimate the exact strength of these militias. Human Rights Watch (2009) for example, estimated that the total number of Mayi Mayi combatants, spread over at least 22 different groups, is around 8,000 to 12,000.

Besides some smaller Mayi Mayi groups (like Mudundu 40) and some other factions, one of the largest Mayi Mayi groups is led by General Padiri. His faction grew in size and popularity with the start of the Second Congo War, to the extent that the group was in partial control over a large swath of territory in Eastern Congo. As a result, General Padiri was recognized as the leader of the Mayi Mayi by various other Mayi Mayi groups and the regime in Kinshasa (Hoffmann 2010: 350). Another large Mayi Mayi group is the so-called Coalition of Patriotic Congolese Resistants (PARECO). This is a coalition of several ethnic-based groups (including the Congolese Hutu, Hunde, and Nande) under the leadership of Colonel La Fontaine. The coalition was brought together in March 2007 (Human Rights Watch 2009). PARECO denounces first and foremost the creation of the mixed brigades in the national army because it believes this will lead to the foundation of a "Tutsi-Land." Since its inception, the Mayi Mayi group has grown rapidly into a significant force. According to Spittaels and Hillgert (2008), PARECO has approximately 3,500 fighters. So far, little human rights violations have been attributed to them (Spittaels and Hillgert 2008: 16). In 2009, many PARECO combatants, particularly the Hutu, joined the official national Congolese army (Human Rights Watch 2009).

The third group, which is important to mention when discussing the Congolese conflict is the Alliance of Democratic Forces for the Liberation of Congo-Zaire (AFDL). This armed group is the former national army of the DRC, originally formed in October 1996, just before the First Congo War. The AFDL was established by a group of Congolese dissidents and disgruntles minority groups, such as Council of Resistance for Democracy (CNRD) and the Alliance Démocratique des Peuples (ADP). However, most of the group consisted of locally recruited children. While some were forcefully abducted, others came willingly or were encouraged by their parents. The AFDL was led by Laurent-Désiré Kabila and supported by Rwanda and Uganda in their fight against the Mobutu regime.

During the First Congo War, the AFDL carried out large-scale killings of civilians, predominantly on Hutu refugees as well as on some Congolese refugees. In addition, the AFDL intentional blocked humanitarian assistance to civilian refugees, which has likely to have resulted in thousands of additional deaths (Human Rights Watch 1997). Following the AFDL's victory, and Kabila's rise to the presidency, the AFDL became the national army of the country. Although, the group was successful in overthrowing Mobutu, the alliance felt quickly apart after Kabila and his Ugandan and Rwandan backers turned on each other, marking the beginning of the Second Congo War in August 1998.

The new national army, the Congolese Armed Forces (FARDC), was created in 2003 and has an estimated strength of 120,000 soldiers, many from former rebel groups and coming from different regions (Human Rights Watch 2009; Spittaels and Hillgert 2008). About half of the Congolese army is deployed in Eastern Congo (Human Rights Watch 2009).

The mixed brigades have been created as the result of negotiations in Kigali (Rwanda) between the government and the different armed movements in December 2006. However, the fact that the new brigades were never mixed beyond Battalion level means that each individual Battalion still retains its own loyalty (Spaettles and Hillgert 2008: 13). Although, the FARDC is the official national army, its soldiers are involved in a considerable number of human rights violations throughout the region. They are especially notorious for their direct and indirect involvement in the illegal traffic in mineral resources and other goods (Spittaels and Hilgert 2008: 13).

Another important actor is the rebel group RCD. It is a movement that was established by Ernest Wambda dia Wamba in the beginning of August 1998, just a few days after the Great African War started (Prunier 2009: 183). The core of the RCD was composed of former ADFL members, who aimed to overthrow president Kabila (Prunier 2009: 183). The group is heavily supported by the Ugandan and Rwandan governments.

In 1999, it became clear that Kabila would not be overthrown and fracture lines began to appear in the organization and Rwanda and Uganda began to struggle over who would control the RCD and its access to natural resources. In May of that year, Wambda dia Wamba left the RCD to establish his own group in the town of Kisangani with support of Uganda (Prunier 2009). His faction is often called, RCD-Kisangani (RCD-K) or RCD-Wamba. The left-over faction was taken over by Dr. Emile Ilunga, which is referred to as RCD-Goma or just the RCD. This latter faction is one of the longest lives and one of the strongest rebel groups and is primarily supported by Rwanda (Global Security 2011).

The two RCD factions met in the battle of Kisangani and the RCD faction under the leader of Wambda dia Wamba was defeated. As a result, his leadership was challenged by Mbusa Nyamwisi, which renamed the faction RCD-Mouvement de Libération (RCD-ML). He took control over the Northern part of North Kivu and the Ituri province. The Rwandan supported RCD faction, the RCD-Goma, retained control of Southern part of North Kivu and some parts of South Kivu under the leadership of Adolphe Onusumba (Vlassenroot 2008).

In the beginning of April 2003, both factions signed a peace accord in Sun City, South Africa. This milestone pact was signed to pursuit the peace and democracy in the DRC and established a two-year transitional government (Prunier 2009). Since the signing of this accord, the RCD have remained in the two eastern provinces. Although, the conflict has not significantly disrupted, the RCD has abused human rights (Turner 2007).

The last armed group that plays an important part in the Congolese conflict is the Rwandan/backed rebel group Congrès National pour la Défense du Peuple (CNDP). It is a recent movement that was launched by the Tutsi Laurent Nkundabatware, better known as General Nkunda during the 2006 elections (Spittaels and Hilgert 2008). At first, the CNDP started out as a movement claiming to protect the interests of all Rwandophones, whether Hutu or Tutsi, in the eastern DRC. However, the CNDP has stopped presenting itself in this manner. It is now generally recognized that Nkunda and his movement serve the interests of (at least a part of) the Tutsi minority in the Kivus (especially in North Kivu) (Spittaels and Hilgert 2008: 6). The organization is said to promote the elimination of the FDLR, defend, protect, and ensure political representation for the several hundred thousand Congolese Tutsi living in Eastern Congo, and some 44,000 Congolese refugees, most of them Tutsi, living in Rwanda (Human Rights Watch 2009). Besides these political points it also seems to protect the specific economic interests of some of its members and sympathizers. For example, it controls the grazing lands used by several rich cattle farmers and two mining areas (Spittaels and Hilgert 2008).

By late 2008, the CNDP was estimated to have between 4,000 and 7,000 troops, including a significant number recruited in Rwanda; many of its officers are Tutsi like General Nkunda (Human Rights Watch 2009). Following a secret agreement between the Congolese president Joseph Kabila and his Rwandan counterpart, President Paul Kagame, a military operation called Umoje Wetu ("our unity" in Swahili) began on January 20, 2009. It resulted in the detention of General Nkunda by the Rwandan authorities. He was ousted by chief of staff, Bosco Ntaganda. Ntaganda, wanted on an arrest warrant from the International Criminal Court, abandoned the three-year insurgency and integrated the CNDP's troops into the government army. On April 26, 2009, the CNDP established itself as a political party (Human Rights Watch 2009).

Data collection: survey research in war-torn societies[1]

Although, collecting information on the level of combatants is necessary to unravel micro-level dynamics underlying civilian abuse, most conventional texts on survey research do not consider the special challenges of conducting research in areas that experience inter or intrastate wars (King 2009). Almost no scholar has recognized and confronted the countless issues that arise around whether, when, and how to undertake research in these areas (Bøås and Hatløy 2006). This lack of attention stems in large part from the presumption that insecurity strongly limits the possibilities of the researcher to collect valid and reliable data. The infrastructure, for example, taken for granted in stable countries is wholly or partly lacking in these settings (i.e., there are many remote areas, people are hiding or fleeing, there are bad roads, and no telephones or printers available). Accounts that do address some of these challenges and dilemmas are mainly focused on how insecurity influence the life of the researcher and respondent; both bear the risk of becoming traumatized, harmed or even killed in these settings (see for example, Nordstrom and Robben 1995). One area of survey literature that remains patchy, however, is the discussion of "danger" and "insecurity" as methodological constraints. Danger and insecurity have an effect on two important elements of field research conducted with the help of face-to-face interviews; the sampling design (the sampling frames and procedures) and the data collection process (the problem of nonresponse and interviewer effect).

Sampling frames and procedures

Before the information can be collected from combatants, it is necessary to select or develop an appropriate sampling frame. These frames are perfect when there is a one-to-one mapping of frame elements to target population elements (Groves *et al.* 2004). Unfortunately, perfect sampling frames do not exist, even not in countries or societies that are not troubled by war and conflict. This imperfectness results in various types of frame errors, which might cause survey estimation problems. Choosing an accurate sampling frame depends not only on the target population (i.e., the combatant population), one's resources and knowledge, but also on the environment where the research takes place.

In general, census records are one of the most often used sources of extracting sampling frames in survey research. When available, they can be used to extract many different frames, such as lists of census enumeration areas or of households. However, scholars should be extremely careful using census records for direct sampling or stratification purposes. Especially in the context of conflict, population estimates change considerably in short periods of time due to substantial changes in population size caused by inner and outer migration, disappearances, and high mortality rates. Nevertheless, using census records, as a source for extracting an appropriate sampling frames is not possible. Like population registers, up-to-date census records are not available for the DRC. Additionally, the possibility to extract sampling frames from geographical area maps that contain geographical units of a country in a hierarchical arrangement, such as province, county, district, ward, and/or village, is also limited. Although, up-to-date geographical maps exist for various countries, including the DRC, the maps are only useful together with information about the distribution of combatants within these units. This latter information might be collected by various demobilization programs, but is for obvious security reasons not available for the public.

Because no appropriate sampling frame is available for the DRC, the choice between the different sampling procedures is limited. Relying on probability sampling procedures, in which each member of the population has a known nonzero probability of being selected (such as cluster sampling and respondent driven sampling), is not a viable option without having a sample frame. For this reason, I relied on convenience sampling, a nonprobability sampling procedure, for selecting combatants for the interviews. This procedure involves the sample being drawn from that part of the population that is available to the researcher. This particular procedure is often employed in conflict divided countries. Especially, convenience sampling via organizations enjoys great popularity among researchers. Riisøen *et al.* (2004), for example, used in their study on child trafficking in Burkina Faso, Ghana and Mali, among others the International Pogramme on the Elimination of Child Labour (IPEC) to get access to their respondents. However, other organizations can also be used for these purposes.

For this study, three welcome centers (financial supported by different NGOs and IGOs) were willing to participate to this study in April and May 2009. These welcome centers provide former (child) soldiers with the first basic needs after they left the armed group. Most of the combatants were released by the groups and taken to these centers. However, some of them escaped or were freed. The first welcome center that participated in the study was Laissez l'Afrique Vivre

(LAV). This center does not only foster former (child) soldiers but also sexually violated woman. Additionally to providing vocational training, this welcome center helps with the reintegration of these children into society by finding an internship for them after they have finished their training. Consequently, some of the interviews were held outside the center at the respondent's working place in the surrounding of Bukavu. The second welcome center, Bureau Volontariat pour les services de l'Enfance et de la Sante (BVES), is focused on fostering (mainly male) former (child) soldiers for some months before sending them back to their families. Consequently, this center does not provide any vocational training. The last center that was willing to participate was the Centre d'Apprentissage Professionnel et Artisanal (CAPA). CAPA is one of the largest centers in Bukavu and is focused not only on the reintegration of former combatants, but also on sexually violated women, and street children. It provides the pupils with a very broad range of vocational training possibilities.

The managers of these three centers selected the (former) combatants for the interviews. However, it is unclear which criteria they used in this selection process. In the case of LAV, the manager of the center allowed us to talk to any former combatant that received his or her training within the center. Additionally, she helped us to get in contact with former combatants that were working in Bukavu or surroundings. The selection criteria of the CAPA center were more ambiguous besides the fact that mostly older former combatants were selected for taking part in this study. This was also the case with BVES.

The sampling procedure applied in this study has then also several non-random aspects. First, combatants were selected from welcome centers in Bukavu, rather than selecting from all welcome centers across the country or a particular region. Consequently, it might be the case that the interviewed combatants differ from those in other welcome centers. Second, it might also be likely that combatants from particular armed groups might be overrepresented in the sample. Perhaps these three centers hosted especially combatants that were active in South Kivu, or in another particular region. Third, besides a possible selection basis due to a focus on a specific area, additional bias might also rise due to the use of welcome centers in order to come in contact with (former) combatants. It might be the case that there is a difference between those (former) combatants that are in these centers and those that are still with their armed group. For instance, it might be likely that those who are still with the group have fewer incentives to leave, i.e., they might have a higher rank, earn more money, are less traumatized, or are crueler than those that decided to escape or leave. Finally, there might also be a selection bias due to the selection process of combatants for the interview by the head of the centers. For example, as Riisøen *et al.* (2004) state, it might be the case that centers choose "the worst cases" or "show cases" in order to influence the media and potential donors.

All together, these non-random aspects of the sampling procedure might cause invalid survey results. However, the exact nature of this bias is hard to estimate, especially since there is not a nation-wide survey on Congolese combatants, with whom I can compare the results of this study. Therefore, one should be careful in making inferences to a population outside the sample. In addition to problems concerning generalization, doing quantitative survey in conflict divided countries might also suffer from nonresponse errors and response errors in the form of interviewer effects. Even the best resourced quantitative survey in "non-conflict" setting carried out by experienced researchers suffers from these two errors. However, facing these two sources of bias in the context of conflict is more challenging.

The problem of nonresponse

Much survey research follows the inferential paradigm that only when all sample elements are measured, probability statements about the population characteristics can be made. However, if only a subset is measured because of nonresponse or other errors, inference becomes difficult. Nonresponse is, therefore, commonly taken as an indicator of the quality of survey data since it can negatively affect both sample estimates and their variance (Dixon and Tucker 2010).

Nonresponse error encompasses both unit and item nonresponse. Unit nonresponse occurs largely because respondents refuse to participate or because researchers cannot contact potential respondents (Dixon and Tucker 2010). In conflict zones this means that respondents have fled to other areas, or they refuse to take part because it increases the potential risk of being associated with the researcher (e.g., Sluka 1990) or of becoming identifiable and traceable (for example, by members of a particular armed group).

I have tried to diminish this form of nonresponse by explaining the purpose and relevance of the study to the respondents with the help of translators. These translators were selected on the basis of three criteria: work experience, experience with interviewing traumatized respondents, and knowledge about different languages (French, Swahili, Lingala, Mashi, and Kinyarwanda). The translators received detailed instructions and the questions in advance, which allowed them to prepare the formulation of some questions and anticipate possible translation problems. With their help, the purpose and relevance of the study was explained to the combatants. This allowed them to weigh the costs of participation against the overall benefits, which generally leads to a reduction of the nonresponse as well as response errors. Additionally, I only interviewed them when they provided me with their informed consent. The consent form that they had to sign before the interview stated that the interview was voluntarily, that they could refuse to answer any questions, that they could leave at any time, that all their responses were treated strictly confidentially (that it would not be possible to identify them in any way later), and that there will be no financial or other direct benefit in exchange for participation (see Appendix 6).

Since decisions to refuse to answer questions (i.e., items) are likely to be related to its topic, it is presumed that the bias of item nonresponse is greater than that of unit nonresponse (Dixon and Tucker 2010). Item nonresponse can either be partial (i.e., respondents end an interview prematurely, which only happened once in this study) or intermittent (i.e., nonresponse scattered throughout the survey). In general, it occurs when a respondent does not answer one or more questions, usually because of unwillingness to provide the information or inability to retrieve it from memory (Dixon and Tucker 2010). This form of nonresponse is particularly present in surveys conducted in conflict zones that involve sensitive questions that trigger social desirability concerns, are seen as intrusive by the respondents, or that raise concerns about the possible repercussions of disclosing information (see Tourangeau and Yan 2007). For example, during the interviews, the Congolese respondents had no problems answering questions concerning the usage of traditional medicines during battles. However, asking questions about the exact ingredients of these medicines were not appreciated. In addition, item nonresponse might be caused by the inability of respondents to retrieve the information from memory. Especially surveys conducted in conflict settings suffer from this form of nonresponse. Many of the respondents in these countries are traumatized and their nonresponse might often be a coping strategy in order to mute flashbacks, nightmares, intrusive thoughts, and arousal (Neuner *et al.* 2008).

Because some sensitive issues were addressed in the interview, like the amount of civilian abuse perpetrated by the combatant, I have attempted to improve the reporting by structuring the questionnaire and by the consciously thinking about the wording of the questions. For instance, all interviews started with some general social and demographic background questions, and slowly moved to detailed questions about the structure of the armed movements. Difficult questions about the experiences of the combatants and their behavior in the armed organizations were placed in the middle of the interview, so that the combatant did not leave the interview with a depressed and sad feeling. Additionally, I decided to read out loud the questions to the respondents and to personally place their given answer in the appropriate answer category. This interview format does not only overcome the problem that some respondents are not accustomed to order their thoughts into pre-constructed answer categories, but it gives also room for the respondent to tell his or her story.

Another way in which I have tried to diminish the amount of item nonresponse was by avoiding asking questions that were hypothetical, excessively complex, and outside the experience of the combatant (e.g., Beatty and Hermann 2002). The survey questions were then also developed with the help of an interdisciplinary team consisting of political scientists and clinical psychologists from the University of Konstanz and the NGO "victim's voice" (vivo). This NGO is specialized in providing mental health care to traumatized refugees in Germany, war-affected youth in Uganda, Rwandan survivors of the genocide, war-affected school children in the north-eastern provinces of Sri Lanka, Ethiopian orphanages and women who have undergone genital mutilation, victims of gender-based violence and demobilized combatants in the DRC, and traumatized survivors of the war and Taliban regime in Afghanistan. Because of their experience, they could help with the wording of questions so that the interviewed combatants did not relive their traumatic experience as a result of the interview (e.g., Neuner *et al.* 2004; Schauer *et al.* 2005).

Interviewer effects

The amount of nonresponse can be diminished by the interviewer, who persuades sample members to participate in the interview, encourages the answering process, and assists when help is needed. However, the interviewer is also seen as one of the principal sources of error in data collected from face-to-face interviews; their verbal and nonverbal presence can increase the variance of the statistics leading to more measurement errors (e.g., Kish 1965; O'Muircheartaigh and Campanelli 1998). However, there is no systematic research conducted to interviewer effects in conflict settings in comparison to survey research in "normal" environments. Notwithstanding, one can assume that also in conflict settings, interviewer effects are present and might result in survey bias.

Visible and non-visible interviewer characteristics are most likely to affect responses to questions that make these characteristics salient or relevant in the interaction, activate stereotype, or evoke the respondent's concerns with affiliation, relative status, and/or deference (Schaeffer *et al.* 2010). This is the case in conflict divided societies in which tension exists about religion, political orientation, race, and/or ethnicity. Although, I did not consciously experience it, the gender of the interviewer might also have an effect on misreporting (see for more information Warren 1988).

Not only does the presence of the researcher have a possible effect on the given answer, but also their local hired staff, such as translators and drivers. While their use can potentially increase the reliability and validity of data by using their local knowledge on the dynamics of the conflict, some problems that are present in conflict zones are worth considering. Using research assistants or translators from the same country or area as the respondent, risks transgressing political, social, or economic fault-lines of which the researcher might not be aware. In highly sectarian conflict countries, like Congo, Rwanda, or Burundi, local staff might be associated by name, appearance, accent, or style of dress, with a group that the respondent fears or despises (Jacobsen and Landau 2003). This will influence the quality of the data collected since it raises the possibility that information will be used against a particular subgroup.

The tenor of survey textbooks is often one that suggests that the problems related to interview effects are so serious that little can be done to improve the matters (Bulmer 1993). This is not always the case. The most essential requirement for dealing with this source of bias is awareness that the quality of data collected in any quantitative survey depends in the last resort upon the capabilities and skills of the interviewer (Bulmer 1993). In this process, certain characteristics may be identified to which careful consideration should be given with a view to reducing cultural and status differences and facilitating easy communication with respondents (Bulmer 1993). During the interviews held for this study, for example, the interviewers and translators tried to blend in as much as possible. The interviewers, for example, never wore clothes that stood out in any way from those wore by the Congolese combatants. In addition, the interviewers worked together with different translators. I worked, for example, with male as well as female translators. This to examine whether combatants, mostly male, would be more eager to talk when there was another male present during the interview. The impression that I got from the interviews was that although it took more time to establish a bond with male combatants, they did not show any hesitation to talk about potentially sensitive topics like sexual violence and the killing and harming of civilians.

The survey

The questionnaire that was used to gather micro-level data on the behavior of the combatants and the different organizational characteristics of the armed groups' active in the DRC consisted of 49 approved mostly closed-ended questions. These questions were taken by vivo to the DRC for a pretest at the end of February and beginning of March 2009. The pretest consisted of 11 interviews held in Bukavu, Goma and Bunyakiri (North and South Kivu).[2] Due to this pretest, the formulation of some questions was changed, some questions were removed from the questionnaire, and others were added. For instance, some open-ended questions, like "What is your most intensive battle experience (when, where, why intensive)?," were removed from the survey since combatants experienced too much negative emotions as the result of this question.

Also questions that dealt with the future of the combatant, such as "If you think about your future, what is your greatest concern?" seemed to be difficult to answer and were consequently removed. The final questionnaire consisting of 54 questions (see for details Appendix 5). It is important to note, that questions were not only asked about their social background, their recruitment into the movements but also about what they experienced during their time in the bush, and how the movement was organized. These questions were directed to gather data on the five independent variables: civilian abuse, recruitment, social density, hierarchy, and commitment.

Civilian abuse

Data on specific actions or the intent of individual combatants are very sensitive, difficult, and especially dangerous to gather. As a result, the survey does not record any individual's acts (or the intent) of violence perpetrated against the civilian population. Rather, information on civilian abuse was collected indirectly, in order to avoid deception. As such, every combatant was treated as an agent; receiving orders rather than giving them. This is based on the assumption that hearing an order implies its execution. This is, of course, a weak proxy for the individual actions against human rights. However, there is no alternative of establishing a measure of individual's actions without further traumatizing the combatants and without them fearing prosecution.

In total, the survey contained five questions, measuring indirectly the amount of civilian abuse perpetrated by the individual combatant:

- Have you ever heard the order to abduct civilians?
- Have you ever heard the order to rape women?
- Have you ever heard the order to kill or harm civilians?
- Have you ever heard the order to attack villages mainly inhabited by civilians?
- In how many battles did you participate?

On the first four questions, the respondent could only indicate "yes" or "no" (of course there was always the possibility not to answer). The last question was formulated on the basis of the idea that civilians are often victimized during a battle (intentionally or as collateral damage). However, during the interviews it became clear that most respondents were not able to count or re-count the exact number of battles. This measure should then also been seen as a subjective indicator, in the sense that when a combatant told that he or she was active in 12 battles, it does not literally mean that the combatants was involved in so many battles. Rather, he or she only re-counts 12 battles, or had the feeling that he or she was involved in so many battles.

Incentives

Depending on whether the respondent was abducted or joined the armed group voluntarily, several questions concerning the recruitment were asked. Some of these questions were only asked to abductees while other questions were only asked to those combatants that joined the armed group on a voluntarily basis. For example, I asked those that joined voluntarily, why they decided to join the armed group.

However, some scholars advise against the use of this particular "why" question, i.e., "why did you join?" or "why did you become involved?" (i.e., Horgan 2008; Cordes 1987). They suggest that the answer to this question may reveal more about the organization's internal use of propaganda and ideological control than anything conclusive about the personnel account (Horgan 2008: 87). Moreover, this open "why" question forces combatants to look back at events that took place earlier, which might increase the nonresponse rate due to necessity of retrospective reasoning. Chai (1993: 100), for example, states that it is unlikely that active or even inactive combatants will admit that their true motives are anything but pure and entirely political. Another major problem, but more practical than the previous two, is the fact that asking this "why" question to abductees is senseless; they did not make the decision to join consciously, rather they were forced. Consequently, using this question as an indicator for combatants' motivation would reduce the sample size significantly. For these reasons, I specifically asked abductees for the reasons why they could not leave (a closed-ended question with several answer categories).

To avoid all the problems related to the "why" question, I induced the motivation for joining from the answers given on several ordinal statements that recorded under which conditions the respondent would take up his or her arms again. In total the respondent was asked to react on 16 statements (see also Appendix 5). The respondent's answer was recorded by an ordinal scale ranging from 1 (strongly disagree) to 5 (strongly agree):

- Other people have told me a couple of reasons and circumstances under which they would take up arms again. Could you please indicate if the following statements are also true for you? For which reasons would you take up arms again? I would take up arms again...
  1   if my comrades ask me for help.
  2   if I am forced by my commander.
  3   if I receive more food, better shelter, etc. than in my own village.
  4   if I can earn more money than outside the group.
  5   if I cannot go back to school.
  6   if I see that the group's political goals are not fulfilled.
  7   if I can protect my family and community by fighting.
  8   if the government fails to implement peace, law and order.
  9   if people in my community do not accept me.
  10   if I have the chance to kill and harm people.
  11   if I have the chance to get women.
  12   if my people continue to suffer.
  13   if my family rejects me.
  14   if I feel that I have nowhere else to go.
  15   if I have the feeling that my life would be more exciting in the bush.
  16   if for other reasons...

Social density

Most conflict researchers working with the concept of social density and its relation to other phenomena have emphasized the role of ethnicity in overcoming collective action problems (see for example, Fearon and Laitin 1996). However, other specific types of interdependence also tie individuals together, not just ethnicity. Social structures can also be, for instance, formed on the basis of friendship or kinship. Since the survey contained no question concerning the ethnicity of the respondent for security reasons and out of fear for priming the successive interview questions, I used other proxies that induced the social environment of the respondent.

I used in total five questions for constructing a proxy measuring the social density of the combatant's environment. Three of these questions were only asked to those combatants that were abducted and the other two were only asked to those combatants that joined on a voluntary basis:

Abductees:
- During your time at in the organization, have you ever seen recruited...?
- In general, did you know anybody active in the organization before you became abducted for the first time?
- In general, were you abducted together with somebody else you?

Voluntarily joining:
- During your time in the organization, have you ever seen recruited...?
- Did you know anybody in the organization before you became involved?

The answer category of all these five questions were nominal scaled: the combatants could indicate whether he or she knew or were abducted with friends, family, people from town/village, fellow school pupils, or did not know anyone or was not abducted/joined voluntarily with some other people the respondent knew before. Multiple answers were of course possible.

Hierarchy

Measuring the amount of hierarchy, to which a combatant is subjected to, is challenging. Unlike regular public or private firms, armed groups operate secretively. Consequently, combatants often do not have knowledge on the rules, regulations, and structures besides that of those within their own unit. In addition, the standardized items, used in the Web survey, to measure the level of hierarchy requires also the ability to think on an abstract level. For most young combatants this is difficult or sometimes even impossible. Therefore, I designed four questions that measure the subjective hierarchical experience of an individual combatant within the unit:

- Think of the superior of your group. How was he appointed? (if the combatant indicated that his or her commander was chosen by a superior commander – it was seen as being an indication of hierarchy).
- Were people from your group punished for disobedience? (if the combatant indicated that he was punished, this was seen as an indication of hierarchy)
- How was it decided what the punishment would be? (if the combatant indicated that the commander alone decided on the punishment – it was considered as being an indication of having a hierarchical top-to-bottom ruling in the armed group).
- Who carried out the punishment? (if the combatant indicated that it was most often members who had a higher rank than the punished person, this was considered to be an indication towards hierarchy.

The answer category of these four questions consisted out of several nominal-scaled answers. For example, the combatant could indicate answering the question "who carried out the punishment?" that the commander carried out the punishment, that a commander from another unit carried out the punishment, that lower-ranked members of the unit, or higher-ranked members carried out the punishment (see Appendix 5 for the exact answer categories of every question). Although these nominal questions do not directly measure the level of hierarchy, they allow for a rough distinction between a more horizontal versus vertical structured armed movement.

Commitment

Commitment was measured with the help of several questions focusing on different aspects of this concept and the intensity in which they prevail during and after the combatant's time in the armed movement. Most of these questions are again based on the standardized OCQ. Some items of this standardized survey were transformed in order to deal with the African context, the fact that we talk about illegal violent organizations, and the fact that I wanted to measure the level of commitment on the individual level.

In total eight questions were used for the construction of the commitment index. The first four questions measured commitment to the armed group, now the combatant is no longer a member of the group. These questions correspond with those asked to the experts in the Web survey:

- Are you proud to tell others you were a part of the armed group?
- Do you care about the fate of the armed group?
- Do you feel very little loyalty to the organization?
- Would you go back to the organization when your comrades ask for help?

However, these questions do not measure the amount of commitment the combatant felt when he or she was in the armed group. To measure this, four other questions were developed:

- I will now ask you some questions about your relationship with different people. Just imagine you are at the very beginning (position 0) of the line, can you show me on this line how close you feel to the following people. The closer you put a cross to your position, the more close you feel to that person. Thinking back to your time in the group, can you please show me how close you felt to:
  - How close did you feel to your friends in the bush?
  - How close did you feel to your family at home?
  - How close did you feel to the organization as a group?
  - How close did you feel to your commander?

In answering these four questions, the combatants received a pencil and were asked to make a little cross on a line. The closer the cross was to the beginning of the line, the closer they felt to friends, family, the organization, or the commander (depending on the question).

Control variables

There are some socio-demographic variables that might have theoretically confounding impact on the level of civilian abuse and are therefore covered in the survey: I noted the gender of the combatants down in the survey, I asked the combatants about their age and about their age at the time of joining (or abduction). In addition, I asked about their level of education. See Appendix 5 for a complete overview of all the socio-economic background questions that I asked the combatants.

Operationalization of the commitment variables

To examine the antecedents of affective organizational commitment among combatants (as described in the theory section of this study), several other independent and control variables are operationalized.

The first HRM strategy that might influence the combatant's level of commitment is the way in which they are recruited. To examine the influence of this possible strategy, I asked the following question:

•   How did you become part of the armed group in question?

The second hypothesis stipulates that socialization in the form of receiving training has a positive effect on a soldier's level of commitment. Training can come in many forms, but in the interviews three kinds stood central: the amount of military training (lessons received on the handling of different kinds of weapons), political training (lessons on the ideology and the political goals of the armed group) and spiritual training (lessons on the use of "traditional medicine," the bible, witchcraft, etc.). Although the latter form of training might seem unrelated to the development of affective organizational commitment, the promotion of spirituality and religion in wartime is often seen as a device to help buttress morale (Keegan *et al.* 1985). To examine the effect of training, the following question was asked:

•   Did you participate in training before fighting? If yes, what type of training (military training, political/ideological training, spiritual training) did you undergo and for how long?

The answers on this question were given in the number of years the combatants enjoyed them.

Another important part of socialization is punishment. Punishing "bad" behavior learns the combatant what behavior is allowed and what not. Punishment is measured with the following question:

•   Were people from your group punished for disobedience?

If the combatant indicated that people were punished, he or she could also indicate how often this occurred (often or sometimes).

The third strategy that might influence the level of commitment of combatants is by the lure of rewards. Combatants were asked to indicate whether they received extra food, money, sex slaves, spiritual objects, or drugs as a reward for participating in fighting (before or after). In total five questions were asked:

- Were you ever given the following things for participating in your unit's operations? And did you receive them before or after a fight?
- Extra food
- Money
- Non-medical drugs (like cocaine, marihuana)
- Woman/Man/Boy/Girl
- Spiritual objects (like holy water or traditional medicine)

The combatant could indicate whether they received these kinds of rewards most likely before, most likely after, whenever available, never at all, or they could decide not to answer.

The last set of strategies that might influence the level of affective organizational commitment of combatants, are those strategies concerning the upward movement of employees, i.e., promotion. Unfortunately, it was difficult to formulate a question measuring the amount of promotion (the combatants often did not recall) nor did I formulate a question measuring the relative amount of promotion combatants received in comparison to others members of the unit. Hence, I constructed a more easy and understandable proxy on the basis of the answers given to questions measuring important factors contributing to promotion. I asked the combatants the following questions, with the answer category ranging from very important to not important at all.

- If you think back to your unit, can you tell me how people were promoted? And how important the following reasons were for their promotion?
    - The person was promoted because he was a friend/relative of the commander.
    - The person was promoted because he was a good fighter during attacks.
    - The person was promoted because he was intelligent or educated.
    - The person was promoted because he was popular in the group.
    - The person was promoted because he was rich, and able to buy a promotion.
    - The person was promoted because he was especially cruel in injuring and killing people.
    - The person was promoted for another reason.

In the next chapter, the information provided by the individual Congolese combatants is analysed in more detail. Besides showing some descriptive tables and figures, the results of the interviews are statistically analysed and presented.

Notes

1 Parts of this section are already published by Haer and Becher (2012). Article can be retrieved from: www.tandfonline.com/doi/abs/10.1080/13645579.2011.597654.
2 Only the questions that remained the same were included in the analyses.

References

Arjona, Ana M. and Stathis N. Kalyvas. 2006. "Preliminary Results from a Survey of Demobilized Fighters in Colombia." Unpublished manuscript. New Haven: Yale University.

Beatty, Paul and Douglas Hermann. 2002. "To answer or not to answer: Decision processes related to survey item nonresponse." In *Survey Nonresponse*, eds. Robert M. Groves, Don A. Dillman, John L. Eltinge, and Roderick J.A. Little. New York: John Wiley & Sons, 71–86.

Bøås, Morton and Anne Hatløy. 2006. *Living in a material world: Children and youth in alluvial diamond mining in Kono District, Sierra Leone*. Research Program on Trafficking and Child Labour. Oslo: Fafo-Research Program on Trafficking and Child Labour.

Buhaug, Halvard. 2010. "Dude, Where's My Conflict?: LSG, Relative Strength, and the Location of Civil War." *Conflict Management and Peace Science* 27(2): 107–128.

Bulmer, Martin. 1993. "Interviewing and field organization." In *Social Research in Developing Countries. Surveys and Censuses in the Third World*, eds. Martin Bulmer, and Donald P. Warwick. London: John Wiley & Sons, 205–217.

Callaghy, Thomas M. 2001. "Life and Death in the Congo: Understanding a Nation's Collapse." *Foreign Affairs* 80(5): 143–149.

Chai, Sun-Ki. 1993. "An Organizational Economics Theory of Antigovernment Violence." *Comparative Politics* 26(1): 99–110.

Clark, John F. 2001. "Explaining Ugandan Intervention in Congo: Evidence and Interpretations." *Journal of Modern African Studies* 39(2): 261–287.

Coghlan, Benjamin, Richard J. Brennan, Pascal Ngoy, David Dofara, Brad Otto, Mark Clements, and Tony Stewart. 2006. "Mortality in the Democratic Republic of Congo: A nationwide survey." *Lancet* 367(9504): 44–51.

Cordes, Bonnie. 1987. "Euroterrorists talk about themselves: A look at the literature." In *Contemporary research on terrorism*, eds. Paul Wilkinson and Alasdair M. Stewart. Aberdeen: Aberdeen University Press.

Dixon, John and Clyde Tucker. 2010. "Survey Nonresponse." In *Handbook of Survey Research*, eds. Peter V. Marsden and James D. Wright. Bingley: Emerald, 593–630.

Emizet, Kisangani N. F. 2000. "The Massacre of Refugees in Congo: A Case of UN Peacekeeping Failure and International Law." *Journal of Modern African Studies* 38(2): 163–202.

Fearon, James D. and David D. Laitin. 1996. "Explaining Interethnic Cooperation." *American Political Science Review* 90(4): 715–735.

Gettleman, Jeffrey. 2008. "Mai Mai Fighters Third Piece in Congo's Violent Puzzle." *The New York Times*, November 20.

Global Security. 2011. "Rassemblement congolais pour la democratie (RCD)." www.globalsecurity.org/military/world/para/rcd.htm (September 20, 2011).

Goodhand, Jonathan. 2000. "Research in conflict zones: Ethics and accountability." *Forced Migration Review* 8: 12–15.

Groves, Robert M., Floyd J. Fowler Jr., Mick P. Couper, James M. Lepkowski, Eleanor Singer, and Roger Tourangeau. 2004. *Survey Methodology*. Hoboken: John Wiley & Sons.

Guichaoua, Yvan. 2009. "Circumstantial Alliances and Loose Loyalties in Rebellion Making: The Case of Tuareg Insurgency in Northern Niger (2007–2009)." MICROCON Research Working paper 20, December 2009.

Gunning, Jeroen 2010. "Scholars, Militants and Conflict Transformation: A Critical Theory reflection on scholarly engagement with armed non-state actors." Paper presented at the International Studies Association conference. New Orleans. February 19.

Haer, Roos and Inna Becher. 2012. "A Methodological not on quantitative field research in conflict zones: get your hands dirty." *International Journal of Social Research Methodology* 15(1): 1–13.

Hoffmann, Kasper. 2010. "The Ethics of Child-Soldiering in the Congo." *Young* 18(3): 339–358.

Horgan, John. 2008. "From Profiles to Pathways and Roots to Routes: Perspectives from Psychology on Radicalization into Terrorism." *Annals of the Academy of Political and Social Science* 618(1): 80–94.

Human Rights Watch. 1997. *What Kabila is hiding. Civilian killings and impunity in Congo*. New York: Human Rights Watch.

Human Rights Watch. 2009. *"You Will Be Punished." Attacks on Civilians in Eastern Congo*. New York: Human Rights Watch.

International Crisis Group. 2009. "DR Congo." www.crisisgroup.org/home/index. cfm?id=1174&l=1 (August 27, 2009).

International Rescue Committee. 2007. "Mortality in the Democratic Republic of Congo." New York: International Rescue Committee.

Investor Relations Information Network. 2006. "DRC: From Protection to Insurgency – History of the Mayi Mayi." March 16. www.globalsecurity.org/military/library/ news/2006/03/mil-060316-irin01.htm (April 19, 2010).

Jacobsen, Karen and Loren B. Landau. 2003. "The dual imperative in refugee research: Some methodological and ethical considerations in social science research on forced migration." *Disasters* 27(3): 185–206.

Kalyvas, Stathis N. 2008. "Promises and pitfalls of an emerging research program: the microdynamics of civil war." In *Order, Conflict, and Violence*, eds. Stathis N. Kalyvas, Ian Shapiro, and Tarek Masoud. Cambridge: Cambridge University, 397–421.

Keegan, John, Richard Holmes, and John Gau. 1985. *Soldiers: A History of Men in Battle*. New York: Elizabeth Sifton.

King, Elisabeth. 2009. "From data problems to data points: Challenges and opportunities of research in postgenocide Rwanda." *African Studies Review* 52(3): 127–148.

Kish, Leslie. 1965. *Survey sampling*. New York: John Wiley & Sons.

Lee, Thomas J., Luke C. Mullany, Adam K. Richards, Heather K. Kuiper, Cynthia Maung, and Chris Beyrer. 2006. "Mortality rates in conflict zones in Karen, Karenni, and Mon states in Eastern Burma." *Tropical Medicine and International Health* 11(7): 1119–1127.

Maedl, Anna. 2010. "Rape as Weapon of War in the Eastern DRC? The Victims' Perspective." *Human Rights Quarterly* 33(1): 128–147.

Ndikumana, Léone and Kisangani F. Emizet. 2005. "The Economics of Civil War: the Case of the Democratic Republic of Congo." In *Understanding Civil War*, eds. Paul Collier and Nicholas Sambanis. Washington: The World Bank, 35–62.

Neuner, Frank, Maggie Schauer, Christine Klaschik, Unni Karunakara, and Thomas Elbert. 2004 "A comparison of narrative exposure therapy, supportive counselling, and psychoeducation for treating post-traumatic stress disorder in an African refugee settlement." *Journal of Consulting and Clinical Psychology* 71(4): 579–587.

Neuner, Frank, Claudia Catani, Martina Ruf, Elisabeth Schauer, Maggie Schauer, and Thomas Elbert. 2008. "Narrative exposure therapy for the treatment of traumatized children and adolescents (KidNET): From neurocognitive theory to field intervention." *Child and Adolescent Psychiatric Clinics of North America* 17(3): 641–664.

Nordstrom, Carolyn and Antonius C.G.M. Robben, eds. 1995. *Fieldwork under fire. Contemporary studies of violence and survival*. Berkeley: University of California Press.

Nzongola-Ntalaja, Georges. 2002. *The Congo from Leopold to Kabila: A People's History*. London: Zed books.

O'Loughlin, John and Clionadh Raleigh. 2008. "Spatial analysis of civil war violence." In *A Handbook of Political Geography*, eds. Kelvin R. Cox, Murray Low, and Jennifer Robinson. Thousand Oaks: Sage, 493–508.

Olsson, Olga and Heather C. Fors. 2004. "Congo: The Prize of Predation." *Journal of Peace Research* 41(3): 321–336.

O'Muircheartaigh, Colm and Pamela Campanelli. 1998. "The relative impact of interviewer effect and sample design effects on survey precision." *Journal of the Royal Statistical Society* 161(1): 63–77.

Prunier, Gérard. 2009. *Africa's World War. Congo, the Rwandan Genocide, and the Making of a Continental Catastrophe*. New York: Oxford University Press.

Raleigh, Clionadh and Henrik Urdal. 2007. "Climate change, environmental degradation and armed conflict." *Political Geography* 26(6): 674–694.

Riisøen, Kari H., Anne Hatløy, and Lise Bjerkan. 2004. *Travel to uncertainty: A study of child relocation in Burkina Faso, Ghana and Mali*. Oslo: Fafo Research Program on Trafficking and Child Labour.

Romkema, Hans. 2007. Opportunities and Constraints for the Disarmament & Repatriation of Foreign Armed Groups in the Democratic Republic of Congo. The Cases of the FDLR, FNL, and ADF/NALU. Washington: The Multi-Country Demobilization and Reintegration Program of the World Bank.

Schaeffer, Nora C., Jennifer Dykema, and Douglas W. Maynard. 2010. "Interviewers and interviewing." In *Handbook of Survey Research*, eds. Peter V. Marsden and James D. Wright. Bingley: Emerald, 437–470.

Schatzberg, Michael G. 1997. "Beyond Mobutu: Kabila and the Congo." *Journal of Democracy* 8(4): 70–84.

Schauer, Maggie, Frank Neuner, and Thomas Elbert. 2005. *Narrative Exposure Therapy (NET) A Short-Term Intervention for Traumatic Stress Disorders after War, Terror or Torture*. Cambridge: Hogrefe and Huber.

Sluka, Jeff A. 1990. "Participant observation in violent social context." *Human Organization* 49(2): 114–126.

Spittaels, Steven and Filip Hilgert. 2008. *Mapping Conflict Motives: Eastern DRC*. Antwerp: International Peace Information Service (IPIS).

Themnér, Lotta and Peter Wallensteen. 2011. "Armed Conflict, 1946–2010." *Journal of Peace Research* 48(4): 525–536.

Tourangeau, Roger and T. Yan. 2007. "Sensitive questions in surveys." *Psychological Bulletin* 133(5): 859–883.

Turner, Thomas. 2007. *The Congo wars: conflict, myth and reality*. London: Zed Books.

Vlassenroot, Koen. 2005. "War and social research. The limits of empirical methodologies in war-torn environments." *Civilisations* 54(1–2): 191–198.

Vlassenroot, Koen. 2008. "Armed Groups and Militias in Eastern DR Congo." Lecture Series on African Security organized by a joint collaboration between the Swedish Defence Research Agency (FOI) and the Nordic Africa Institute (NAI). (January 2012).

Vlassenroot, Koen and Frans van Acker. 2001. "War as Exit from Exclusion? The Formation of Mayi-Mayi Militias in Eastern Congo." *Afrika Focus* 17(1–2): 51–78.

www.nai.uu.se/research/nai-foi%20lectures/calendar2009/vlassenroot.pdf

Warren, Carol A. B. 1988. *Gender Issues in Field Research*. Newsbury Park: Sage Publications.

7 Combatant analyses and results

In total, I interviewed 95 (former) combatants from different armed groups active in Congo. Rather than relying on information received by the head of the centers, I started the interview by asking the former combatants whether they were a member of an armed group and if so, from which group. Figure 7.1 shows the distribution of the interviewees across the different armed group. As is shown, the 95 combatants were active in more than one group (on average they indicated to have participated in 1.167 groups, with a maximum of 4 armed groups). Consequently, the dataset consists of 139 observations; the number of respondents per armed group.

As Figure 7.1 illustrates, most of the combatants were members of the different Mayi Mayi factions. This is an armed group that is especially active in North and South Kivu, the provinces in which all the interviews were held. In addition, it shows that few former FDLR combatants were interviewed. This is not surprising, given the fact that most members of this armed movement have the Rwandan nationality and when caught, escaped, or released are directly sent back to Rwanda.

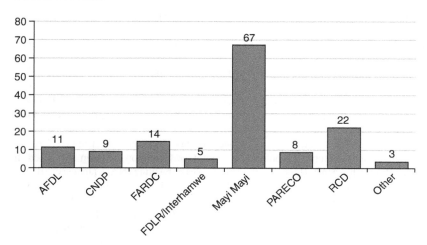

Figure 7.1 Aggregated number of respondents per armed group.

Civilian abuse

The most important variable for testing the formulated hypotheses is the dependent variable: civilian abuse. This was measured with four questions concerning hearing particular orders (have you heard the order to attack civilians, to abduct children, to attack villages, and to rape) and a question measuring the number of battles that the combatants experienced. Since this last question was very subjective and had a huge variance, I only used the four abuse variables for making the index. Table 7.1 shows the summary statistics of these abuse variables. As this table shows, the nonresponse on these four questions was minimal; only few respondents did not answer the questions. This was especially the case when asking whether they had ever heard the order to rape. One possible reason might be that male combatants might find it awkward to admit to have ever heard this order to female interviewers and translators. However, when looking at the mean answer on this particular variable (0.810), it seems that the majority of those combatants that answered this question had no problems admitting to having heard this particular order. Consequently, although relatively few respondents answered this question, the given answers seem not to be biased.

Figure 7.2 shows the percentage of respondents that confirm to have heard a particular order. On average, between 25 percent and 35 percent of the combatants indicated to have heard the order to abduct, to kill and harm civilians, and to attack villages. However, more than 85 percent (98 respondents) of the combatants heard the order to rape. This percentage confirms the idea that Congo is the worst country to live in as a woman (Human Rights Watch 2009).

Figure 7.3 displays the distribution on these four variables across armed groups. The figure shows that especially members of the FDLR/Interahamwe and the RCD have heard the order to attack villages, abduct civilians, and to kill and harm innocent civilians. In contrast to other armed groups, however, members of the FDLR have not heard the order to rape civilians. This might be due to the fact that most interviewed FDLR members were females. Another important thing to note is that members of all groups have heard these particular orders, not one armed group in particular. What is especially striking when looking at the figure is the fact that all combatants who were a member of the FARDC, indicated that they have heard the order to rape civilians. This is especially shocking, considering the fact that the FARDC is the official national army of the DRC. Moreover, members of PARECO and the Mayi Mayi, which are groups that claim to protect civilians, have also heard orders to abuse human rights.

Table 7.1 Summary statistics of the abuse variables

Variable	*Obs.*	*Mean*	*Std. Dev.*	*Min*	*Max*
Abduction	130	0.308	0.463	0	1
Attack villages	131	0.262	0.441	0	1
Kill and harm civilians	139	0.302	0.461	0	1
Rape	129	0.810	0.394	0	1

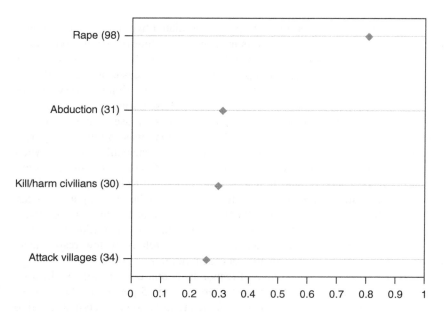

Figure 7.2 Percentage of respondents hearing different orders.

Note
The figure displays the absolute number of respondents answering "yes" on the question whether they heard the different orders.

The responses to the four dichotomous abuse questions were turned into an index following a logistic distribution, resulting from a Rasch analysis. Rasch analysis is regarded as a one-parameter Item Response Theory model, which models the probability of a specific response as a function of person ability to answer the question and item parameters. The Rasch analysis produces Rasch scores that correspond to the raw scores of each individual on the items. These scores can be put on a ratio scale, allowing the comparison of people with each other independent of which item may be used within the set of items assessing the same variable (see for more information on the Rasch model, Bond and Fox 2007). Table 7.2 shows the descriptive statistics of this variable. The constructed Rasch index ranges from −1.23 (low level of civilian abuse) to 3.92 (high level of civilian abuse).

To allow specialists on the DRC conflict and their armed groups to evaluate the validity of this index as compared with their view on the armed group behavior acquitted with other approaches, I plotted the mean and standard deviation of the level of civilian abuse per armed group in Figure 7.4. Although an analysis of variance is not possible because of a serious difference in group size, the figure shows that especially combatants of those armed groups that are supported by foreign powers, such as the RCD and the FDLR are those that score high on

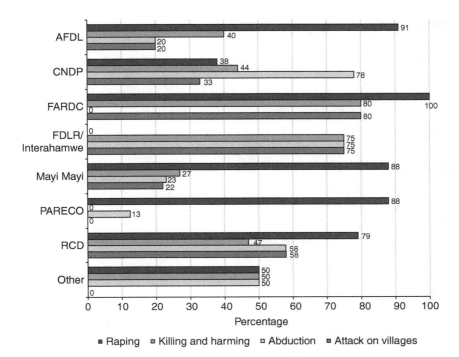

Figure 7.3 Distribution of civilian abuse across armed groups.

Table 7.2 Motivation for voluntarily joining

Motivation for joining	Frequency	Percentage	Cumulative percentage
Political reasons	19	21.35	21.35
Income	25	28.09	49.44
Revenge	8	8.99	58.43
Personal safety	17	19.10	77.53
Nowhere else to go	7	7.87	85.39
Love for soldier profession	4	4.49	89.89
Other	9	10.11	100
Total	89	100	

this index. Those groups that score relatively low on this index, such as PARECO and the FARDC, are those that profile themselves as being a self-protection militia (in the case of PARECO) or are the national army of the DRC (in the case of the FARDC). These results are also confirmed by different NGO reports (e.g., Human Rights Watch 2005; 2009) and by the UCDP One-sided Violence datasets (version 1.3 2010b and 2011; see Eck and Hultman 2007).

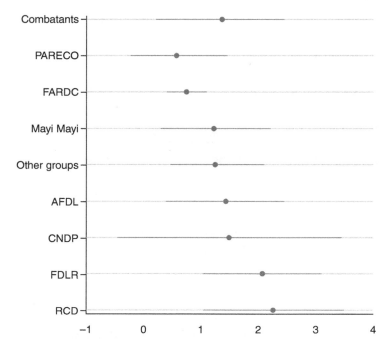

Figure 7.4 Dotchart of the level of civilian abuse per armed group.

There is, however, one major difference between this information on the level of abuse and the information collected on the level of the armed groups: the ranking of the AFDL. As Figure 7.5 shows, this armed group has only perpetrated a medium level of civilian abuse according to the Congolese combatants compared to all other armed groups. However, the UCDP One-sided Violence datasets have estimated that the AFDL's amount of perpetrated civilian killings exceeds those of the RCD, FDLR, and CNDP (see Eck and Hultman 2007). This difference can be due to many different factors. First of all, my measure of civilian abuse is a subjective measure based on a non-random sample. Second, it might be due to the fact that my index does not measure the direct amount of civilian abuse (killing and harming) since it is focused rather on the received orders. Lastly, the UCDP datasets are largely based on written news reports. It might be the case that there are, relatively to other groups, many reports written about the actions of the AFDL, especially because the march of the AFDL to Kinshasa was an exceptional event in African history.

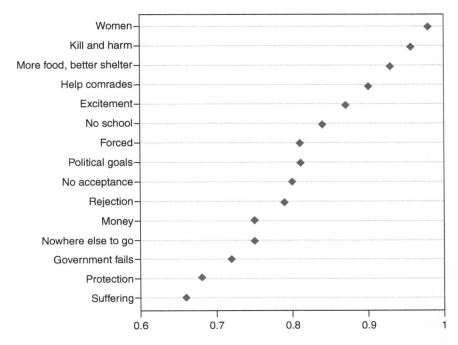

Figure 7.5 Percentage of combatants disagreeing on taking up arms.

Incentives

Although I decided to not use the answers of the famous "why" question, i.e., "why did you join?" in the upcoming analysis, it is interesting to see what the combatants answered. Table 7.2 shows the distribution of given answers on this question. Answers like "I wanted to kick out the Rwandans" or "The Tutsis are occupying our country" were coded as being political motivations. Some other combatants indicated that they were primarily motivated by economic incentives: "I needed to earn money so I could go to school" or "I earn more in the army than I did with selling bananas." Again, others said to have joined out of revenge. A female combatant, for example, told that she joined because she wanted to take revenge on the commander for killing her father. Others did not see any other choice than joining, otherwise they would have been killed or abducted by other armed groups. These motivations were summed under the header "personal safety." Only few combatants joined the armed group because they had no family anymore and no one took care of them, and also only few indicated that they joined because they always wanted to become a soldier because they love the uniform and the weapons.

Although these answers are not used to induce greed or grievance incentives of the individual combatant, I think using this particular question is not such a problem as is portrayed by some authors (e.g., Horgan 2008): the given answers by the combatants significantly varied. Moreover, it seemed that the interviewed combatants did not have any problems in admitting that they simply joined because they needed the money. An alternative possibility would have been using the following question: "why would you not leave the armed group?" However, this question did not result in much variation, around 70 percent of, for instance the abductees indicated that they were afraid to be killed or harmed. In addition, the answers to this particular question made clear that there is a strong difference between the motivations for joining and the motivations for staying.

Consequently, I used the 16 statements, measuring under which circumstances former combatants would take up their arms again. Figure 7.5 shows the percentage of respondents that indicated to "disagree" or "strongly disagree" on the different items. The figure illustrates that relatively few combatants agreed with the statements "I would take up my arms again if I can get more women" or "I would take up my arms again if I have the chance to kill and harm people" compared to the statements "I would take up my arms again if I can protect my family and community by fighting" or "I would take up my arms again if my people continue to suffer." The mean value of the latter two statements is lower than that of the first two.

Since some scholars have pointed out that it is very unlikely that only one type of incentive to rebel is present (Herbst 2000), two variables are constructed on the basis of these 16 items. The first variable measures the extent to which the respondent is motivated by material benefits, i.e., whether he is motivated by greed. Two statements are used to construct this measure: (1) I would take up my arms again if I receive more food, better shelter, etc. than in my own village, and (2) I would take up my arms again if I can earn more money than outside the group. On the basis of these two statements, I constructed a simple unweighted additive index that I divided by the amount of missings per respondent. The constructed greed instrument ranges from 0 (low level of greed motivation) to 1.25 (high level of greed as a motivational factor) with a mean of 0.48 and a standard deviation of 0.25. See also Table 7.5 for the summary statistics of this variable.

The second index measures the amount of grievance motivators per respondent. Again, the statements mentioned above are used to construct this index. However, I am aware of the fact that the statements do not capture all elements put forward by the deprivation theory. For this index, three statements were used that captured the main grievance factors that are offered by the theory: (1) I would take up my arms again if I see that the group's political goals are not fulfilled, (2) I would take up my arms again if the government fails to implement peace, law, and order, and (3) I would take up my arms again if my people continue to suffer. Like the greed index, I made on the basis of these three statements an unweighted additive index that takes into account the amount of missings on these statements per respondent. The created ordinal measure ranges from 0 (low level of grievances) to 0.55 (high level of grievances) with a mean of 0.23 and a standard deviation of 0.14. See Table 7.5, for additional descriptive statistics on this measure.

Social density

In total, I used five questions for constructing a proxy measuring the social density of the combatant's environment. The combatant could indicate during the interview who they already knew in the armed group, whether they were abducted together with school children or friends, and whether family members were already active in the particular armed groups (see Appendix 5 for a more detailed overview of the questions and their answer categories). The mode answer category of the questions was friends, i.e., combatants indicated that they, in most cases, knew some friends that were active in the armed group before joining. Only on the question "during your time in the organization, have you ever seen recruited…?" asked to abductees, the respondents indicated that they most often saw people from town or their village and not so many friends. Also unexpected was the answer on the question, whether the combatant was abducted with people that they knew. From other countries, such as Uganda, it is known that armed groups often find new recruits by abducting whole school classes (Ehrenreich 1998). However, although the answer category on this particular question included the item "other schoolchildren," only 15 percent of the combatants indicated that they were abducted together with people from school.

Although these questions are not specifically focused on ethnicity, it measures the density of the social environment of the combatant. Figure 7.6 shows the distribution of the given answers on these five questions. Those questions that start with an "A," are those asked to abductees. Those questions that begin

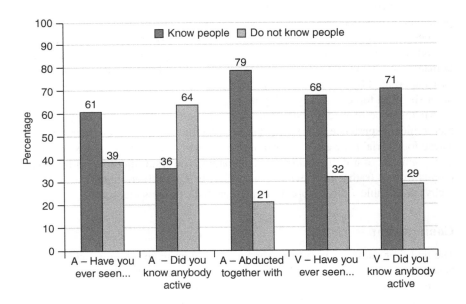

Figure 7.6 Percentage of respondents knowing or not knowing people.

with a "V," are those questions asked to those combatants that joined the armed group on a voluntarily basis. As the figure shows, 61 percent of the abducted combatants indicated that during their time in the armed group that they have seen people that they knew from before. What the figure also shows is that most abductees (79 percent) were abducted together with people that they knew. Many combatants knew also already people in the armed group before they decided to join on a voluntarily basis (71 percent).

Each of these five nominal questions was transformed into a dichotomous question (a value of 1 means a higher social density – the combatant knew more people and a value of 0 means the combatant did not knew anyone). These 5 dichotomous variables were thereafter used to construct an additive index that was again weighted by the amount of missing values per respondent. The constructed social density proxy ranged from 0 (low level of social density) to 0.75 (high level of social density) with a mean of 0.24 and a standard deviation of 0.19. See Table 7.5 for more descriptive measures of this variable.

Hierarchy

For measuring hierarchy, I asked four questions, from which three dealt with punishment; whether they were punished for being disobedient, how it was decided what the punishment would be, and who would carry out this punishment. More than 76 percent of the combatants answering the question on the amount of punishment indicated that they were often punished. Whenever they were punished, 95 percent of combatants indicated that the exact nature of the punishment was decided upon by the commander. However, it was most often (35 percent) carried out by combatants that had a lower rank than the punished person. Only few combatants indicated that it was the commander himself that punished the combatants (15 percent). The commander was also almost in all cases appointed by a superior commander (95 percent). Only in a few instances he or she used force to receive a higher rank.

All the four hierarchy variables were dichotomized (value 0 means a less hierarchical experience in the armed group and the value of 1 more hierarchical). These four variables were then also used to construct an additive index weighted by the amount of missing values per combatant. The resulting proxy of hierarchy ranges from 0 (rather low level of hierarchy) to 4 (relatively high level of hierarchy). See Table 7.5 for more descriptive statistics of this measure.

Commitment

The first four questions measuring the level of commitment of an individual combatant dealt with concepts like being proud, whether they care about the fate of the group, loyalty towards the group, and whether they would go back if former comrades asked for help. Table 7.3 shows the descriptive statistics of these four variables. All these questions had a five point answer category scale in which the value 1 means "strongly agree" and the value 5 means "strongly disagree." As the table

Table 7.3 Summary statistics of the commitment variables

Variable	Obs.	Mean	Std. Dev.	Min	Max
Proud	132	3.20	1.24	1	5
Fate	131	3.45	1.22	1	5
Little loyalty	125	2.73	1.23	1	5
Closeness	102	3.44	1.17	1	5

illustrates, on average most combatant disagree (although not much) with most statements, i.e., the mean value on the statements is above 3. However, the negative formulated question tapping the amount of loyalty of the respondent has an average of 2.73, meaning combatants slightly agree with the statement, indicated that they are no longer loyal to the armed group in which they were active.

What the table also shows is that the mean of the 4 elements of commitment (proud, fate, loyalty, closeness) does not change significantly. This is confirmed by the Cronbach's alpha, measuring the scale reliability between the four commitment variable. The alpha is 0.60, meaning that the different variables are reliable and closely related to each other.

In addition, to these four questions, I asked whether the combatant could indicate how close he or she felt towards his or her friends in the armed group, family at home, to the organization in general, and to the commander during the time that they were in the armed group active. Table 7.4 shows the descriptive statistics of these four variables. The answers are measured in millimeters. The fewer millimeters, the closer the combatant felt to his or her friends, family, commander, or the armed group in general. The table illustrates that, on average, combatants felt closer to the armed group and their friends than to the commander or their family, i.e., the mean values are lower.

From these 4 millimeter variables, three were used in the final constructed index measuring the level of commitment per respondent. The family variable, measuring the closeness of the combatant to his or her family while he or she was active in the armed group was not used because the literature on organizational commitment only minimal mentions the role of the family. In contrast, much attention is devoted in the military literature on the closeness of the commander, the military in general, and the fellow unit members.

These 3 millimeter variables were rescaled into five categories, matching those categories of the first four variables measuring the different elements of

Table 7.4 Summary statistics of the identity variables

Identity variables	Obs.	Mean	Std. Dev.	Min.	Max.
Friends	91	47.41	60.69	0	161
Family	92	97.04	65.69	0	173
Organization	94	64.69	63.53	0	169
Commander	95	50.78	64.12	0	167

commitment. Thereafter, a simple additive index was constructed (the variable measuring the amount of loyalty was reversed), weighted by the amount of missing values per respondent. The final index ranges from 0 (low level of commitment) to 4 (high level of commitment). See Table 7.5 for more descriptive information on this measure.

To allow specialists on the DRC conflict and their armed group to evaluate my collected data, I plotted the mean and standard deviation of the level of commitment per armed group in Figure 7.7. Although, commitment does not vary significantly across the major armed groups active in the conflict troubling the eastern provinces of the Congo ($F(7, 131) = 1.24$, $p=0.2839$), we can see that combatants who were a member of the old national army (the AFDL) and the newly formed national army (the FARDC) show a somewhat lower level of loyalty than those who were active members of the several non-state armed groups. This effect is partly explained by the fact that both armies are established by integrating existing non-state armed groups.

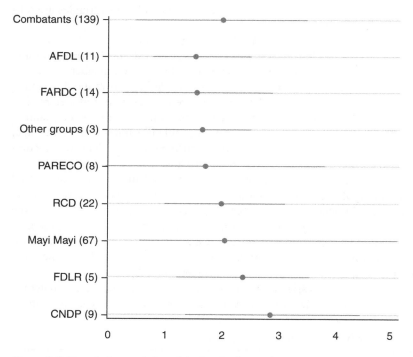

Figure 7.7 Descriptive statistics of the level of commitment per armed group.

Note
Absolute number of respondents in brackets.

Control variables

Besides measuring these major independent variables, I also asked some basic of demographic indicators, such as age, gender, and educational level. On average, the interviewed combatants were 22 years old, with a minimum age of 14 and a maximum age of 49. At first glance, this seems not very young given many publications emphasizing the use of very young children as child soldiers (e.g., Haer *et al.* 2011). However, very young combatants were not selected to take part in this study to prevent further traumatization and because some of the questions were difficult to comprehend for youngsters. Besides their age at the time of the interview, I asked about the age at the time that they joined the group. On average, combatants joined or were abducted into an armed group around the age of 15. Those combatants that joined on a voluntarily basis were somewhat older, namely 16 years old when they joined (with a standard deviation of 5.13 years). Those that were abducted into an armed group where on average younger: they were 14 years old (with a standard deviation of 5.00). See Table 7.5 for more descriptive information on the age of the combatants.

Another important socio-demographic variable that might have confounding impact is the level of education. Because most combatants were very young when they were recruited by the armed group, it is no surprise that most of them received only a few years of primary education or just finished this education. Only four combatants finished their secondary school and had some further education, and 11 respondents did not even go to school in the first place. See Table 7.5 for more descriptive information on the level of education of the respondents.

Most of the other possible socio-demographic control variables are highly correlated with one of the independent variables or suffer from a lack of variance. For example, the duration or tenure of a combatant in an armed group is highly correlated with the level his or her organizational commitment. Also gender is often used as a control variable. Gill and Horgan (2013: 440) find for instance, in their work on the PIRA, that perpetrators of violent crimes are most likely to be males between the age of 15 and 25. Also Silke (2008: 107) find that it is especially young males that are attracted to become involved in illicit activities, including

Table 7.5 Summary statistics of the independent and control variables

Variable	Obs.	Mean	Std. Dev.	Min	Max
Civilian abuse	139	1.28	1.25	−1.23	3.92
Greed	139	0.48	0.25	0	1.25
Grievances	139	0.23	0.14	0	0.55
Social density	139	0.24	0.19	0	0.75
Hierarchy	139	2.98	0.99	0	4
Commitment	139	1.04	1.22	0	4
Age of joining/abduction	131	15.60	5.10	6	38
Education	84	2.82	1.23	1	6

political violence. Although, most of the interviewed former combatants were indeed male (95 percent), due to our non-random sample design I cannot confirm these findings for the entire conflict. Moreover, due to a lack of variance, including these control variables in the analyses will lead to a large sample error of the partials that might lead to inaccurate calculations and conclusions. Consequently, in the following analyses the number of control variables is limited to two: age and education.[1]

Organizational commitment

Besides the general variables created to measure organizational commitment, I also collected information that might explain this level of commitment. First, I asked whether the combatants were abducted or whether they joined the armed group(s) voluntarily. Most of the interviewed combatants indicated that they joined the armed group on a voluntarily basis. From the 139 observations, only 50 (36 percent) indicated to be abducted. Figure 7.8 shows a mosaic plot of the distribution of the abductees and combatants that joined voluntarily per armed group. The plot shows that the RCD, the FDLR, and to a lesser extent the CNDP,

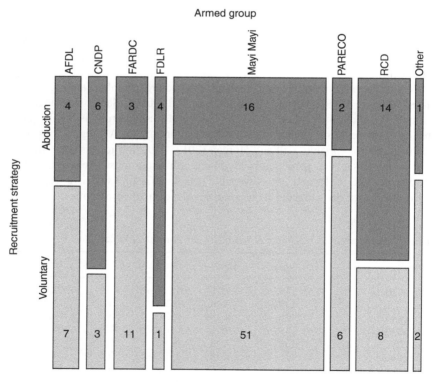

Figure 7.8 Mosaic plot of the recruitment strategy per armed group.

abduct relatively the most number of combatants. These are the armed movements that are supported by Rwanda and Uganda (except for the CNDP).

The FARDC, the Mayi Mayi, and PARECO, are the armed groups that abduct few people and primarily attract recruits on a voluntary basis. This result is not surprising considering the fact that the FARDC is the official national army of the Congo and that the Mayi Mayi and PARECO are both armed movements that profile themselves as being a Congolese militia organized to protect the Congolese civilian population.

Another potential factor that influences the level of commitment is training. Figure 7.9 shows the distribution of the different training forms per armed group. Large variations exist between the different armed groups. The combatants in the RCD received, for example, much military training compared to those of the CNDP. In general, political training was not so much given, with the exception for the CNDP. Spiritual training especially occurs in the national army. Although not asked systematically, from the interviews it was clear that members of the national army were obliged to read the bible (before fighting, after fighting, and on Sundays). The members of the Mayi Mayi on the other hand, were more often trained about the use of traditional medicines to become invisible for the enemy or bullet proof. Table 7.6 shows the descriptive statistics of these three training forms and the overall training variable.

A third potential factor is punishment. Punishment is a tool for socializing; it can teach the combatant the difference between "good" and "bad" behavior. In examining this potential factor, I asked how often they were punished. Table 7.6 shows the distribution of this variable. Most of the combatants indicated that they were often punished for bad behavior. Only two respondents indicated that they were never punished for their actions.

Besides punishments, rewards as a socialization tool can promote "good behavior" and in turn, might increase the level of organizational commitment.

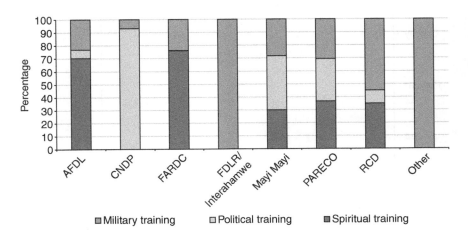

Figure 7.9 Distribution of training per armed group.

To examine this potential variable, I asked whether the combatants received rewards, and if so which rewards they received and when. The combatants indicated that most rewards were given before the actual action took place. For example, more than 49 percent of the combatants indicated that they received some spiritual objects before going to battle. Also non-medical drugs were most often distributed before fighting. However, rewards were not something that they received on a regular basis. For example, although some combatants indicated that they received sometimes food as a reward for participating in fighting, they indicated that the amount of food generally given was not enough and that they were often hungry (63.91 percent).

On the basis of these five variables which measured rewards (see Appendix 5 for more information), dichotomous variables were created, measuring per reward whether the combatant received them (before or after) or not. With the help of these dichotomous variables, an additive index was created weighted by the amount of missing values per combatant. The constructed variable ranges from 0 (no rewards were received) to 4 (many rewards were received). See Table 7.6 for more descriptive statistics. Notice that the constructed reward index only focuses on tangible rewards. Estimating received intrinsic rewards is more difficult and outside the scope of this study.

Lastly, I asked them about receiving promotion in the armed group and whether particular factors were important for this. Figure 7.10 shows the percentage of combatants indicating that particular factors are "important" or "very

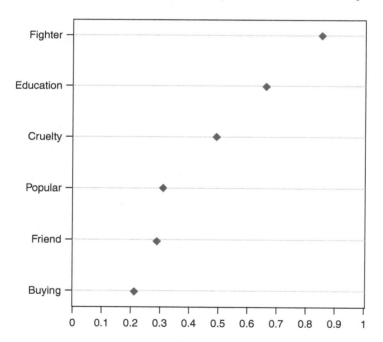

Figure 7.10 Percentage of respondents indicating importance of promotion factors.

important." For example, 85 percent of the combatants indicated that to get promotion it was important or very important to be a good fighter. And only 20 percent indicated that to get promotion they needed to pay a particular amount of money.

In order to make a proxy on the basis of these variables that measures the amount of promotion per respondent, I made the assumption that combatants who were never promoted were not able to answer these questions. This is of course a very strong assumption, but a better proxy for the amount of promotion is not available. Hence, I counted the missing values per respondent per item and turned it into a dichotomous variable. See Table 7.6 for the average, minimum, and maximum value of all independent variables.

It is assumed that affective organizational commitment can be enhanced with the above-mentioned HRM practices. However, previous research reveals that the level of commitment is also determined by three general antecedents: personal variables, job and role characteristics, and structural factors (Smeenk *et al.* 2006). Most of the variables that fall into one of these three categories do not seem to be of relevance when applying to armed groups, such as working hours, job challenge and social involvement. However, in order to control for the most robust antecedents, I decided to include the *age* of the respondent when they joined the armed group (as is discussed in the previous section) and for the organizational tenure or *duration*, measured in the number of years of membership. Both age and organizational tenure are generally positively related to the level of organizational commitment in public and private organizations, albeit weakly (e.g., Mathieu and Zajac 1990). See Table 7.6 for the descriptive statistics of these two variables.

Analyses

As discussed in the previous section, patterns in a population can only be estimated from a carefully drawn random sample or other probability-based model. From a sampling perspective, the held interviews are called convenience

Table 7.6 Summary statistics of the commitment variables

Variable	Obs.	Mean	Std. Dev.	Min	Max
Commitment	139	1.04	1.22	0	4
Training total	139	0.70	1.56	0	12.33
Military training	129	0.28	0.48	0	3
Spiritual training	101	0.39	1.48	0	12
Political training	99	0.26	0.96	0	8
Punishment	133	1.76	0.46	0	2
Rewards	139	0.94	0.97	0	4
Promotion	139	0.09	0.28	0	1
Duration	137	2.59	2.20	0	12
Age of joining/abduction	131	15.60	5.10	6	38

samples. Because of the possibility of having a sample bias, it is not possible to make any inference about the entire population of combatants with standard empirical methods. A technique able to manage this problem is the Bayesian approach, which provides inferences that are conditional on the data and are exact, without reliance on normality approximations based on large sample asymptotes (Congdon 2003).

For the micro-level models tested in this study, I extended the Bayesian inference into a linear regression with Gaussian errors method. To facilitate the implementation of this Bayesian model, a random walk Metropolis algorithm is employed. In addition, I assume that the predictors have equal prior probabilities, by choosing an improper prior distribution (with a mean of zero and a large variance). With these prior probabilities, three chains of 30,000 MCMC iterations initiating from mostly over dispersed starting values, discarding the first 2,500 iterations as burn-in. Additionally, I checked for convergence and non-convergence, autocorrelation problems and cross-correlation problems. None of the tests shows that there is any problem and that a Bayesian model cannot be applied.

Table 7.7 provides the posterior mean and the standard deviation for each of the variables in the adverse selection model, i.e., those strategies that the principal can employ before signing the contracts, together with the set of control variables. For readers who prefer figures, I also report the 95 percent credible intervals of this posterior distribution in the same table. Since this study has an X-centered focus, i.e., I examine the effect of the different control mechanisms on the level of civilian abuse rather than trying to explain the total amount of abuse, the table does not report any model-fit statistics (Ganghoff 2005).

Table 7.7 Parameter estimation results of the adverse selection model

Variables	Adverse selection model		
	Mean	SD	Credible intervals 95%
Constant	0.9122	0.4813	
Greed	0.0470	0.6912	
Grievance	−0.9613	1.1920	
Social Density	1.4905	0.5494	
Age	0.0007	0.0249	
Education	0.00479	0.1019	
N	139		

Note
The presented coefficients are produced by Bayesian Gaussian Linear Regression, using the Gibbs sampler.

Table 7.7 shows the results of the Bayesian analysis of the first two strategies that the leader of an armed group can employ to increase her control over her troops. I hypothesized that by providing the recruits with the right incentives and by recruiting them from a socially dense network, the principal could overcome the problem of adverse selection. Overcoming this problem would not only increase her control but also make it more likely that her troops follow her orders, i.e., kill more civilians when ordered.

I hypothesized that those combatants motivated by grievance factors are more likely to perpetrate civilian abuse than combatants motivated by greed factors. This due to differences in time horizons between the groups. However, the negative coefficient of grievance (−0.9613) shows that there is a negative relationship between grievance incentives and civilian abuse. In other words, those combatants that said that they are primarily motivated by grievance factors (e.g., protecting to country) are less likely to kill civilians in their quest. However, the figure next to the coefficient shows that the 95 percent credible interval includes the zero and I can therefore not definitive reject the hypothesis. The effect is simply not statistically reliable.

Looking at the greed incentives and how this relates to civilian abuse, the positive coefficient indicates that combatants motivated by greed factors (e.g., earning money or looting) are more inclined to kill civilians. However, like with the grievance factors, the figure show that this effect is statistically not reliable, since it crosses the 0 line, and that we cannot make any definitive conclusions. This lack of results (for both indicators of incentives) might corroborate with the idea that the distinction between greed and grievance is not terribly useful either in explaining the motivations or persistence of civil wars (Berdal 2005). Recruitment for example, might also be motivated by push factors such as the desire to escape violence, repression and suffering. However, due to a lack of data this idea cannot be tested. At the same time, it might be the case (as it was also suggested in the previous chapter analyzing the results of the armed group analysis) that those recruits that are motivated by grievances are inclined to do whatever is needed to make sure that the armed group survives. Consequently, they will be more likely to kill civilians in their quest due to the fact that this might hurt the armed group existence.

I also hypothesized in the theory chapters that the leader of an armed group can increase her control over her troop by recruiting her members from the same social network. This might make communication easier (orders are understand) and it can also make it easier to detect "bad" behavior since norms and values are pretty much the same. To test this possibility, I asked the combatants (abducted or not) whether they knew people in the armed group from before they got recruited. Table 7.7 shows the result and the linkage between social density and civilian abuse. The positive coefficient of 1.4905 indicates that there is indeed a relationship between social density and civilian abuse (or having heard the order to abuse civilians). The figure next to the coefficient shows that this effect is statistically reliable, since the 95 percent credible interval does not include zero. In other words, the second hypothesis is confirmed in this analysis:

when combatants are together in a unit with friends, family members, or other people that they know from before they were recruited, the probability that they heard the order to rape, kill civilians, attack settlements, and abduct children increases.

Two control variables were included in the analysis: age and the educational level. Other potential confounding factors, such as gender, were not included because they were highly correlated with the main independent variables or showed not too much variation (as was the case with gender). The positive coefficient of age indicates that the older a person was, the more likely it was that this person heard the orders to abuse civilians. This might be due to the fact that the older a person is, the more likely he or she was involved with more than one armed group. This in turn, might increase the likelihood of having heard these orders of abuse. Second, the positive coefficient of 0.00479 indicates that the higher a combatant was educated, the more likely he or she heard the orders to abuse the civilian population. It might be likely that especially higher educated combatants were challenged to "prove" themselves on the battlefield and as such were more likely to hear these orders. However, future research should definitely spend some time and energy to examine this potential relationship. It is important to note, however, that the figure shows that for both of these control variables, the 95 percent credible interval includes the zero.

Table 7.8 provides the posterior mean, the standard deviation, and the credible intervals of the variables connected to overcoming the problem of moral hazard. This problem surrounds the idea the leader of the armed groups cannot really see and control the actions of every individual combatant. In other words, the combatants might free ride and not follow the orders of the principal. To overcome this particular agency problem, the leader has to increase her monitor and sanctioning capacities. In the theoretical chapters I argued that one way to

Table 7.8 Parameter estimation results of the moral hazard model

Variables	Moral Hazard Model		
	Mean	*SD*	*Credible intervals 95%*
Constant	2.0451	0.5930	
Commitment	0.1710	0.0862	
Hierarchy	−0.3454	0.1212	
Age	−0.0023	0.0255	
Education	0.0252	0.1000	
N	139		

Note
The presented coefficients are produced by Bayesian Gaussian Linear Regression, using the Gibbs sampler.

do so is to structure the armed group more hierarchical and to create organizational commitment among her fighters.

The idea behind the commitment strategy was that when the leader creates commitment among the fighters, that they are more likely to cross personal boundaries and to follow orders, even though these orders go against personal norms and values, such as killing or the abduction of children. The positive coefficient of 0.1710 indicates that there is indeed a positive link to be found: combatants that are highly committed are more likely to hear orders to abuse the civilian population. This effect is statistically reliable, since the credible interval does not include the zero. In other words, the hypothesis is statistically confirmed. However, the effect of commitment on the level of civilian abuse is not that strong. The mean coefficient of the posterior distribution of the commitment variable indicates that one unit change in the commitment index is associated with an increase of about 2 percent in the level of civilian abuse.

In the third row of Table 7.9, one can see the effect of hierarchy on civilian abuse. It was argued that making the armed group more hierarchical might make it easier for the principal to detect free riding behavior of the individual combatants, since everyone is responsible for a pre-defined part of the organization. The negative coefficient of –0.3454, however, does not confirm at all this hypothesized positive link. Rather, this coefficient shows that the less hierarchical the armed group is structured, the more orders are heard to abuse civilians. As the figure next to the coefficient shows, this negative effect of hierarchy is statistically reliable. Consequently, the formulated hypothesis is rejected. Moreover, the analysis shows that the reality is reversed: the more network-like the armed group is structured, the more likely orders are heard that call for the abuse of the civilian population. It might be likely, however, that hierarchical structured armed groups, although killing fewer civilians, are perpetrating more attacks. Notwithstanding, this idea cannot be tested with the available data.

Like in the previous analyses, as is shown in Table 7.8, the age of joining/ abduction and the level of education are included. There is a slight negative effect of age on civilian abuse; the younger a combatant is, the more likely he or she will have heard the orders to abuse civilians. However, the credible interval includes a zero, i.e., the effect is not statistically reliable. Also the effect of the level of education on the likelihood that a combatant heard the orders to abuse civilians is not statistically reliable. However, the mean of the parameter shows that there might be a positive relationship between the level of education and civilian abuse: like in Table 7.8, higher educated combatants are more likely to hear the orders in comparison to those combatants with little education.

Although the combatants seemed to be able to distinguish between the different groups during the interviews, it might be the case that some observations are dependent on each other since some combatants were member of more than one armed group. To control for this possible bias in a straightforward way, I sampled 10 different datasets with each 95 observations (each respondent was only once included in each of dataset). For those respondents that were more than once in the dataset, it was randomly chosen which observation was included. The Bayesian analyses performed on these datasets did not result in any significant difference. The direction and average effect of all independent and control variables were the same. Nevertheless, because of the considerable decrease in the number of observations (from 139 to 95 observations), some effects became – as expected – less significantly reliable.

Another possible objection to this analysis is the subjective determination of the prior distribution of the parameters, as is done in all Bayesian analyses. However, most Bayesians reply to this objection by arguing that they make subjective priors transparent as opposed to the apparent objectivity of frequentists' statistics (Hangartner *et al.* 2007). To make sure that the results of the Bayesian models are robust, I changed the priors used in the analyses. Instead of having an uninformative prior with a mean of zero and a large variance in order to let the data speak for itself, I randomly chose two other priors: one with a small variance (0.0001) and one with a different mean (5). The change of priors did not seem to change the results. Again, the impact of greed and grievances on the level of civilian abuse is minimal. Social density of the unit and the level commitment of the combatant have a positive influence, while the level of hierarchy in the unit has a negative impact.

Analyzing the origins of organizational commitment[2]

In the previous section, I showed that the level of organizational commitment of the individual combatant is positively related to the amount of civilian victimization: those fighters that are highly committed are those that perpetrate the most one-sided violence. This result seems to be robust across models and alternative specifications. However, it is important to explore this relationship in further detail, especially because organizational commitment is not a feature that all combatants share.

In order to explore what determines the level of organizational commitment additional Bayesian analyses are ran. Like in the first analyses of this study, I extent the Bayesian approach to an ordered probit model, in which the dependent variable is the ordinal variable organizational commitment of the combatant. In the following analyses, I assume that the predictors have equal prior probabilities, by choosing for an improper prior distribution. Again, three MCMC chains are ran each of 30,000 iterations (simulations) initiating from randomly chosen starting points, discarding the first 2,500 iterations as burn-in. All the formal convergence and non-convergence tests, including measures of autocorrelation and cross-correlation, show that each chain has reached its stationary distribution and is fast mixing.

Table 7.9 provides the posterior mean and the standard deviation for each of the independent variables associated with the tested HRM strategies together with the set of control variables. Moreover, the asterisk in the table shows which relationship is statistically reliable. I used asterisk for space saving reasons. However, it is important to note that most Bayesian theorists do not approve it because it might bring confusion about the exact interpretation of the coefficients. Just to make it

Table 7.9 Parameter estimation results of the origins of commitment

Variable	Recruitment strategy	Training strategy (1)	Training strategy (2)	Rewards strategy	Promotion strategy
Constant	1.1603***	0.5664	0.38717***	0.8372***	0.8586***
	(0.3720)	(0.5360)	(0.1680)	(0.3669)	(0.3513)
Abduction	-0.5637***				
	(0.2078)				
Training		-0.1470***			
		(0.0892)			
Military training			-0.7771***		
			(0.3415)		
Political training			0.0275		
			(0.1117)		
Spiritual training			-0.6214***		
			(0.3188)		
Punishment		0.1494			
		(0.2191)			
Rewards				0.0867	
				(0.1052)	
Promotion					-0.2813
					(0.3651)
Age	-0.0345*	-0.0337*		-0.0400**	-0.0388***
	(0.0214)	(0.0220)		(0.0210)	(0.0210)
Duration	-0.0837**	-0.0367		-0.0660	-0.0718*
	(0.0489)	(0.0542)		(0.0482)	(0.0487)
Gamma2	0.5562***	0.5762***	0.5730***	0.5542***	0.5553***
	(0.0971)	(0.1006)	(0.1181)	(0.0954)	(0.0954)
Gamma3	1.1255***	1.1390***	1.1686***	1.1010***	1.1017***
	(0.1391)	(0.1394)	(0.1649)	(0.1353)	(0.1333)
Gamma4	1.9493***	1.9139***	2.1207***	1.8542***	1.8470***
	(0.2172)	(0.2092)	(0.2796)	(0.2038)	(0.2047)

Note
The first coefficient is the mean of the parameter. The standard deviations are in parentheses. * the credible interval of 90% does not include a 0; ** the credible interval of 85% does not include a 0; *** the credible interval of 95% does not include a 0.

clear, an asterisk in Table 7.9 does not indicate statistical significance, but rather that there is a 95 percent, 90 percent or 85 percent probability that the credible interval contain the mean of the parameter.

The first factor that might have impact on the level of commitment of an individual combatant is how they were recruited. It was argued that when they would join on a voluntarily basis, rather than being abducted, it is more likely that their level of commitment is higher. In the second column of Table 7.9, you see the statistically reliable result. The negative coefficient of –0.5637 shows that those combatants that were abducted into the armed group show a higher level of affective organizational commitment in comparison to those who joined voluntary. This result stands in sharp contrast to the formulated hypothesis and the hypothesis is, therefore, rejected.

Even though this result appears counterintuitive, it becomes more comprehensible when taking the negative coefficient of the age into account (–0.0345). This coefficient indicates that specifically young combatants show a high level of commitment, which confirms again the idea that recruiting children as soldiers – even by force – is in general an effective strategy.[3] Not only are they cheap – as children make up more than half of the population in many developing countries – they are easy to replace, to manipulate, to model and to indoctrinate (Haer *et al.* 2011; Schauer and Elbert 2010). Consequently, they are more likely to get abducted.

The next set of hypotheses set forth that the socialization process, in the form of training and punishment should have a positive influence on the level of organizational commitment felt by the combatant. The results, which can be found in the third column of Table 7.9, exhibit that training has indeed an effect; the 95 percent credible interval does not include the zero. However, in contrast to the hypothesis, the effect of training is negative, as is shown by the negative coefficient of –0.147. This means that if a combatant were to increase the amount of training with one extra year, his or her ordered log-odds of being in a higher commitment category would decrease by 0.147, while the other variables in the model are held constant. To look more into this negative relationship, I also examine the effect of the individual components of training (military, political and spiritual training). The analysis shows that this negative but statistical reliable effect of training is mainly due to the influence of military and spiritual training, the two forms of training especially used on the battlefield. The more military and spiritual training a recruit received, the less committed he or she becomes. The coefficient of –0.7771 for military training, for example, indicates that with one year extra military training, the combatants' ordered log-odds of being in a higher category of commitment would decrease by 0.771. The effect of spiritual training is somewhat lower; see the coefficient of –0.6214. Political training, although the effect is not statistical reliable, has on the other hand a positive effect on commitment. This confirms at least partly the idea that indoctrination of soldiers might be crucial for the establishment of commitment among fighters.

These negative effects of training on the level of commitment might be explained by the fact that the more combatants receive this particular training, the more likely they are used in battles in which they experience life threatening events that not only might influence them physical (e.g., getting harmed) but also mentally. This possible burn-out effect can in turn negatively influence their loyalty towards the armed group. However, when controlling for the possibility of a curvilinear relationship between training and commitment, no statistical reliable burn-out effect could be detected. Additionally, it might be the case that training is offered selectively to the combatants because of cost reasons; only those combatants that need it (i.e., those that have a low level of commitment in the first place) will receive it. However, during the interviews no indication was given that the use of training as a strategy was offered selectively.

In addition to the influence of training, I examine the influence of punishment on the level of commitment showed by the combatants. I hypothesized that punishment is positively related to commitment, since combatants learn what is regarded to be good and bad behavior. This positive relationship is confirmed by the Bayesian analysis. Nevertheless, the relationship between punishment and commitment might be curvilinear; those combatants that receive less punishment might have a high level of commitment, and at the same time, those combatants that experience much punishment have a high level of commitment. Testing the possibility of this curvilinear relationship requires a more fine graded measurement of punishment than is currently available.

I also hypothesized that receiving rewards has a positive influence on the level of affective organizational commitment of the individual combatant. The linkage between the two concepts can be found in Table 7.9, when looking at the positive coefficient of 0.0867. This coefficient indicates that the more rewards an individual combatant receives, the higher his or her level of affective organizational commitment becomes. Although this confirms the hypothesis, this effect is not statistical reliable in the Bayesian analysis. This might be due to the proxies that were used to measure this particular variable: receiving rewards was measured by counting the missing values on the survey questions. However, this mixed effect, i.e., positive but not statistical reliable, can also be found in HRM studies in the public and private sector. For example, Paul and Anantharaman (2004: 78) conclude that among various HRM practices, rewards have the greater influence on organizational commitment, while a recent meta analyses conducted by Smeenk *et al.* (2006: 2039) conclude that the level of compensation is found to have no significant influence on any form of organizational commitment. Although rewards have no reliable effect, the control variable of age has it. Age is, as expected, negative related to the level of commitment and statistical reliable at the 95 percent credible interval.

The last column reports the effect of the promotion strategy on the level of commitment. I formulated in the theory chapters two contrasting hypotheses on the influence of promotion on the level of organizational commitment of combatants. The first hypothesis expected a positive relationship between promotion and commitment, considering promotion as a kind of reward. The second formulated hypothesis regarded a negative relation between promotion and commitment, based on the idea that promotion has to be something special and unique before it affects the level of commitment. The negative coefficient of –0.2813 in the sixth column of the table indicates that this latter hypothesis is confirmed. To be more precise, the coefficient indicates that when combatants receive somewhat more promotion (a difference of 1 category in the variable) the log-odds of being in a higher commitment category decrease with 0.28. What I was not able to test due to a lack of data, is the relative influence of promotion. It might be the case that receiving promotion has only an impact if every other combatant does not receive it. However, for testing this idea I need information on the general promotion policies per unit, which is not available and probably also not known by most combatants.

Like in all other columns of the table, the last column also shows the effect of age and the duration on the level of affective organizational commitment. Although it seems to depend on the calculated model whether the effect of these two control variables on the level of organizational commitment is statistically reliable, both do not seem to switch from direction. Across all models there is a negative impact of age on the level of affective organizational commitment: the younger a combatant is the more committed they are. Moreover, the negative coefficient of duration seems also to indicate that when combatants are just active in the armed group for a short period of time, it is more likely that their level of commitment is higher. These results seem to indicate the presence of a burn-out effect; the longer/older one is, the more likely one becomes dissatisfied with what they see and experience.

Alternative specification and robustness checks

Four alternative specifications were made to control for robustness of the above findings. An obvious robustness check is the calculation of the full model including ever strategy. Some of the parameters in the full model lost some statistical significance. This is mainly due to the decrease of the number of freedom. However, the direction and average effect of all independent and control variables where the same as in each individual model.

Additionally, as in the previous analyses, eight datasets were samples each 95 observations (each respondent was only once included in each dataset). I recalculated the above models by running them through all of the eight datasets and averaging their coefficients. This procedure helps to check for a possible dependency of observations problem. However, the results did not point towards any significant difference. The direction and average effect of all independent and control variables were the same. Nevertheless, because of the considerable decrease in the number of observations, some effects became – as expected – less significantly reliable.

In addition, to check the robustness of the measurement of the dependent variable, I made an alternative measure of commitment. The commitment measure used in the above analyses was based on eight questions. Some of these questions are closely related to each other. For instance, it might have been difficult for some combatants to determine the difference between the present-tense question: "I still feel close to my friends in the group" and a reflective question that asked about their feelings during the time in the armed group: "how close did you feel to your friends in the bush?" Hence, a new measure of commitment was made, excluding the latter question. However, the results of the Bayesian analyses using this new measure did again not differ substantially from the original analyses, perhaps with the exception of a minor change in the effect of training. In the Bayesian calculations with the new measure, the effect of training on commitment becomes less strong, which is due to an incline in the effect of military training. With the removal of a measure that tapped the bonding between friends during their time in the armed group, the effect of the military training on the level of commitment declined. This is no surprise, given the fact that in the military there is a very strong relationship between the fighting spirit of combatants and the bonding that takes place within a unit (Keegan *et al.* 1985).

Lastly, the priors used in the Bayesian analyses were changed. Instead of having an uninformative prior with a mean of zero and a large variance, two randomly chosen other priors were employed; one with a small variance (0.0001) and one with a different mean value (3). Again, the results seem to be robust. Abducted combatants show the highest level of commitment, training (especially military and spiritual training) has a negative reliable effect on the level of affective commitment among combatants, rewards do still not have a statistically reliable effect and the effect of promotion is still significantly reliable.

Notes

1 Besides these socio-demographic control variables, there is also a possibility control for possible interview and translator effect. These effects are mostly examined with the help of a Heckman model (similar to a two-stage model). However, the calculated models did show that the coefficients are no different than the Heckman corrections. In other words, the interviewer and translator do not have a significant impact on the given answers.
2 Note that part of this analysis is already published in Haer (2011).
3 Additional analyses suggest that there is a linear relationship between age and commitment. Hence, the level of commitment does not seem to change per age group.

References

Berdal, Mats. 2005. "Beyond greed and grievance – and not too soon...." *Review of International Studies* 31(4): 687–698.
Bond, Trevor G. and Christine M. Fox. 2007. *Applying the Rasch Model. Fundamental Measurement in the Human Sciences.* New York: Routledge.
Congdon, Peter. 2003. *Applied Bayesian Modelling.* Chichester: John Wiley & Sons Ltd.
Eck, Kristine and Lisa Hultman. 2007. "One-Sided Violence Against Civilians in War: Insights from New Fatality Data." *Journal of Peace Research* 44(2): 233–246.
Ehrenreich, Rosa. 1998. "The Stories We Must Tell: Ugandan Children and the Atrocities of the Lord's Resistance Army." *Africa Today* 45(1): 79–102.
Ganghof, Steffen 2005. "Vergleichen in qualitativer und quantitativer Politikwissenschaft: X-zentrierte versus Y-zentrierte Forschungsstrategien." In *Vergleichen in der*

Politikwissenschaft, eds. Sabine Kropp and Michael Minkenberg. Wiesbaden: VS, 76–93.

Gill, Paul and John Horgan. 2013. "Who were the Volunteers? The Shifting Sociological and Operational Profile of 1240 Provisional Irish Republican Army Members." *Terrorism and Political Violence* 25(3): 435–456.

Haer, Roos. 2011. "Commitment among Fighters: A Research Note." *Peace Economics, Peace Science and Public Policy* 17(1): 1–6.

Haer, Roos, Lilli Banholzer, and Verena Ertl. 2011. "Creating Compliance and Cohesion – How Rebel Organizations Manage to Survive." *Small Wars & Insurgencies* 22(3): 415–434.

Hangartner, Dominik, André Bächtiger, Rita Grünenfelder, and Marco R. Steenbergen. 2007. "Mixing Habermas with Bayes: Methodological and Theoretical Advances in the Study of Deliberation." *Swiss Political Science Review* 13(4): 607–644.

Herbst, Jeffrey. 2000. "Economic Incentives, Natural resources and Conflict in Africa." *Journal of African Economies* 9(3): 270–294.

Horgan, John. 2008. "From Profiles to Pathways and Roots to Routes: Perspectives from Psychology on Radicalization into Terrorism." *Annals of the Academy of Political and Social Science* 618(1): 80–94.

Keegan, John, Richard Holmes, and John Gau. 1985. *Soldiers: A History of Men in Battle*. New York: Elizabeth Sifton Paul, A.K. and R.N. Anantharaman. 2004. "Influence of HRM practices on organizational commitment." *Human Resource Development Quarterly* 15(1): 77–88.

Mathieu, John. E. and Dennis M. Zajac. 1990. "A review and meta-analysis of the antecedents, correlates, and consequences of organizational commitment." *Psychological Bulletin* 108(2): 171–194.

Schauer, Elisabeth and Thomas Elbert. 2010. "The Psychological Impact of Child Soldiering." In *Post-Conflict Rehabilitation: Creating a Trauma Membrane for Individuals and Communities and Reconstructing Lives after Trauma*, ed. Erin Martz. New York: Springer, 311–360.

Silke, Andrew. 2008. "Holy Warriors: Exploring the Psychological Processes of Jihadi Radicalization." *European Journal of Criminology* 5(1): 99–123.

Smeenk, Sanne G.A., Rob N. Eisinga, Christine Teelken, and Hans Doorewaard. 2006. "The effects of HRM practices and antecedents on organizational commitment among university employees." *International Journal of Human Resource Management* 17(12): 2035–2054.

8 Conclusion and discussion

The central objective of this study was to advance the theoretical and empirical understanding of the occurrence of civilian abuse. In theoretical terms, I was especially interested to what extent organizational characteristics of armed groups relate to the level of perpetrated civilian killings. In this study, this linkage between organizational characteristics of armed groups and their behavior is established with the help of the principal–agent theory. Based on the literature on genocide and mass killing, I started with the assumption that civilian abuse is the result of a rational strategic decision from the principal and that the faithful execution of this order depends on the amount of control she can exercise over her troops.

I argued in the theory chapters of this book that the amount of control that she has over her troops depends on her abilities to overcome two problems inherit in any delegation relationship: the problem of adverse selection and the problem of moral hazard. To overcome the problem of adverse selection (i.e., the principal does not know the intentions and beliefs of the agents before they are hired for the job), the principal has to improve her selection and recruitment strategy in order to attract the right recruits for her armed group. Insights from conflict research indicate that the incentives offered by the principal have influence on the type of combatants the armed group attracts. I hypothesized in this study that by offering non-material incentives (rather than material incentives) recruits are attracted that are more interested in the survival of the organization than in their personal gain. And that they, consequently, are more likely to follow the principal's order to kill civilians. Another factor that might improve the recruitment and selection strategy of the principal is if she attracts members from the same social network. These kinds of networks have often their own practices, language, and enforcement methods, which makes overcoming the collective action problem more likely. Consequently, I hypothesized in Chapter 2 that armed groups composed out of members coming from the same social network are more likely to harm civilians than those groups that recruit their members from different networks. For the micro-level part of this book, I then also hypothesize that combatants coming from the same social network are more likely to resort to violence.

The second problem underlying the relationship between the leader and her troops is the problem of moral hazard. It refers to the problem that the principal is unable to observe the individual actions of her agent. To overcome this particular delegation problem, the principal has to improve her monitoring and sanctioning mechanisms. In Chapter 3, I argued that one important way to improve these mechanisms is to structure the armed group in a more hierarchical way: in hierarchical organizations free riding behavior can be earlier detected and punished. Consequently, I hypothesized that hierarchical armed groups and combatants active in more hierarchical structured armed groups perpetrate more civilian abuse. An additional strategy that the principal can employ to improve her monitoring and sanctioning mechanisms is to create organizational commitment among her troops. In the literature it is argued that organizational committed combatants are willing to give something of themselves in return for the well-being of the armed groups (e.g., Meyer and Allen 1991). These combatants are then also more inclined to overstep personal boundaries and should have fewer problems with the faithful execution of the order to kill or harm the civilian population. Consequently, I hypothesized that armed groups that are composed primarily out of highly committed members are more likely to abuse the civilian population than those who are not composed of committed members.

For testing these hypotheses on the level of the armed groups and combatants, systematic and empirical information was needed on the internal structure of the armed groups and about the combatants themselves. Since there was no dataset readily available, I decided to collect my own data for both levels of analyses. To test these hypotheses on the level of the armed groups, I collected systematic and comparative data on the organizational structure of 71 armed groups via a Web survey among experts. For the analysis on the level of the individual combatants, I collected systematic information during quantitative fieldwork in Congo. In total, I interviewed 95 (former) combatants on the day-to-day behavior of their armed group, the orders that they received, and whether they heard the order to abuse the civilian population.

The Bayesian analyses of the collected information showed that in contrast to the hypotheses, armed groups composed primarily out of greed-motivated combatants were more likely to resort to violence than those armed groups composed of combatants that were attracted by social endowments. Furthermore, the analyses showed that more socially dense armed groups are more likely to kill civilians and combatants that are active in more socially dense armed groups are also more inclined to overstep personal boundaries and abuse the civilian population. Also the hypothesis concerning the level of hierarchy was confirmed, although only at the armed group level. The individual analysis showed that combatants active in less hierarchical environments are perpetrating more abuses than those active in hierarchical groups, which stands in contrast with the formulated hypothesis. Lastly, the analyses showed that armed groups composed primarily out of highly committed combatants are less inclined to abuse the civilian population, while organizational commitment plays an important role on the individual level. Table 8.1 summarizes the hypotheses on the two levels of analyses and whether the hypotheses are accepted or rejected in the analyses.

Table 8.1 Overview of the results

Independent variables	Expected linkage with civilian abuse	Armed group level result	Combatant level results
Greed	−	+	+
Grievances	+	−	−
Social density	+	+	+
Hierarchy	+	+	−
Commitment	+	−	+

The table shows two important things: it displays the differences between the formulated hypotheses and the results of the analyses and it displays whether there are differences in results between the levels. For instance, the table shows that the hypotheses on the effect of greed and grievances on the level of civilian abuse are not confirmed on both levels. Although, this stands in contrast with the hypotheses, the results are consistent across the two levels of analysis, which might be an indication that the underlying assumption, linking incentives to civilian abuse, is wrong. I assumed in the theory chapters that recruits motivated by grievances are more likely to follow the orders of the leader because they are more likely to have longer time horizons. However, the results showed that although grievance motivated armed groups and combatants have longer time horizons, this does not automatically result in following the leader's order. Instead, the results seem to indicate that these combatants are aware that killing civilians is in the long run counter-effective; it can complicate future support, can have negative impact on post-conflict settings, and can have severe consequences for the survival of the armed group in general.

The positive linkage between greed and civilian abuse (i.e., armed groups and combatants that are primarily motivated by material rewards) also provides evidence that Humphreys and Weinstein (2006: 433) were right to argue that civilian abuse produces private rewards for the individual combatant but at a social cost of the armed group. They hypothesized that combatants who are attracted by material rewards are more likely to kill civilians in their quest for material rewards than those that are in pursuit of social endowments like the establishment of democracy. Unfortunately, however, my survey among combatants did not include any question linking looting activities with civilian abuse. Future research and field studies might, therefore, want to explore this relationship in more detail to establish a clearer linkage between the type of incentives and civilian abuse.

The table also shows mixed result for the variables hierarchy and commitment. On the armed group level, the analyses suggest that armed groups primarily composed of highly organizational committed combatant are less likely to perpetrate human rights abuses. However, on the level of the combatants, this negative relationship becomes positive. At the same time, the analyses also suggest that hierarchical armed groups are more likely to kill civilians, but that combatants active in more hierarchical armed groups are refraining from this behavior. The fact that the results differ between the levels of analysis does imply that the individual perception of hierarchy and commitment is different from that observed at the armed group level. Those combatants that are, for instance, active in more hierarchical groups might have another idea on what hierarchy entails than experts that evaluate the hierarchical level of the whole group. Additionally, it might be the case that there are confounding factors influencing the perception of commitment and hierarchy on the individual level, which are not present on the armed group level. Further research should examine the existing differences between the group and individual level.

Besides these two broad analyses, an additional analysis was conducted on the origins of organizational commitment on the individual level. The effects of several management practices were examined. It was hypothesized that combatants that joined armed group on a voluntarily basis, that received much training, that were often punished, and that received much rewards, were more likely to become committed to the armed group. The Bayesian analyses show that in contrast to what these management practices prescribe, abducted combatants and those combatants that did not make consciously the choice of joining the armed group, are more likely to be committed to the armed group. This can partly be explained by the fact that most often younger persons are abducted and they are much more easily to indoctrinate or to influence. Also the years in training, especially in military and spiritual areas, had a negative influence on the level of commitment. This counter-intuitive result is probably due to the fact that the more they receive this form of training, the more often they are exposed to the horrors of the battlefield, which in turn is more likely to reduce the level of commitment. The last practice that seemed to have influence on the level of affective organizational commitment is whether combatants were promoted or not. The results show that the less often a combatant received promotion, the more he or she valued and appreciated the armed group.

Besides these theoretical new insights, important issues and implications emerge from this study. Most of these implications are of a scholarly nature. This study, for instance, proves that although the internal characteristics of armed groups are often ignored in the literature on human right abuses, they play an important role in the explanation of these cruel acts against the civilian population. In addition, combining the armed group level with the level of the individual combatants can give unique insights in the causal mechanism that are in place and the problems that might occur when applying broad theories to the micro-level. Notwithstanding, there are some avenues for further research. I mention a couple of them. First, it is highly likely that the data collected for both levels of analyses suffers from sample bias. Therefore, the conclusions that are drawn should be very carefully interpreted. Further research should clarify whether relationships found in this study are generalizable to more armed groups outside the sample and to combatants outside the Congolese context. Only then, we can know for sure that the found relationships are robust and generalizable.

Second, future research should connect the different facets of the internal characterizations of armed groups to different dependent variables. The structure of these groups might also influence, for instance, their behavior on the battle-field (their number of attacks or battles) or on the negotiation table. Furthermore, it would be fruitful to combine both levels analysis (the meso and micro-level) in a multi-level analysis, in which the answers of the individual combatants are linked to the general characteristics of their armed groups in one analysis. However, this asks for the collection of more systematic and precise data. Especially collecting the data on the level of the combatants might be problematic. However, conflict scholars often forget that at the fundamental, it should be the individual that stands central in their analysis. When they are not prepared to collect data until the guns fall silent, research agendas will become smaller and some countries will even be understudied.

Third, the analyses showed that among others, greed and grievance endowments do matter for the behavior of rebel groups towards the civilian population. This is a first indication that the resource capabilities of an armed group play an important role. However, what is so far not yet examined is the behavior of armed groups that receive external support towards the civilian population. It might be likely, in light of the presented evidence, that those groups that receive external support, and have therefore much resources available, are less likely to kill civilians than those who are not. At the same time, focusing on the resource base of the armed group and its leader might also make the principal–agent model, as is presented in the theory chapters more realistic. The model that is currently presented, assumes indirectly that the leader of an armed group could transform the group in such a way that its members would be more likely to follow orders. As such, it discards the actual capabilities of the leader. However, when including the influence of external support, the model is extended to a situation with several principals (those that pay the leader of the armed group and the leader herself). Consequently, the leader of an armed group becomes an agent herself, and the game becomes more complicated. This might significantly change the dynamics between the leader and her recruits, and as such have consequences for the behavior of the armed group on the battlefield.

Another potential fruitful research avenue that should be examined is the idea that the characteristics of the leader influence the structure of her armed group. So far, the characteristics and the capabilities of the leader are to a certain extent dismissed. I have only argued that some leaders might be constrained in their actions by the unavailability or availability of resources. However, future research might look at the characteristics of the leaders of an armed group and how this relates to the organizational structure of her group and the strategies employed on the battlefield. For instance, it might be highly likely that charismatic leaders have less problems attracting recruits, and as such do not have to offer much material awards.

Besides these issues and these potential avenues for future research, it is important to note that this work is the first that attempts to shed light on how the internal structure of an armed group influence their behavior (and of combatants) on the battlefield and in particular how they treat the civilian population during conflict. Apart from contributing to a young branch of research, the generated knowledge can assist the policy community. When talking about the behavior of armed groups in conflict and conflict resolution, the analyses indicate, for example, that hierarchical armed groups are dangerous for the civilian population. If the policy community wants to prevent civilian abuse on a large scale, they might want to focus on decapitation as a counter strategy. By removing the principal in hierarchical armed groups, the international community removes the focal point of the organizations. This in turn might lead to the dissolvent of the group. However, future research should establish the connection between the level of hierarchy and the effect of decapitation on the level of perpetrated violence.

The policy implications of the micro-level part of this study are somewhat easier to pinpoint. In the development of, for example, DDR programs, attention should especially be devoted to not only the influence of the incentives but also to the social environment of the combatant. In other words, in the analysis I show that combatants, motivated by material benefits are more likely to target civilians in their quest. An effective DDR program should then also pay especially attention to help the combatant in finding alternative sources of money than joining the armed groups. For example, they should offer vocational training, assist with finding internships, and jobs. Only then is it possible to make sure that they will not rejoin and again perpetrate these kinds of human rights abuses. Another potential implication might be that DDR programs should initially focus on those combatants that show a high level of commitment and on those that were active in a socially dense armed group. All in all, understanding how rebel organizations integrate and control their combatants is an important step towards understanding how to disintegrate them.

References

Humphreys, Macartan and Jeremy M. Weinstein. 2006. "Handling and Manhandling Civilian in Civil War." *American Political Science Review* 100(3): 429–447.
Meyer, John P. and Natalie J. Allen. 1991. "A three-component conceptualization of organizational commitment." *Human Resource Management Review* 1(1): 61–89.

Appendix 1

Organizational Commitment Questionnaires (OCQ)

15-item OCQ version

1 I am willing to put in a great deal of effort beyond that normally expected in order to help this organization be successful.
2 I talk up this organization to my friends as a great organization to work for
3 I feel very little loyalty to this organization.
4 I would accept almost any type of job assignment in order to keep working for this organization.
5 I find that my values and the organization's values are very similar.
6 I am proud to tell others that I am part of this organization.
7 I could just as well be working for a different organization as long as the type of work was similar.
8 This organization really inspires the very best in me in the way of job performance.
9 It would take very little change in my present circumstances to cause me to leave this organization.
10 I am extremely glad that I chose this organization to work for, over others I was considering at the time I joined.
11 There's not too much to be gained by sticking with this organization indefinitely.
12 Often, I find it difficult to agree with this organization's policies on important matters relating to its employees.
13 I really care about the fate of this organization.
14 For me this is the best of all possible organizations for which to work.
15 Deciding to work for this organization was a definite mistake on my part.

9-item OCQ version

1 I am willing to put in a great deal of effort beyond that normally expected in order to help this organization be successful.
2 *I talk up this organization to my friends as a great organization to work for.*
3 I would accept almost any type of job assignment in order to keep working for this organization.

4   I find that my values and the organization's values are very similar.
5   I am proud to tell others that I am part of this organization.
6   This organization really inspires the very best in me in the way of job performance.
7   I am extremely glad that I chose this organization to work for, over others I was considering at the time I joined.
8   I really care about the fate of this organization.
9   For me this is the best of all possible organizations for which to work.

8-item OCQ version

1   I am willing to put in a great deal of effort beyond that normally expected in order to help this organization be successful.
2   I talk up this organization to my friends as a great organization to work for.
3   I find that my values and the organization's values are very similar.
4   I am proud to tell others that I am part of this organization.
5   This organization really inspires the very best in me in the way of job performance.
6   I am extremely glad that I chose this organization to work for, over others I was considering at the time I joined.
7   I really care about the fate of this organization.
8   For me this is the best of all possible organizations for which to work.

Appendix 2
Measurement of hierarchical structure

Specialization

1   Are the following activities performed by specialists – i.e., those exclusively engaged in the activities and not in the line of chain of authority?
    a   activities to develop, legitimize, and symbolize the organizational purpose (e.g., public relations, advertising).
    b   activities to dispose of, and service the output (e.g., sales, service).
    c   activities to obtain and control materials and equipment (e.g., buying, stock control).
    d   activities to devise new outputs, equipment, process (e.g., R&D, development).
    e   activities to develop and transform human resources (e.g., training, education).
    f   activities to acquire information on the operational field (e.g., market research).
2   What professional qualifications do these specialists hold?

Standardization

1   How closely defined is a typical; operative's task (e.g., custom, apprenticeship, rate fixing, work study)?
2   Are there specific procedures to ensure the perpetuation of the organization (e.g., R&D programs, systematic market research)?
3   How detailed is the marketing policy (e.g., general aims only, specific policy worked out and adhered to)?
4   How detailed are the costing and stock control systems (e.g., stock taking: yearly, monthly, etc,: costing: historical job costing, budgeting, standard cost system)?

Standardization of employment practices

1   Is there a central recruiting and interviewing procedure?
2   Is there a standard selection procedure for foreman and managers?
3   Is there a standard discipline procedure with set offenses and penalties?

Formalization

1   Is there an employee handbook or rulebook?
2   Is there an organization chart?
3   Are there any written terms of reference or job descriptions? For which grades of employee?
4   Are there agenda and minutes for workflow (e.g., production) meetings?

Centralization

1   Which level in the hierarchy has the authority to
   a   decide which supplies of materials are to be used?
   b   decide the price of the output?
   c   alter the responsibilities of areas of work of departments?
   d   decide marketing territories to be covered?

Configuration

1   What is the chief executive's span of control?
2   What is the average number of direct workers per first-line supervisor?
3   What is the percentage of indirect personnel (i.e., employees with no direct or supervisory responsibility for work on the output)?
4   What is the percentage of employees in each functional specialism (e.g., sales and service?

Appendix 3

Web survey

* *Welcome screen*

Welcome to the survey on the Organizational Structure of Armed Movements (OSAM)!

The survey contains around **30 questions** about the motivations of the members, their level of commitment, and the level of hierarchy of the **Armed Group's name** in the **last two decades**. Although we understand that this group is highly dynamic in this period of time, the questions are of general nature. If it is not possible to answer the questions in a general way, please answer the questions with regard to its current state. Your opinion as an expert is highly appreciated and filling out the survey will take approximately **10 minutes**.

Your personal information will not be given to any third persons. If you have any questions about the study or your right as a participant please e-mail to: osam.survey@uni-konstanz.de

Yours sincerely,
Roos Haer
Junior Research Fellow
Chair of International Relations and Conflict Management
University of Konstanz.

* *Header: Recruitment*

The first few questions concern the way in which the **Armed Group's name** recruits new members. Does the **Armed Group's name** select particular persons? What are the recruits' motivations for joining the **Armed Group's name**? How many of them are forcefully abducted into the group?

* *Recruitment*

1 In general, are members of the Armed Group's name abducted or did they join voluntarily?
   * All of them are abducted, none of them joined voluntarily
   * Most of them are abducted, few joined voluntarily

- Some of them are abducted, some joined voluntarily
- Very few are abducted, most of them joined voluntarily
- None of them are abducted, all of them joined voluntarily
- I do not know
- I choose not to answer

2 Some armed groups recruit their members for a lifetime, i.e., once they join they are expected to stay forever with the group. In general, are members of the Armed Group's name recruited for life?
- Always
- Usually
- Occasionally
- Rarely
- Never
- I do not know
- I choose not to answer

3 Some armed groups try to recruit potential members from specific ethnic and/or religious groups. To what extent does the Armed Group's name try to attract recruits with the same ethnic and/or religious backgrounds?
- Always
- Usually
- Occasionally
- Rarely
- Never
- I do not know
- I choose not to answer

4 To you knowledge, does the Armed Group's name have clear defined political goals, such as separation of a particular territory, replacing the government, or implementing particular laws?
- Yes
- No
- I do not know
- I choose not to answer

5 *Filter*: To what extent do you think "regular" members are aware of these political goals?
- Extremely aware
- Moderately aware
- Somewhat aware
- Slightly aware
- Not at all aware
- I do not know
- I choose not to answer

6 Some people join an armed group because they experience political repression and/or political exclusion. How important do you think are these political reasons for the recruit's decision to join the **Armed Group's name**?
Very unimportant ○ ○ ○ ○ ○ Very important

- I do not know
- I choose not to answer

7 Some people join an armed group because they experience inter-ethnic and/ or inter-religious hatred. How important do you think are these ethnic and religious reasons for the recruit's decision to join the **Armed Group's name**?

Very unimportant ○ ○ ○ ○ ○ Very important
- I do not know
- I choose not to answer

8 Some people join an armed group because they seek to revenge past humiliations and defeats. How important do you think revenge is for the recruit's decision to join the **Armed Group's name**?

Very unimportant ○ ○ ○ ○ ○ Very important
- I do not know
- I choose not to answer

9 Some people join an armed group because they are discontent about existing economic inequality. How important do you think economic inequality is for the recruit's decision to join the **Armed Group's name**?

Very unimportant ○ ○ ○ ○ ○ Very important
- I do not know
- I choose not to answer

10 To your knowledge, are recruits offered material benefits such as money, drugs, food, and/or livestock in return for joining the **Armed Group's name**?
- Always
- Often
- Sometimes
- Rarely
- Never
- I do not know
- I choose not to answer

11 To your knowledge, how often is the **Armed Group's name** engaged in plundering?
- Constantly
- Frequently
- Sometimes
- Hardly ever
- Never at all
- I do not know
- I choose not to answer

12 *Filter*: Is plundering promoted by the commanders of the **Armed Group's name**?
- Always
- Often
- Sometimes

- Rarely
- Never
- I do not know
- I choose not to answer

- *Header Hierarchy*

The next couple of questions concern the internal organization of the **Armed Group's name**. How hierarchical is the group organized? Do individual members have any influence on the day-to-day decision making in the **Armed Group's name**? Are they often punished? If so, by whom?

- *Hierarchy*

13 In general, how hierarchical do you think the **Armed Group's name** is organized?
    Not at all hierarchical ○ ○ ○ ○ ○ Very hierarchical
    - I do not know
    - I choose not to answer
14 In some armed groups there are rules written down that prescribe how a recruit should behave in particular situations. Do such written rules exist for the **Armed Group's name**?
    - Yes
    - No
    - I do not know
    - I choose not to answer
15 In some armed groups there are standard procedures for hiring new recruits. For instance, recruits are interviewed by one of the commanders or they have a kind of trial-period. To your knowledge, does such a standard procedure exist in the **Armed Group's name**?
    - Yes
    - No
    - I do not know
    - I choose not to answer
16 To your knowledge, how are commanders of the **Armed Group's name** generally appointed?
    - They appoint themselves by means of force
    - They are appointed by their unit
    - They are appointed by their superiors
    - They are appointed another way, namely . . .
    - I do not know
    - I choose not to answer
17 Does the **Armed Group's name** make use of military language for their ranks, such as "officer," "sergeant," or "general"?
    - Yes
    - No

- I do not know
- I choose not to answer

18 To what extent do you think that individual members of the **Armed Group's name** can make their own decisions concerning the use of violence against other armed groups?
- Always
- Frequently
- Occasionally
- Rarely
- Never
- I do not know
- I choose not to answer

19 To your knowledge, are members of the **Armed Group's name** punished for disobeying orders?
- Yes
- No
- I do not know
- I choose not to answer

20 *Filter*: How is the punishment decided upon?
- The commander alone decides
- A commander from another unit decides
- There are trials within the unit
- There are public trials in front of civilians
- Other, namely...
- I do not know
- I choose not to answer

21 *Filter*: Who, generally, carries out this punishment?
- The commander
- A commander from another unit
- Armed group members with a lower rank than the punished person
- Armed group members with a higher rank than the punished person
- Other, namely...
- I do not know
- I choose not to answer

- *Header Commitment*

Another aspect of armed groups is whether their fighters are committed or not. Are they proud to be a part of the **Armed Group's name**? Are they willing to sacrifice much of their own in fulfilling the groups' goals? Are they loyal to the group? Can recruits leave whenever they want to leave?

- *Commitment*

22 To what extent do you think that members of the **Armed Group's name** are committed to the organization?

Not at all committed ○ ○ ○ ○ ○ Extremely committed
- I do not know
- I choose not to answer

23 Some armed groups forbid their members to have contact with their family members, friends, and/or other people that are not part of the group. To what extent do members of the **Armed Group's name** have contact with people from outside the armed group?
- Always
- Often
- Sometimes
- Rarely
- Never at all
- I do not know
- I choose not to answer

24 In general, how hard is it for members to leave the **Armed Group's name**?
- Impossible
- Very hard
- Somewhat hard
- Not really hard
- Not hard at all
- I do not know
- I choose not to answer

25 If members have left the **Armed Group's name**, to what extent have they still contact with their former comrades?
- Always
- Often
- Sometimes
- Rarely
- Never
- I do not know
- I choose not to answer

26 Do members care about the fate of the **Armed Group's name**?
- Extremely
- Very
- Somewhat
- Slightly
- Not at all
- I do not know
- I choose not to answer

27 How proud are members to be part of the **Armed Group's name**?
- Extremely proud
- Very proud
- Somewhat proud
- Slightly proud
- Not at all proud

- I do not know
- I choose not to answer

28   To what extent are members loyal to the **Armed Group's name**?
- Extremely loyal
- Very loyal
- Somewhat loyal
- Slightly loyal
- Not at all loyal
- I do not know
- I choose not to answer

- *Header: Behavior towards civilians*

The last few questions concern the way in which the **Armed Group's name** behave towards the civilian population. Does the armed group provide public services like healthcare? Are civilians intentionally killed or harmed by the armed group? How often does this happen?

- *Public services*

29   Some armed groups are engaged in the provision of public services to civilians. They provide for instance healthcare and education. Is the **Armed Group's name** engaged in such public services?
- Yes
- No
- I do not know
- I choose not to answer

30   Is the **Armed Group's name** official affiliated with a political party?
- Yes
- No
- I do not know
- I choose not to answer

31   To your knowledge, does the **Armed Group's name** harm or kill civilians intentionally?
- Yes
- No
- I do not know
- I choose not to answer

32   *Filter*: How often do you think are civilians targeted by the **Armed Group's name**?
- All the time
- Often
- Sometimes
- Rarely
- Never at all
- I do not know
- I choose not to answer

33   *Filter*: To what extent do you think that members of the **Armed Group's name** use violence against civilians because they have been given orders to do so?
- Always
- Often
- Sometimes
- Rarely
- Never
- I do not know
- I choose not to answer

- *Header: Other expert*

If you know the names and/or e-mail addresses of other experts on the **Armed Group's name**, who might be willing to fill out this survey, we would be grateful if you provide us the contact details in the box below.

_____

_____

_____

_____

In addition, if you are interested in being kept informed about the release of this dataset and

- *Header: Further contact*

If you have any comments or suggestions that you would like to share, please let us know in the box below.

_____

_____

_____

_____

- *Header: Thank you*

Thank you for participating in this survey!
Your responses help to further understand the armed group's organizational settings. We greatly appreciate your time and feedback!

Yours sincerely,
Roos Haer

Appendix 4

Case selection

No.	Armed group	Comments	No. invited experts	No. experts who completed
1	AAH	Not included – experts found but no e-mail addresses.	–	–
2	Abu-Hafs al-Masri Brigades	Not included – no experts found and doubts about its existence.	–	–
3	ACCU	Not included – no experts found.	–	–
4	ADF	√	4	1
5	AFDL	√	4	2
6	AFL	Not included – the AFL are the national forces of Liberia.	–	–
7	al-Aqsa Martyrs' Brigades (AMB)	√	7	2
8	al-Gama'a al-Islamiyya	√	10	3
9	Al-Shabaab	√	6	2
10	Al-Mahdi Army	√	5	2
11	al-Qaida (The Base)	√	5	1
12	Ampatuan militia	Not included – no experts found	–	–
13	ANC (Umkhonto we Sizwe (MK))	ANC is a political group with its military wing Umkhonto we Sizwe (MK).	10	5
14	Ansar al-Islam	√	7	2
15	AQIM	√	4	4
16	ASG	√	5	2
17	ATTF	√	1	0
18	AUC	√	9	4
19	AWB	√	2	1
20	Bakassi boys	√	5	3
21	BLA	√	2	0
22	BLTF	√	3	1
23	Buxton Gang	Not included – no experts found.	–	–
24	Caucasus Emirate	Not included – actors are too unspecific.	–	–
25	Chechen Republic of Ichkeria	Not included – actors are too unspecific.	–	–
26	CNDD (FDD)	√	3	1
27	CNDP	√	4	2
28	Cobras	√	5	3
29	CPI-M	√	3	1
30	CPN-M (PLA)	CPN-M is a political party with its armed wing PLA.	4	3
31	CPP (NPA)	√	6	2
32	Croatian Republic of Bosnia and Hercegovina	Not included – actors are too unspecific.	–	–
33	DHD	√	2	1
34	DHD-BW	Not included – is a faction	–	–
35	ELN	√	4	0

No.	Armed group	Comments	No. invited experts	No. experts who completed
36	FAPC	Not included – no experts found.	–	–
37	FARC	√	10	6
38	FARDC	Experts indicated he could fill the survey out for this group.	1	1
39	FARF	√	4	1
40	FDLR	√	8	5
41	Fedayeen Islam	Not included – no experts found.	–	–
42	FIAA	√	2	1
43	FNI	√	2	0
44	FPR	√	4	1
45	FRPI	Not included – no experts found.	–	–
46	GAM	√	6	0
47	Gazotan Murdash	Not included – no experts found.	–	–
48	GIA	√	3	2
49	GICM	√	2	0
50	HAMAS	√	9	2
51	HPC	√	1	1
52	Hutu rebels	Not included – actors are too unspecific.	–	–
53	IFP	Not included – the IFP is a political party that was involved in election violence, which is unintentional violence.	–	–
54	Indian Mujahideen	Not included – is a faction of SIMI.	–	–
55	INPFL	√	3	2
56	Interahamwe	√	6	3
57	ISI	√	2	0
58	Jamaat Jund al-Sahaba	Not included – no experts were found and the group is now part of ISI.	–	–
59	Janjaweed	√	6	5
60	JEM	√	8	5
61	Jemaah Islamiya (JI)	√	9	1
62	Jondullah	Not included – no experts found.	–	–
63	JSS/SB (Shanti Bahini)	√	6	1
64	JVP	√	4	2
65	Kashmir insurgents	Not included – actors are too unspecific.	–	–
66	KNU	√	5	3
67	KR	√	5	1
68	KRA	Not included – no experts found.	–	–
69	Lashkar-e-Jhangvi	√	6	1
70	Lashkar-e-Taiba	√	4	1
71	Laskar Jihad	Not included – no experts found.	–	–
72	Los Zetas	√	4	0
73	LPC	Not included – no e-mail addresses found.	–	–
74	LRA	√	19	14
75	LTTE	√	8	3
76	LURD	Not included – no experts found.	–	–
77	MAGRIVI	Not included – no experts found.	–	–
78	Mara Salvatrucha (MS-13)	√	5	1
79	Mau Mau	Included in pretest.	2	2
80	Mayi Mayi	√	10	6
81	Mayi Mayi-Chinja Chinja	Not included – is a faction.	–	–
82	Mayi Mayi-Complet	Not included – is a faction.	–	–
83	Mayi Mayi-Ngilima	Not included – is a faction.	–	–
84	MCC	√	6	2
85	Medellín cartel	√	4	1
86	MFDC	√	8	7
87	MFDC-FN	Not included – is a faction.	–	–
88	MILF (BIAF)	√	8	2
89	MNJ	Experts indicated he could fill the survey out for this group.		1
90	MPCI	√	1	0

No.	Armed group	Comments	No. invited experts	No. experts who completed
91	MPGK	√	2	2
92	MPIGO	Not included – no experts found.	–	–
93	Mungiki	√	5	2
94	NDFB	√	1	1
95	NDFB-RD	Not included – is a faction.	–	–
96	NLFT	√	1	1
97	NPFL	√	5	1
98	NSCN	Included – instead of the NSCN-IM faction, just the NSCN is included.	4	3
99	NSCN–IM	Not included – is a faction.	–	–
100	Ntsiloulous	Not included – no experts found.	–	–
101	ONLF	√	5	4
102	OPC	Included in pretest	5	1
103	PAC (APLA)	PAC is political group with its military wing APLA.	2	2
104	Palipehutu-FNL	Not included – no experts found.	–	–
105	PARECO	Not included – no experts found.	–	–
106	Patani insurgents	Included – the largest Patani insurgent is the PULO	9	2
107	Paz y Justicia	Not included – no experts found.	–	–
108	PIJ	√	5	3
109	PKK	√	7	4
110	PWG	√	3	2
111	Ranvir Sena	√	3	1
112	Rastas	Not included – no experts found.	–	–
113	RCD	√	4	3
114	RCD-CP	Not included – is a faction.	–	–
115	RCD-K-ML	Not included – is a faction.	–	–
116	RCD-LN	Not included – is a faction.	–	–
117	RCD-ML	Not included – is a faction.	–	–
118	RCD-N	Not included – is a faction.	–	–
119	Renamo	√	7	4
120	Republic of Abkhazia	Not included – actors are too unspecific.	–	–
121	Republic of Nagorno-Karabakh	Not included – actors are too unspecific.	–	–
122	RRA	Not included – no experts found.	–	–
123	RTC	Not included – no experts found.	–	–
124	RUF	√	6	3
125	Sendero Luminoso (SL)	√	7	2
126	Salafia Jihadia	√	3	2
127	Sikh insurgents	Not included – actors are too unspecific.	–	–
128	Serbian Republic of Bosnia and Hercegovina, Serbian irregulars	Not included – actors are too unspecific.	–	–
129	SIMI	√	5	1
130	SNA	Not included – no experts found.	–	–
131	SLDF	√	4	0
132	SLM/A	Not included – no experts found.	–	–
133	SLM/A-MM	Not included – is a faction.	–	–
134	SPLM/A	√	13	9
135	SPM	√	1	0
136	SSDF	√	4	1
137	Taliban	√	7	1
138	Tawhid wal Jihad	Not included – no experts found.	–	–
139	TTP	√	3	1
140	UIFSA	√	1	0
141	ULFA	√	5	3
142	ULIMO	Not included – no experts found.	–	–
143	ULIMO-J	Not included – is a faction.	–	–
144	ULIMO-K	Not included – is a faction.	–	–

No.	Armed group	Comments	No. invited experts	No. experts who completed
145	UNITA	√	7	1
146	UNRF II	Not included – no experts found.	–	–
147	UPA	Not included – no experts found.	–	–
148	UPC	Not included – no experts found.	–	–
149	UPDS	Not included – no experts found.	–	–
150	USC	√	2	0
151	VHP	√	4	0

Appendix 5

Combatant survey

Name Interviewer: _____ Name Interpreter: _____

Date: _____ Place:_____

General Armed Group Survey (GAGS)

In the following survey some questions are asked concerning your experiences in the armed group in which you were actively involved. If you do not feel comfortable answering any of the following questions, please let the interviewer know, and we will move to the next question.

Background

Name or Acronym of the Interviewee: _____

Gender: ❏ Male   ❏ Female

Date of birth: _____ day _____ month _____ year.

Age: _____ years old.

Place of birth: _____

Language(s): _____

What is your highest level of education?

- No school
- A few years of primary school
- Completed primary school
- A few years of secondary school
- Completed secondary school
- Went to further education e.g., evening school, trainings
- Went to university
- Completed university, which degree _____
- Dk/Na

Did you have a job and a regular income before you joined the armed group?

- Yes, I had a regular income of_____ $ a month. My occupation was:

  _____
- No
- Dk/Na

Name of the armed group(s): _____

If known, the name of the brigade(s) or unit(s):_____

Note for the interviewer:
When the interviewee was or is a member of different organizations – all of the following questions should be answered per organization! The best thing is to use one survey form per group or indicate the different answers per question.

General – Recruitment

Now, I will ask you some questions concerning your recruitment. I will ask questions concerning your time spend in the organization, but also some questions concerning how you left this organization.

1   How did you become part of the armed group in question?
- I was abducted   Go to question 12
- I joined voluntarily the organization in the year(s):_____.
- My armed group was integrated into another group.
- Dk/Na
- Other, please specify_____

Questions, if voluntarily joining

2   If you joined voluntarily, could you please tell me in a few sentences, why you joined the organization?

   _____

   _____

   _____

   _____

3   Did you join the same organization more than once, and why?

   _____

   _____

   _____

4   What was the longest period you have stayed in the organization? If you do not know the exact period, please tell me your best guess.

- I stayed _____ day(s)/month(s)/year(s).
- Dk/Na

5   How old were you when you joined the armed group? If you joined the organization voluntarily more than once, please think back to the longest period you were involved.

- When I joined the armed group, I was _____ years old.
- Dk/Na

6   Did you ever tried to leave the group?

•	Yes, _____ times.	Go to question 7
•	No	Go to question 9
•	Dk/Na	Go to question 9

7   If you have tried to leave the group, could you please tell me in one or two short sentences, why you decided to leave?

_____

_____

_____

_____

_____

_____

8   How did you leave the group? If you joined the organization voluntarily more than once, please think back to the longest period you were involved.
- I just left without problems.
- I escaped on my own.
- I was freed by MONUC.
- I was released by the organization
- Dk/Na
- Other, please specify_____

9   Others, told me a couple of reasons why they could or would not leave the organization. Please tell me which of the following reasons are also true for you

	I could or would not leave the organization, because…	Yes	No
1	I was afraid of being killed when trying to flee	❑	❑
2	I felt safe inside the group	❑	❑
3	I had friends in the group	❑	❑
4	I received more food, better shelter, etc. than I had in my own village	❑	❑
5	I supported the group's political goals	❑	❑
6	Other, please specify:	❑	❑

10 Did you know anybody in the organization before you became involved? More than one answer possible.
    •   Yes, some family members were involved.
    •   Yes, some friends were involved.
    •   Yes, some people from my village/town were involved.
    •   I did not know anyone, who was involved.
    •   Other, please specify _____
    •   Dk/Na

11 During your time in the organization, have you ever seen recruited ... More than one answer possible
    •   Family members
    •   Friends
    •   People from your village/town
    •   None of them
    •   Other, please specify_____
    •   Dk/Na

Go to question 21

Questions, if Abduction

12 How often were you abducted?
    •   1 time
    •   2 times
    •   3 times
    •   More than 4 times
    •   Dk/Na

13 How long were you abducted each time? If you do not know the exact time, please indicate your best guess.
    •   1st time, I was abducted for _____ day(s)/month(s)/year(s).
    •   2nd time, I was abducted for _____ day(s)/month(s)/year(s).
    •   3rd time, I was abducted for _____ day(s)/month(s)/year(s).
    •   Dk/Na

14 How old where you, at the time of abduction? If you do not know your exact age at that time, please tell me your best guess.
    •   1st time, I was _____ old.
    •   2nd time, I was _____ old.
    •   3rd time, I was _____ old.
    •   Dk/Na

15 Did you try to escape? If yes, how many times?
    •   Yes, _____ times.
    •   No
    •   Dk/Na

16 How did you leave the bush each time?
    •   The **1st time**, I was
    •   Freed by the government.

- Escaped on my own.
- Released by the organization.
- With the help of MONUC.
- Dk/Na
- Other, please specify_____
- The **2nd time**, I was
- Freed by the government.
- Escaped on my own.
- Released by the organization.
- With the help of MONUC.
- Dk/Na
- Other, please specify_____
- The **3rd time**, I was
- Freed by the government.
- Escaped on my own.
- Released by the organization.
- With the help of MONUC.
- Dk/Na
- Other, please specify_____

17 I will now sum up some reasons why you could or would not leave the organization. Please tell me which **two** reasons are the most important ones.
- I was afraid to be killed when trying to flee.
- I felt safe inside the group.
- I had friends in the group.
- I received more food, better shelter, etc. than I had in my own village.
- I supported the group's political goals.
- Dk/Na
- Other, please specify_____

18 In general, were you abducted with somebody else you knew at the same time? More than one answer possible.
- Yes, with family members
- Yes, with friends
- Yes, with other people from my village
- Yes, with other schoolchildren
- No, I was not abducted together with other people I knew.
- Other, please specify_____
- Dk/Na

19 In general, did you know anybody active in the organization before you became abducted for the first time? More than one answer possible.
- Yes, I knew that some family members were involved.
- Yes, I knew that some friends were involved
- Yes, I knew that some people from my village/town were involved.
- No, I did not know anyone who was involved.
- Dk/Na
- Other, please specify _____

20 During your time at in the organization, have you ever seen recruited ... (more than one answer possible)
- Family members
- Friends
- People from your village/town
- None of them
- Other, please specify_____
- Dk/Na

21 Other people have told me a couple of reasons and circumstances under which they would take up arms again. Could you please indicate if the following statements are also true for you?

   For which reasons would you take up arms again? I would take up arms again...

		Strongly disagree	Disagree	Neither nor	Agree	Strongly agree	Strongly disagree
1	If my comrades ask me for help.	❏	❏	❏	❏	❏	❏
2	If I am forced by my commander.	❏	❏	❏	❏	❏	❏
3	If I receive more food, better shelter, etc. than in my own village.	❏	❏	❏	❏	❏	❏
4	If I can earn more money than outside the group.	❏	❏	❏	❏	❏	❏
5	If I cannot go back to school.	❏	❏	❏	❏	❏	❏
6	If I see that the group's political goals are not fulfilled.	❏	❏	❏	❏	❏	❏
7	If I can protect my family and community by fighting.	❏	❏	❏	❏	❏	❏
8	If the government fails to implement peace, law, and order.	❏	❏	❏	❏	❏	❏
9	If people in my community do not accept me.	❏	❏	❏	❏	❏	❏
10	If I have the chance to kill and harm people.	❏	❏	❏	❏	❏	❏
11	If have the chance to get women.	❏	❏	❏	❏	❏	❏
12	If my people continue to suffer.	❏	❏	❏	❏	❏	❏
13	If my family rejects me.	❏	❏	❏	❏	❏	❏
14	If I feel that I have no where else to go.	❏	❏	❏	❏	❏	❏
15	If I have the feeling that my life would be more exciting in the bush.	❏	❏	❏	❏	❏	❏
16	Other, please specify:	❏	❏	❏	❏	❏	❏

Military organization

Now I will ask you some general questions concerning your ideas about the goals of your organization, the training and weapons you have received.

22 Could you please tell me in one or two short sentences what you think is the most important aim of the organization? There is no wrong or right answer, you should answer according to what you think is the most important aim.

_____

_____

_____

_____

23 Did you participate in training before fighting? If yes, what type of training did you undergo and for how long? More than one answer possible.
   - No, I did not have had any training.
   - Yes, I have had military training for _____ days/months/years.
   - Yes, I have had political/ideological training for _____ days/months/years.
   - Yes, I have had spiritual training for _____ days/months/years.
   - Other, please specify _____
   - Dk/Na

24 When did you receive your first weapon?
   - Directly after I was abducted/joined voluntary.
   - Directly after my training.
   - Just before my first combat experience.
   - I have not received any weapon during my time in the organization.
   - Other, please specify _____
   - Dk/Na

25 What was the first kind of weapon that you received?
   - Traditional weapons, like spears and axes
   - Pistol/revolver
   - Automatic rifles, such as AK 47
   - Other, please specify _____
   - Dk/Na

26 What weapon did you have just before you left the organization?
   - Traditional weapons, like spears and axes
   - Pistol/revolver
   - Automatic rifles, such as AK 47
   - Other, please specify _____
   - Dk/Na

27 What happened to your weapon when you left the bush?
   - I took it with me, and I still have it
   - I left it behind

- • I buried it
- • I sold it
- • I handed it over to the government
- • I handed it over to the DDR program
- • Dk/Na
- • Other, please specify _____

28 Can you tell me what your highest rank/position was each time in the organization? Were you a military commander? If so, how many people where in your unit? If you did not receive any rank or you did not command a unit, please tell me than the number of people that were together with you in your unit.
   - • **1st time,** _____ rank/position; _____ people where in my unit.
   - • **2nd time,** _____ rank/position; _____ people where in my unit.
   - • **3rd time,** _____ rank/position; _____ people where in my unit.
   - • Dk/Na

This is to be placed at right of question 28, see author's original file

Private
Corporal
Sergeant
Lieutenant
Captain
Major
Colonel Brigadier
General

END

29 Can you tell me the name of your commander(s):

   _____

Promotion

Now we will ask some questions on how and why you get promoted in the organization.

30 If you think back to your unit, can you tell me how people were promoted? And how important the following reasons were for their promotion?
- • The person was promoted because he was a friend/relative of the commander
   - • Very important
   - • Important
   - • Not important
   - • Dk/Na
- • The person was promoted because he was a good fighter during attacks

- Very important
- Important
- Not important
- Dk/Na
- The person was promoted because he was intelligent or educated.
  - Very important
  - Important
  - Not important
  - Dk/Na
- The person was promoted because he was popular in the group.
  - Very important
  - Important
  - Not important
  - Dk/Na
- The person was promoted because he was rich, and able to buy a promotion.
  - Very important
  - Important
  - Not important
  - Dk/Na
- The person was promoted because he was especially cruel in injuring and killing people.
  - Very important
  - Important
  - Not important
  - Dk/Na
- The person was promoted for another reason, please specify _____
  - Very important
  - Important
  - Not important
  - Dk/Na

31 Think of the superior of your group (if you are abducted or joined more often, pick the abduction period that was the longest). How was he appointed?
- He appointed himself by force.
- He was chosen by one or two people in your unit.
- Your unit voted for him/her.
- He was chosen by a superior commander.
- Other, please specify _____
- Dk/Na

Rewards and punishments

The following questions deals with the possible rewards and punishments given by fellow members of your organization.

32   Were you ever given the following things for participating in your unit's operations? And did you receive them before or after a fight?
*   Extra food
    *   Most likely before.
    *   Most likely after.
    *   Whenever available, it did not depend on an action.
    *   Dk/Na
*   Money
    *   Most likely before.
    *   Most likely after.
    *   Whenever available, it did not depend on an action.
    *   Dk/Na
*   Non-medical drugs (like cocaine, marihuana)
    *   Most likely before.
    *   Most likely after.
    *   Whenever available, it did not depend on an action.
    *   Dk/Na
*   Woman/Man/Boy/Girl
    *   Most likely before.
    *   Most likely after.
    *   Whenever available, it did not depend on an action.
    *   Dk/Na
*   Spiritual objects (e.g., holy water)
    *   Most likely before.
    *   Most likely after.
    *   Whenever available, it did not depend on an action.
    *   Dk/Na

33   Was the food that you received from the organization enough? Or, did you have to find other sources?
*   Yes, it was enough for me.   Go to question 35
*   No, it was not enough and I was forced to find other ways to survive.
*   Dk/Na

34   **If you did not** receive enough food, how did you get hold of food?
*   I stole food from other group members
*   I stole food from civilians
*   I bought food
*   Other, please specify? _____
*   Dk/Na

35   Were people from your group punished for disobedience?
*   Yes, often   Go to question 37
*   Yes, sometimes   Go to question 37

- No, never   Go to question 39
- Dk/Na   Go to question 39

36 **If yes**, how was it decided what the punishment would be? More answers possible
- The commander alone would decide on the punishment.
- A commander, from outside your unit, would decide on the punishment.
- There were trials within our unit.
- There were public trails in front of civilians.
- Other, please specify_____
- Dk/Na

37 Who carried out the punishment?
- The commander of the unit.
- A commander from another unit.
- Members of the unit, who had lower rank than the punished person.
- Members of the unit, who had a higher rank than the punished person.
- Others, please specify_____
- Dk/Na

Action

I will now ask you some questions that deals with your actions in the organization. If you do not feel comfortable answering these questions, please let me know, and then we move on to the next question.

38 You indicated previously that you were abducted/joined the organization voluntarily _____ times. How often were you involved in fight during these times? If you can not recount the exact number, please write down your best guess.
- **1st time**, I was involved _____ times.
- **2nd time**, I was involved _____ times.
- Dk/Na

39 How many times were you active in fighting during a regular week?
- Every day/night
- Every other day (3–4 times a week)
- Once or twice a week
- Dk/Na
- Other, please specify_____

40 What is your most intensive battle experience (when, where, why intensive)?

41 Were people in your unit ordered to attack settlements for the organization?
- Yes
- No
- Dk/Na

42 Were people in your unit ordered to abduct children for the organization?
- Yes

- No
- Dk/Na

43 Were people in your unit ordered to injure/kill innocent civilians for the organization?
- Yes
- No
- Dk/Na

44 Were people in your unit ordered to rape civilians?
- Yes
- No
- Dk/Na

45 In general, against whom did you most fight?
- Civilians
- The Congolese Army
- Other armed organizations
  - CNDP – Nkunda
  - FDLR – Interahamwe, Ex-FAR
  - RCD
  - NALU
  - Mai-Mai
  - Other armed groups, please specify_____
- Dk/Na

Identification and commitment

I will now ask you some questions about your relationship with different people. Just imagine you are at the very beginning (position 0) of the line, can you show me on this line how close you feel to the following people. The closer you put a cross to your position, the more close you feel to that person.

46 Thinking back to <u>your time in the group,</u> can you please show me how close you felt to:
    i   How close did you felt to your friends in the bush?

_____

(You)
    ii How close did you felt to your family at home?

_____

(You)
    iii How close did you felt to the organization as a group?

_____

(You)
    iv How close did you felt to your commander?

_____

(You)

47 Do you agree or disagree with the following statements:
   i   I am proud to tell others that I was part of the organization.
- Strongly agree
- Agree
- Neither agree nor disagree
- Disagree
- Strongly disagree
- Dk/Na

   ii   I really care about the fate of the organization.
- Strongly agree
- Agree
- Neither agree nor disagree
- Disagree
- Strongly disagree
- Dk/Na

   iii I feel very little loyalty to the organization.
- Strongly agree
- Agree
- Neither agree nor disagree
- Disagree
- Strongly disagree
- Dk/Na

   iv I would go back to the organization when my comrades ask for my help.
- Strongly agree
- Agree
- Neither agree nor disagree
- Disagree
- Strongly disagree
- Dk/Na

   v   I still feel close to my friends in the group.
- Strongly agree
- Agree
- Neither agree nor disagree
- Disagree
- Strongly disagree
- Dk/Na

Contact with other groups

I will now ask you some questions concerning the contact that your organization had with other armed groups.

48   Did you have friends who were fighting in other armed organizations?
- •   Yes, they were active in _____
- •   No, I did not had friends who were active in other armed groups.

O Dk/Na
- •   Other, please specify_____

49   Did you ever saw a meeting between your commander and a commander of another armed group? If yes, from which group was the other commander and how often did you saw them together?
- •   I did not saw any meeting.
- •   My commander had a meeting with the commander of _____ (name of armed group) _____ times.
- •   Dk/Na
- •   Other, please specify_____

50   Did you ever fought together with another organization against your enemy?
- •   Yes, I fought together with _____
- •   No, my group always fought without assistance of any other group
- •   Dk/Na
- •   Other, please specify _____

Current Situation

I am also interested in your current situation, how you feel and which help you would like to receive. This is important so that aid programs can be effective.

51   If you think about your future, what is your greatest concern?
- •   My lack of education
- •   That I will not have a job and income
- •   That I will feel unprotected
- •   That I do not know where to go
- •   That the goals of my armed group will not be fulfilled
- •   That people will not accept me anymore
- •   Other, please specify_____

52 How important do you consider the following aid programs for you?

		Very important	Important	Not important	Dk/Na
1	Medical Care	❑	❑	❑	❑
2	Psychological Counselling	❑	❑	❑	❑
3	Economic Support (cash, utilities etc.)	❑	❑	❑	❑
4	Social Activity Programs (music, dancing, football club)	❑	❑	❑	❑
5	Traditional ceremony, please specify:	❑	❑	❑	❑
6	Family Tracing	❑	❑	❑	❑
7	Schooling or Vocational Training	❑	❑	❑	❑
8	Other, please specify:	❑	❑	❑	❑

53 Are you planning to go back to school?
   • Yes   Interview is finished
   • No   Go to question 55
54 If you do not plan to go to school, could you tell me from the following list
   of reasons, which one applies for you?

	I do not plan to go to school, since...	Yes	No
1	I am too old	❑	❑
2	I had finished school before joining the armed group	❑	❑
3	No schools are available	❑	❑
4	I have no money for fees/uniform	❑	❑
5	It is not worthwhile to continue	❑	❑
6	I do not like school	❑	❑
7	I need to earn cash	❑	❑
8	I have a good work opportunity	❑	❑
9	I do not want to repeat a grade	❑	❑
10	I have difficulty concentrating	❑	❑
11	Other, please specify:	❑	❑

Instrumental Aggression Questionnaire

	Strongly disagree	Disagree	Neither nor	Agree	Strongly agree
1 When I am angry, I can always control my feelings.	☐	☐	☐	☐	☐
2 I have been more aggressive than others.	☐	☐	☐	☐	☐
3 I have only attacked others when I was threatened.	☐	☐	☐	☐	☐
4 I have encouraged others to come with me to fight.	☐	☐	☐	☐	☐
5 During combat, I felt like a hunter.	☐	☐	☐	☐	☐
6 When I harmed others, I was mostly well prepared.	☐	☐	☐	☐	☐
7 Whenever I have gone to fight, I have mostly expected to win.	☐	☐	☐	☐	☐
8 When someone makes me seriously angry I hit back on the spot.	☐	☐	☐	☐	☐
9 I have felt the need to fight.	☐	☐	☐	☐	☐
10 Once you start beating another person it is difficult to stop.	☐	☐	☐	☐	☐
11 I have hurt others because I wanted to do so.	☐	☐	☐	☐	☐
12 Fighting is a part of human life.	☐	☐	☐	☐	☐
13 Once a person has been cruel, they will want to be cruel the next time.	☐	☐	☐	☐	☐
14 When I have to defend myself or others, I can be a serious fighter.	☐	☐	☐	☐	☐
15 Inside your body you can feel when it is time for fighting.	☐	☐	☐	☐	☐
16 Once you have harmed others, attacking becomes more and more important in your life.	☐	☐	☐	☐	☐
17 Sometimes I have had the need to fight even if I knew it could be life-threatening.	☐	☐	☐	☐	☐
18 When I am threatened I defend myself and do not avoid a fight.	☐	☐	☐	☐	☐
19 When I see a dead person I want to look at the wounds.	☐	☐	☐	☐	☐
20 When I see a dead person I try to imagine the act of killing.	☐	☐	☐	☐	☐
21 The defeated person must bleed.	☐	☐	☐	☐	☐
22 The defeated person must scream.	☐	☐	☐	☐	☐
23 It can be satisfying to harm others.	☐	☐	☐	☐	☐
24 I have only harmed or killed in order to be accepted in my group.	☐	☐	☐	☐	☐
25 I have only attacked others because I was forced to do so.	☐	☐	☐	☐	☐
26 The pleasure of harming others was greater when it was difficult to defeat the victim.	☐	☐	☐	☐	☐
27 It is exciting when your victim suffers.	☐	☐	☐	☐	☐
28 I like to listen to other people to tell me stories of how they killed others.	☐	☐	☐	☐	☐
29 Attacking humans has made me feel sexually aroused.	☐	☐	☐	☐	☐
30 When I am harassed, I strike back instantly.	☐	☐	☐	☐	☐
31 I would love to go on a hunt to kill animals.	☐	☐	☐	☐	☐

Drug use in DRC

	Drug 1	Drug 2	Drug 3	Drug 4
Drug name(s): Language: Classification, e.g., alcohol	_____ _____ _____	_____ _____ _____	_____ _____ _____	_____ _____ _____
(1). What does it look like? Color:	❑ powder ❑ liquid ❑ pill form ❑ paste-like ❑ crystal (like sugar)	❑ powder ❑ liquid ❑ pill form ❑ paste-like ❑ crystal (like sugar)	❑ powder ❑ liquid ❑ pill form ❑ paste-like ❑ crystal (like sugar)	❑ powder ❑ liquid ❑ pill form ❑ paste-like ❑ crystal (like sugar)
(1). How do you use it? Comment:	❑ drink it ❑ inhale it ❑ inject it ❑ eat it ❑ sniff it ❑ place it on skin/in scar ❑ place it in mouth	❑ drink it ❑ inhale it ❑ inject it ❑ eat it ❑ sniff it ❑ place it on skin/in scar ❑ place it in mouth	❑ drink it ❑ inhale it ❑ inject it ❑ eat it ❑ sniff it ❑ place it on skin/in scar ❑ place it in mouth	❑ drink it ❑ inhale it ❑ inject it ❑ eat it ❑ sniff it ❑ place it on skin/in scar ❑ place it in mouth
(2). How is the effect?	❑ I get awake ❑ it calms me down ❑ I get happy/euphoric ❑ I get sexually stimulated ❑ it takes away pain ❑ it takes away hunger ❑ I easily get aggressive ❑ I feel powerful/mighty ❑ it takes away my fears ❑ I hear/see things that others do not hear/see	❑ I get awake ❑ it calms me down ❑ I get happy/euphoric ❑ I get sexually stimulated ❑ it takes away pain ❑ it takes away hunger ❑ I easily get aggressive ❑ I feel powerful/mighty ❑ it takes away my fears ❑ I hear/see things that others do not hear/see	❑ I get awake ❑ it calms me down ❑ I get happy/euphoric ❑ I get sexually stimulated ❑ it takes away pain ❑ it takes away hunger ❑ I easily get aggressive ❑ I feel powerful/mighty ❑ it takes away my fears ❑ I hear/see things that others do not hear/see	❑ I get awake ❑ it calms me down ❑ I get happy/euphoric ❑ I get sexually stimulated ❑ it takes away pain ❑ it takes away hunger ❑ I easily get aggressive ❑ I feel powerful/mighty ❑ it takes away my fears ❑ I hear/see things that others do not hear/see
(3). When do you use it?	❑ before combat ❑ after combat ❑ at night ❑ in the morning ❑ cerem./rituals/prayers ❑ during leisure time	❑ before combat ❑ after combat ❑ at night ❑ in the morning ❑ cerem./rituals/prayers ❑ during leisure time	❑ before combat ❑ after combat ❑ at night ❑ in the morning ❑ cerem./rituals/prayers ❑ during leisure time	❑ before combat ❑ after combat ❑ at night ❑ in the morning ❑ cerem./rituals/prayers ❑ during leisure time

continued

	Drug 1	Drug 2	Drug 3	Drug 4
Drug name(s):	_____	_____	_____	_____
Language:	_____	_____	_____	_____
Classification, e.g., alcohol	_____	_____	_____	_____
(5). How often have you used it last week?				
(6). How do you get it?				
(7). Would it be possible to buy it?				
(8). With whom do you use it?	❑ alone ❑ with comrades ❑ with other friends	❑ alone ❑ with comrades ❑ with other friends	❑ alone ❑ with comrades ❑ with other friends	❑ alone ❑ with comrades ❑ with other friends
(9). Why do you use it?	❑ it protects me (e.g., from bullets) ❑ it makes me healthy ❑ it gives me magical powers ❑ it makes my sex better ❑ I can fight better ❑ I can endure the stress better ❑ it helps me to forget the war	❑ it protects me (e.g., from bullets) ❑ it makes me healthy ❑ it gives me magical powers ❑ it makes my sex better ❑ I can fight better ❑ I can endure the stress better ❑ it helps me to forget the war	❑ it protects me (e.g., from bullets) ❑ it makes me healthy ❑ it gives me magical powers ❑ it makes my sex better ❑ I can fight better ❑ I can endure the stress better ❑ it helps me to forget the war	❑ it protects me (e.g., from bullets) ❑ it makes me healthy ❑ it gives me magical powers ❑ it makes my sex better ❑ I can fight better ❑ I can endure the stress better ❑ it helps me to forget the war

Appendix 6

Consent form interview

My name is Roos Haer

This is _____ (s)he will interpret everything because I don't speak your language).

   I would like to learn more about your current life and what has happened to you and your people in the past, what you have experienced and how you feel about it today. The information collected will help to understand the condition and needs of people that face difficult situations in Congo and will help to improve our understanding of the current civil wars. By participating in this study you will contribute a lot to my work and I am very grateful for that. Thank you.

   I would like to ask you to participate in an interview (me plus the interpreter). There are no correct answers to the questions. I am interested in your personal history, your emotions and your points of view, so I ask you to answer each question as honestly as you can. (The interpreter and) I will keep all of your responses strictly confidential. It will not be possible to identify you in any way later. No personal data will be available to anyone.

   If anything I ask is unclear or if you need me to repeat any of the questions as we go through the interview, please stop me. Also if you feel uncomfortable at any time, please stop me and we will talk about your feelings.

Unfortunately there will be no financial or other direct benefit for you. Your participation is voluntary. You may refuse to answer any question and you may choose to leave the discussion anytime. Do you have any questions? You may ask questions about this study at any time.

I have read the consent form to the participant and the participant agreed to take part in the study:

——————————— (interviewer's signature) ————————— (translator's signature)

I agree to take part in this study: ————————————— (participant's signature)

Do you agree that I could use your picture for educational purpose (in the university, for awareness raising purpose and for publications (homepage or articles)? If you do not agree for us to use for photograph, you can still take part in the interview and in the study.

I agree that my picture may be used for the purpose listed above:

_____

(participant's signature)

Index

Page numbers in *italics* denote tables, those in **bold** denote figures.